Revolution and Improvement

Also by John Roberts

Europe 1880–1945
The Mythology of the Secret Societies
The Paris Commune from the Right

Revolution and Improvement

The Western World 1775–1847

JOHN ROBERTS

UNIVERSITY OF CALIFORNIA PRESS

BERKELEY AND LOS ANGELES

University of California Press
Berkeley and Los Angeles
ISBN: 0-520-03076-1
Library of Congress Catalog Card Number:
75-17288
© 1976 John Roberts
Printed in England

Contents

CONTENTS

Book IV The New Worlds of the Nineteenth Century

Illustrations

Jonathan Hull's steam tugboat, after the specification for his patent (*Mary Evans Picture Library*)

The *Comet*, a contemporary sketch (*Radio Times Hulton Picture Library*)

The hopes and disappointments of German emigrants to the United States, contemporary German print (*H. Roger Viollet*)

The causes of emigration in Ireland, cartoon from *The Lady's Newspaper*, 1849 (*Radio Times Hulton Picture Library*)

Holeing a cane-piece in Antigua, from R. Bridgens's *West Indian Sketches*, 1851

Cartoon satirizing the American attitude to slavery, 1848 (*Radio Times Hulton Picture Library*)

The taking of Missolonghi by Ibraham Pasha, engraving by Mauro and Vautrin (*Bibliothèque Nationale, Paris; H. Roger Viollet*),

French cartoon on the opium trade in China, by Grandville, lithograph by Forest (*H. Roger Viollet*)

Power looms in a cotton factory, engraving, c. 1845 (*Radio Times Hulton Picture Library*)

Michael Faraday lecturing at the Royal Institution, contemporary print (*The Royal Institution*)

Railway travellers to the Epsom races, 1847, contemporary engraving (*Radio Times Hulton Picture Library*)

'*Galop Chromatique*', a caricature of Liszt by Grandville, 1843 (*Bibliothèque Nationale, Paris*)

Picture research by Ann Mitchell.

Maps

The maps were designed by Tony Garrett.

Foreword

This book does not pretend to be a complete account of the Western World between 1775 and 1847 (nor of anything else, for that matter). It was shaped to fit into a series of volumes interpreting different phases of the history of an evolving entity, the Western World. This explains both the dates which provide its chronological limits and the selection of topics discussed in it. Publishing difficulties, unfortunately, have brought the series to an end but these considerations have left their mark on the book which must now stand on its own. Because of its genesis, it is, I am afraid, somewhat idiosyncratic in approach. It dwells on some matters which seem to me especially revealing, and ignores others which some of my colleagues and readers might well expect to find here. But I have assumed (and hoped) that readers who wanted to know more, whether because tantalized by how little they were told or exasperated by the views expressed, would be willing to turn to other books to do so. What they will find here is in the nature of a personal essay or series of reflections on Western history between 1775 and 1847. The main organizing principle is the contrast in efficacity presented by the facts I have chosen to designate as Revolution and Improvement. But for all the impressiveness of the changes we can attribute to these abstractions, I have often felt that at the end of the day the last word often belongs to the sheer inertia of the inherited past; I hope this strikes my readers, too. If so, this book may have a minor usefulness, in leading people to read other books with slightly different assumptions in mind from those which usually dominate our interest in these much-studied years.

I wish to acknowledge a number of debts of gratitude: to Mr Christopher Falkus for first suggesting to me that I should write this book, to Miss Jenny Ashby for the agreeable way in which she handled the editorial work and to Miss Clare Bass for her help with the typing of the manuscript. A more particular word of thanks is due to Mrs N. Sissons; her contribution both in preparing material for inclusion and in scrutinizing the result was invaluable. Finally, I am most grateful to Professor M. S. Anderson, who was good enough to read and comment on the entire manuscript. His observations were of great utility, but, of course, neither he nor any of my other helpers bears any responsibility for whatever shortcomings this book contains.

Merton College, Oxford   JMR

Book I

Beginnings and Boundaries

1 Signs of the times

Somewhere between 1775 and 1847, the fate of the world was settled by the West. India passed almost completely under British rule. The door to China was kicked open and her long march into revolution began. A new nation and a future super-power came into existence which spread across the North American continent and established its first footholds on the Pacific coast. Meanwhile, in the European heartland of Western civilization there was a great political revolution and the first experience of what industrial society might be, two changes which would in the next age, when the world domination of Western civilization was completed, transform the lives of most of the inhabitants of the globe.

Few men in the West grasped the significance of any of these transformations, and their total impact escaped everyone. Yet of change itself, whether it was feared or welcomed, men were more conscious than ever before. Two variations of it particularly struck them, revolution and improvement. They run through all serious discussion of human affairs in the years covered in this book. Both were inseparably wedded to the notion that things might get better, and both were extended to cover so wide a range of facts that the distinction between them is often blurred. Yet they are still the best keys to what was going on.

For over a century people have talked about industrial and agricultural 'revolutions' whose crucial phases fall inside these years. They still do this because such sweeping changes are involved that only the dramatic idea of revolution does them justice. 'Improvement' is a less familiar word nowadays, but it was once used very frequently. Its sense was originally confined to agriculture, but then it was stretched to cover many more examples of progressive change by the application of knowledge, skill, enthusiasm and capital. In eighteenth-century England the idea of improvement moved from the countryside to the towns; 'improvement schemes' were launched in them with 'improvement commissioners' to supervise them. The idea had already been extended to the moral life. The busy bee, the great hymn-writer and religious poet Isaac Watts had long before observed, *improved* each shining hour, and soon men pointed out that manners could be not only reformed but *improved* by attention to them. *Improving* literature became conventional reading. There were to be many other applications of the word. Something of a culmination of the idea and a recognition of its indispensability came in the claim with which Macaulay opened his great narrative history of England. It was self-evident, he thought, that 'the history of our country during the last hundred and sixty years is eminently the history of physical, of moral, and of intellectual improvement.'

Yet revolution and improvement are not the whole story. They leave out a huge, nearly silent area of history. For most of these years there was no obvious change in the lives of millions of men. The acceleration of history in this three-quarters of a century would not have been noticed by most of the world's inhabitants, nor, indeed, by all of Europe's. A child born in 1775 who survived to 1847 would certainly have seen a great deal of change, had he grown up to be a French lawyer, or a Lancashire millhand, or a Virginia slave-owner. But were he a Russian peasant, or a Norwegian fisherman, or a Canadian trapper, he would probably not have done. Millions of people (probably most) in the middle decades of the nineteenth century still wore clothes such as their parents wore when it began; they ate the same foods, worked to the same rhythms, respected the same authorities, laughed and wept at the same old stories, observed the same festivals and worshipped at the same shrines. These things shaped their lives as they had for centuries shaped those of their forbears. Such stability is no longer thinkable in the West and now is ceasing to be thinkable over more and more of the world. Even our parents – let alone our grandparents – stand on the other side of great gulfs of discontinuity, so much has history speeded up since their day.

Familiarity with change may be one reason why we look for it in history, but it is not the only explanation of our tendency to look for changes as, in some sense, the 'real' story of the past. It is also simply easier to observe the passage of time when it is marked by conspicuous transformation than to remember the huge inertia of the past, the sheer weight of inherited conglomerates of ideas and practices which have always been the great enduring forces of history. 'A thirteenth-century peasant would visit many of our farms without much astonishment,' wrote a Frenchman in the middle of the nineteenth century, contemplating the agriculture of his day. The steam-engine had a century and a half of life behind it in 1847, and the first locomotive had run forty years earlier, but millions of Europeans had by then still not seen a stationary engine, let alone a railway.

This suggests that a historian should think about *whose* history he is writing when he talks of something as comprehensive as a 'Western World'. A pushing British engineer of 1847 saw his world and its past in a way quite differently from, say, a Spanish peasant, but even distinctions within individual societies blur differences of locality and tradition. The industrialist probably did *not* see the world in the same way as a contemporary Oxford don.

This suggests, too, the artificiality of talking about Europe in general terms at any date; how much more unreasonable, then, it must be to talk about a 'Western World'. Yet one existed already in 1775. The societies forming part of it can be seen clearly enough as historical entities when they are contrasted with others – with China, or India, for example – because their origins and traditions shaped them to be the carriers and cradles of a distinctive civilization which was in the end to shape the history of all mankind. But not all Western societies shared in this civilization in the same way or to the same degree. Some expressed it at its peak and might be called 'advanced' or 'developed'; such were, say, France or Great Britain in 1800. Russia and large parts of the Habsburg dominions, on the other hand, were not then in this position and were closer to great traditional societies in other parts of the world than they were to be a century later. Yet they indubitably shared much of the Western heritage and had already begun to take a hand in shaping it. Here is another question about subject-matter: is the history of the Western World the history of its advanced sectors, or of all its components? The answer must surely be that it is both. The Western World was the interplay of its components with one another; they released some possibilities in one another and contained others. They, too, are different facets of a larger entity.

These are not trivial points, for they define approaches and subject-matter. They also justify the choice of a period. At some moments in history, a date helps in delimiting great processes, but neither 1775 nor 1847 is such a one. They are not decisive years, but between them lies a decisive zone. In it can be discerned new forces, not always new in that they have never existed before, but new in that they are for the first time exercising determining weight. They are the source of irreversible change in world history as well as in the history of the Western World. But the danger of giving the impression that something 'began' in a certain year has to be avoided. All that need be said for starting a book with the last quarter of the eighteenth century is that in 1775 and 1776 a few events took place which coincidentally already suggest many of the themes of history for the next seventy or so years.

3

They are striking symptoms of what was to come and what had to go.

One can be dated very precisely. During the night of 18 April 1775, a detachment of British soldiers marched out of the Massachusetts port of Boston. They were going to the village of Concord, about eighteen miles away, to seize arms and ammunition gathered there by local patriots who feared and sometimes hoped that quarrels then going on with the British government might force Americans to fight to defend their interests. By the morning, when it was light but misty, the British were marching into Lexington, rather more than half-way to their objective. There, something happened which has never been completely explained, for firing began when they encountered a hastily assembled detachment of militia organized by the American patriots. Eight Americans were killed. The British force pushed on to encounter much more formidable opposition later that morning in a long action at Concord bridge before the march back to Boston began. All the way the British were sniped at and harried, and suffered over two hundred casualties. But what had happened was more important than even this figure suggested, for the War of American Independence had begun.

This was one of those rare moments in world history when great processes and issues run together to be crystallized briefly in a single incident. Later, an American poet wrote of the shots at Concord bridge being heard round the world, and hyperbole for once seems appropriate: this scuffle announced the birth of what was to become the most powerful nation in the world. Few could have seen this coming, but many people had long been expecting to hear the shots. A succession of irritations and grievances had bedevilled relations between the colonies and the mother country for a decade. The most radically minded Americans exploited them until in 1774 things were so bad that Boston, one of the greatest American ports, was occupied by a British garrison and was closed to commerce. A 'Continental Congress' met in Philadelphia and formulated proposals to be put to the British government for the pacification of the colonies which went very far. Something like the Dominion status of a later British Empire was envisaged, with only external commerce and strictly imperial concerns left to British legislation.

Soon, radical-minded Americans were able to go much further than this. After the Continental Congress which they dominated there appeared a clearly illegal and revolutionary 'Association' to enforce economic sanctions against the British and therefore to supervise much of the daily life of Americans. This was the background of the Concord skirmish. A few weeks later, the British soldiers found themselves bottled up in Boston, besieged by swarms of colonial militiamen dug in on the hills and shores surrounding the city.

When, on 10 May, the Continental Congress met, again it was reminded by a delegate from Virginia that 'the war is actually begun.' Revolt was breaking out everywhere. The law-abiding and moderate who still sought a solution at least under the rule of King George had lost control to the radicals. Congress could only recognize this fact; a 'Declaration on the Causes and Necessity of Taking up Arms' was agreed. Still, the final step to independence was not yet taken, though Congress appointed a commander-in-chief of the forces of the 'United Colonies'. A British force was bloodily handled at Bunker Hill on 17 June and an American attack was launched on Quebec, the key to former French Canada. But the British government was not disposed to be conciliatory even without such irritations. The radicals continued to fan the flames provided by the propaganda use they could make of American casualties, a process which had begun at once at Lexington, whose eight dead 'minutemen' were depicted as helpless victims of unprovoked attack. The British therefore proclaimed the colonies to be in a state of rebellion. General Washington, commander of the colonies' forces, ran up a new flag – of red and white stripes – at his HQ on 1 January 1776. Yet the king's health was still drunk in the officers' mess over which he presided.

In May 1776 Rhode Island was the first colony to declare itself independent. A new Continental Congress at Philadelphia appointed a committee to draft constitutional arrangements for a union of the colonies. There were important divisions about the way ahead. By and large, the radicals wanted the units which were now emerging from the colonial structure to stay as independent as possible; they had on their side the indisputable fact that the states – as we may now call them – of the future nation had come into existence before the Union between them. Conservatives, on the other hand, favoured a stronger central authority. This question was to take years to settle. Meanwhile, the constitutional fate of a new nation would be shaped not only by the ideas and assumptions inherited from the Anglo-Saxon past but by the play of parties, the course of hostilities with Great Britain and a public opinion now broadly committed to independence.

On 4 July Congress approved one of the key documents of modern history, the Declaration of Independence, the ideological justification of a new nation. The Virginian Jefferson, who did most of the drafting, claimed that it was 'an expression of the American mind', a statement of what was already accepted by American common sense. In part the Declaration was a narrative of the misdeeds of George III (his parliament's role was all but ignored) as evidence of an attempt to establish a tyranny. This historical case was then used to justify independence, on the basis of a political theory whose essence was the revolutionary claim that governments are set up in order to secure to men their possession of certain rights and that their just powers are derived only from the consent of the governed to this end. For the first time, a major state was to be based wholly on a contractual theory and on popular sovereignty. There would be no place in it for the prescriptive rights which were so important in the jurisprudence and political theory of every other state in the Western World, and it would be a doctrine which would go the round of the globe.

The war, meanwhile, had to be fought and won if American independence was to survive. Although they suffered a grave and decisive defeat at Saratoga in 1777, the advantage long appeared to lie with the British, who were able to press the Americans hard and had many sympathizers among the colonists (some eighty thousand 'loyalists' eventually emigrated to remain under the British flag and many more than this number must have existed in 1776). The colonies' governments did not co-operate easily and were reluctant to pay for defence when not directly menaced, too. Balancing these advantages, on the other hand, was geography – British strategy had to be carried out in a huge and widely dispersed group of theatres at the end of more than three thousand miles of oceanic communications – the enormous costs of campaigning at such a distance and the nature of the war to be fought. The British had to recover lost dominions; fighting a battle for the hearts and minds of men, they could not terrorize the local population. Destroying the 'Continental Army' commanded by General Washington would eliminate the military problem but still leave the political.

Periodically after 1776 each side made gestures towards some settlement which would preserve a formal link between the two largely Anglo-Saxon communities, but the war went on. In the end it was decided by the entry to it of the French in 1778, prompted by the American victory at Saratoga. The Spanish and the Dutch later joined France. Great Britain was the greatest naval power of the age, but this was too great a threat for her fleet to contain while preserving her communications with North America. The end came when a French fleet arrived off the coast of Virginia, where, in October 1781, the British army was bottled up on land by Washington. The siege of Yorktown ended on 17 October, when the British commander surrendered.

Though the war still went on, Yorktown was an event of huge importance. Only seven thousand or so British troops surrendered –

about half a modern division – but it was the greatest military disgrace suffered by Great Britain until 1941. It ended a ministry in London and led George III to draft a message of abdication, though, fortunately, he did not use it. Peace negotiations now began. Hostilities ended at the beginning of 1783, and peace was signed at Paris in the following September.

The new nation had been organizing itself for years. Several states had quickly given themselves constitutions in the greatest burst of political creativity since the days of the English Commonwealth. Two of them were submitted to popular ratification, thus establishing the characteristic American model of distinguishing between constitutional and ordinary legislation, by giving the formulation of the first to a special Convention and then having it approved by some kind of referendum. On the whole, the state constitutions reflected colonial experience. In two instances they were simply colonial charters renewed. Though republican in form, they retained governors who exercised the executive power and two legislative chambers. Usually, the electorate was limited.

At the national level it had soon been obvious, above all in foreign affairs and commerce, that Congress had to exercise some central authority. Articles of Confederation were drawn up, but they were not accepted by all states and effective until 1781. These Articles clearly left the preponderant weight with the individual states; a Congress of Confederation was set up with the same powers already enjoyed by the Continental Congress. But new issues had increased tension between those who favoured more centralization and those who favoured the rights of the states. In particular, they arose over the future use and relation to the new nation of Western lands, and over the weight to be given politically to slaves in computing the representation to be given to states. The Articles of Confederation had just sustained the government in war but proved barely adequate even for that. It was more true that the British had lost the war than that the Americans had won it.

Post-war difficulties seemed to show that the Continental Congress could neither tax the states nor control their monetary policies in a time of economic difficulty and thus restore public credit, nor provide force to uphold the law when a state asked for it. For many Americans the crucial evidence that a new Constitution was needed came in 1786 when a rebellion of Massachusetts farmers against the deflationary policies of their state revealed that Congress was powerless to help. It seemed that the break up into anarchy which was the fate often predicted for the new republic was now about to take place. It was time for a change.

A Constitutional Convention met at Philadelphia in May 1787. Debate was long and difficult. It was also, so far as incomplete records reveal, of a remarkably high standard. The central issue was the power to be given to the national government. From the start, those who sought a strong national focus took the initiative but they had to relinquish many of their hopes. On the other hand, the federal government which emerged from the deliberations of the Founding Fathers reflected their wishes more than those of their opponents. A league of states was transformed into a nation, the device of delimiting the areas of action of the national government and that of the states being the key to this solution. The smaller states which had feared that the larger states would have too much weight in a stronger union were reassured by concessions made to them. The whole structure was negotiated, realistic, a compromise. Though one state was to hold out until 1790, a sufficient majority had ratified the Constitution for the first presidency of the United States, that of George Washington, to be inaugurated on 30 April 1789.

The Constitution was to prove astonishingly successful. Through interpretation and amendment, it was able to regulate the transformation of the United States from an agrarian to an industrial society and from a scatter of weak and isolated little republics to a nation of global power. The success it enjoyed can be measured by its durability; only the British constitution – which can be argued to have undergone much more change since 1789 than the American – and the Papacy have a longer continuous history. Gradually, its example and influence would be felt worldwide, though this would take a long time. The device of a written constitution, as opposed to the charter of liberties or privileges, was an American invention (the forerunners of the English seventeenth century had failed to take root). Because of this its fundamentals were especially important, above all the principle of popular sovereignty. Yet the Founding Fathers deployed it not to draw up a scheme of government for Utopia but to meet pressing needs, as the opening words of the Constitution show: 'We the People of the United States, in order to form a more perfect union, establish Justice, insure domestic tranquillity, provide for the common defence, promote the general Welfare, and secure the Blessings of Liberty to ourselves and our Posterity, do ordain and establish this Constitution for the United States of America.'

Of course, more was at stake in principle than whether treaties could be honoured or debts collected. It is now taken so much for granted that it is easy to overlook the supremely important point that the Constitution was republican. This implied a great experiment. One of the leading members of the Convention said a great and true thing when

8

he reminded his colleagues at one moment that they were to decide the fate of republican government. Its prestige in modern times dates from the foundation of the United States. It was perhaps the turning-point in the long history of the republican idea when it was settled that the new nation, unique among great powers, would maintain republican institutions. Whatever antiquarian respect republics might command in Europe, in practice they suggested at that moment only the weakness, disunity and decay of Venice and Genoa, or the limited effectiveness of Swiss cantonal government, successful only within a very narrow geographical area and unsuited to the needs of a great state.

Thus in fourteen years the American Revolution had come a long way. Yet the events that followed Concord also constituted a strangely limited change, for all their expense and bloodshed and huge future implications. The essence of the revolution, like that of 1688 in England, was that it replaced one set of political arrangements with another, but did so without concomitant social or economic upheaval, though such upheaval might later be made possible by what had happened. The revolution was also conservative in another sense. Whatever individual Americans might think then and later about their country's duty to uphold abroad the principles on which it rested, the American revolution was unaggressive and for a long time bred few missionaries. Geography helped; the new union was a far-off country with little interest in what went on in Europe. The achievement of the American revolution opened the way to nationhood for Americans. Its exemplification of certain political principles was to be very important in the long run in shaping ideals elsewhere, but the direct importance of the American Revolution was that it made a nation and changed the history of a hemisphere, not that it had ideological repercussions elsewhere. It was to preserve an imperial authority rather than a different ideology that the British had fought and that their soldiers had, as their epitaph at Concord bridge puts it, come three thousand miles to die 'to keep the Past upon its throne'.

At the time of the Concord skirmish the leading minister of the King of France – Controller-General of Finances, as he was called – was a professional civil servant in his late forties, Anne-Robert-Jacques Turgot. He came of a distinguished legal family long associated with royal service, had shown exceptional intelligence as a student and was known as a writer on many topics; he translated Hume and Berkeley and contemplated writing a huge history of human progress. He had rejected the career as a cleric which had been planned for him, which reflects well on his scrupulousness: there were many Frenchmen who

9

found the dogmas of Catholic Christianity as unacceptable as he who yet took orders in order to qualify themselves for the material prospects opened by an ecclesiastical career. Turgot instead turned to the law, but this, too, was not to absorb his energies and interests fully. His intellectual power and public spirit could be satisfied only by governing men. After being *intendant* of Limoges, he was called in 1774 to be a royal minister, first at the Admiralty, and then as Controller-General.

This was the climax of Turgot's career. In so far as finance is the mainspring of government and the determinant of policy, he ruled France, but this statement must be heavily qualified. Turgot was in no sense a 'prime minister'. Indeed, even the idea of such a minister was often said to be repugnant to the French constitution in his day. He was personally responsible only to the king, like all other ministers who took part in the royal councils and had independent access to him. Everything depended, therefore, on Turgot's retention of his king's confidence and the royal authority which alone could turn policy into law.

The tone and general bearing of Turgot's policies can in large measure be inferred from his earlier interests and intellectual formation. Louis XVI appears at first to have thought that he might have views too advanced to be respectable; while still hesitating over advice to appoint him minister, he remarked that Turgot was said to be closely linked to the 'encyclopaedists', the thinkers and writers who took their name from the great Encyclopaedia, which was the symbol of progressive thought in the later eighteenth century. Turgot shared many of the ideas of these men: he was to be the first French statesman who attempted to turn into policy the ideas of the first European *avant-garde* (a term not yet given an intellectual and cultural sense). Earlier ministers usually meant by reform essentially limited and practical concerns, such as the balancing of books, the encouragement of efficiency and the rooting-out of corruption and peculation. Turgot looked to do something more. He wished to bring about the general improvement of French society, to insert France into the flow of human progress with a decisive acceleration from which there would be no recession.

A new reign had itself generated hopes; at the news of Louis XV's death in 1774 someone had put a placard on the statue in Paris of Henry IV, the Bourbon whose memory traditionally enjoyed great popularity, bearing the word *resurrexit*. Though his views on policy were not known, the new king was young, well-intentioned and anxious to rule well. On the other hand, there was no evidence that he could do so. One observer cautiously judged him 'a child-king of twenty, in whom no one has yet seen any trace of a capacity for government'.

Under this master, Turgot opened his ministerial career with a number
of economies and minor fiscal reforms. There was always room for
economy when the personal and public expenses of the Crown were
hardly to be distinguished. People had spoken of a hoard of royal
treasure running to hundreds of millions, but at Louis xv's death it
turned out to be non-existent. Turgot set a good example by refusing
financial benefits which were customary in his office and brought a
new liberalism to its routine in some months of minor but useful
technical reform. He also projected reforms of the system by which the
taxes were farmed out to financiers, but like talk of economies in the
royal household (the most conspicuous centre of extravagance) they
came to naught. Unlike most Controllers-General, Turgot was not in
fact primarily interested in finance. What mattered to him, it soon
appeared, was the economy as a whole.

He faced the paradox that the French state and people were always
poor, yet France was a rich country. Somehow her wealth had to be
deployed so as to benefit the monarchy and the people. Turgot thought,
too, that this wealth should be increased; he was sure that if it were
other necessary benefits would follow.

The fundamental social fact of eighteenth-century France was that
population was growing just a little faster than food supply. In good
years this could be endured, for the margin was narrow; in bad years,
grain had to be imported to avoid famine. The trend brought a continuing rise in prices and a long, slow worsening of the lot of the poor.
They ate less, and they ate worse, as the century went on.

It was in the early nineteenth century that the epigram was coined
that 'Man is what he eats'. Most readers of this book probably eat
more than they need, but only very recent changes have made this
likely. Most people in the world today probably still feel that they could
do with more. This is as things have always been and as they were in
most of Europe at the end of the eighteenth century. It was obvious
in the starved faces of the beggars and vagrants who swarmed on the
roads of France and infested her cities, or in the foundlings abandoned
on the doorsteps of churches. In the countryside, though not so obvious
to the traveller, poverty was often even more biting. Hunger was the
universal social fact and when a harvest failed, it quickly became
famine. Then the hospitals and religious houses of the towns which
succoured the poor were besieged by emaciated crowds of country-
dwellers who had come to the only source of relief.

The horizons of the hungry are narrowed by the harsh definition
imposed by the need to get a living. Even if they were aware of them,
which they can only rarely have been, the comings and goings of
eighteenth-century statesmen and kings would have been irrelevant

to them except when they sought scapegoats. This should remind us that most of what happened is unwritten in most books of history; it is the story of countless unrecorded lives of people unaware of the great events of their national histories. Yet administrators never despaired of doing something for these millions and strove to do so for very good reasons of self-interest. Hunger was too important a fact of government not to be legislated about.

In eighteenth-century France, *subsistances* – food-supply – was a technical term of administration. Diet was much less varied than it is today, even for townsmen, and its most important constituent was bread – coarse, nourishing, filling stuff, in France by then sometimes made from wheat, but in many countries only from maize, rye or other grains. Only in a few places could this central dependence be supplemented by such foods as chestnuts or pulses. Bread prices, which depended on grain prices, were the best index of hard times. Buying bread took up something over half of a family's income in good times. The tiny disposable margin of the wage-earner's budget could thus be obliterated by even a small rise in the price of flour. This was why the control of the grain trade was properly reckoned by writers on government to be a part of that side of public affairs comprised under the French word *police*, another technical term of administration, comprising almost all the day-to-day executive action needed for the maintenance of good order. It was not charity which concerned them, but government.

A steady supply of grain at reasonable prices was not easy to maintain. Transport difficulties, tradition and legal arrangements fragmented France (like other countries) into many local markets. There were no national prices because there was no nationwide commerce in grain. The most important markets served large towns – of which the most important was Paris – by collecting and transferring to them the produce of a near-by agricultural region. Local administrations were concerned that there should be no disruption of supplies, and their concern locked the economy even more firmly to its fragmented foundations.

So inelastic a system could produce great inequalities and sudden movements of prices: bread could treble and quadruple in price in a matter of months. What made this worse was the encouragement the system gave to speculation. Market-rigging was always suspected when shortages occurred, with reason. In an economy lacking many other outlets for private investment, holding grain stocks for a rise in the market had been common since the seventeenth century, however it might be deplored. Government was supposed to prevent this and sometimes steps were taken to do so, but when it could be rumoured that even the king speculated in grain, such efforts can hardly be taken very seriously.

It is only a small exaggeration to say that when Turgot took office, he was obsessed with the grain trade. He saw its reform as a key which would make all other things possible. He had grappled with famine as an *intendant*. Already before that he had attentively followed the great intellectual debate which went on through the middle decades of the eighteenth century about the wisdom of removing restrictions on free trade in grain. He was convinced that consumer and producer alike – to say nothing of the economy as a whole – would benefit if the price mechanism of a free market were allowed to propel grain towards the place where it was needed at the time when the need was felt.

In September 1774 a royal edict had given expression in policy to these ideas. Its main provisions were directed against the regulations which had formerly entangled the actual operation of markets. Growers had not been allowed to sell their own corn, sales had been permitted only in public markets on market-day, the holding-back of grain from sale for more than a limited period had been forbidden, and individual buyers for consumption had been given priority over bakers and merchants. Such restraint and much more was swept away. The free movement of grain between markets was now not to be interfered with, with the exception of Paris, whose special provisioning arrangements were to be maintained, and the retention of controls on export. Though a step towards liberalization, this was by no means revolutionary. No doubt this explains some of the acclaim with which the decree was granted. It was not too alarming. Yet it was a triumph for the most up-to-date economic thinking of the day.

What followed had its source in one of the most powerful of all the social mechanisms of the *ancien régime*, bad harvests. Those of 1773 and 1774 had been disappointing. They assured that the new policy would be launched in a context of rising prices for which it is scarcely surprising that free trade came to be blamed. As usual, the outcome of hard times was violence.

There were riots and disturbances over rising prices in many towns in April 1775. But in some parts of northern France there appeared briefly a more impressive phenomenon, which won itself the name of the 'Flour War' (*guerre des farines*). It began on 27 April (nine days after Lexington) at a little town on the Oise, to the north-west of Paris. From there it spread through the traditional granary of the capital – the Ile-de-France, part of the Orléanais and Brie, and from there into the suburbs and eventually the centre of Paris itself as well as to the north-east. Its forms were always much the same. Trouble usually began on a market-day, with attacks on merchants or rich peasants who had grain to sell, and then spread by way of attacks on bakeries and flour-merchants' stores in the towns, on grain in transit by road or river and on the stocks of millers, peasants, landlords and even the clergy in the countryside. The aim of these movements was not, as might be expected, loot. Such cases of outright pillage as occurred seem exceptional. What usually happened was that those who had grain, flour or bread were forced to bring it out and sell it at what was felt to be a just price. This was always somewhat lower than current market-prices in conditions of free sale. It was a popular form of price control in an inflationary situation, appealing to people because it embodied a balm for their consciences in the idea that the owner of the property thus distributed was not being robbed but only being made to conform to what the community regarded as a just price. Some people even seem to have believed rumours that these operations were being carried out by royal command.

Nothing could have been less true. When the disturbances spread to Versailles – the royal doorstep, so to speak – a well-meaning young nobleman who was governor of the town tried to handle the situation by imposing price-controls himself. He was promptly disavowed by the government. There was a dramatic scene at the palace itself, where the young king could not make himself heard as he strove to pacify a huge crowd which had invaded his courtyard. Turgot was not con- ciliatory and the government decided to support him by force if necessary; it assembled the soldiers needed to meet any emergency. Yet after a climax on 3 May, when something like a thousand bakers' shops were sacked, there was no further important trouble at Paris. Within ten days the movement, though it had spread very far, had fizzled out elsewhere, too. Local authorities who had acquiesced in its demands when their backs were to the wall were rebuked or even punished; imprisonment in the *Bastille* for a few months was a powerful reminder of what was expected of officials. Guards were mounted at bakers' shops and markets in Paris until October (the official responsible for police there had resigned during the crisis, being unhappy about the policy of repression) and there were even two people hanged from among some hundreds arrested. In the autumn, prices began to come down; the harvest had been plentiful and the guards were withdrawn as the danger subsided.

There is every sign that Turgot and those who admired him mis- read the meaning of this upheaval. Voltaire produced a pamphlet denouncing the priests who, he said, had incited the mobs. This is nonsense. There were a few country clergy among those arrested, it is true, but understandably so, for they could not be indifferent to a plight they often shared with their parishioners and they were as deeply attached to traditional views of the social control of the economy as their flock. What was happening was that the people – by no means only the poorest – were acting spontaneously in defence of traditional practice and ideas. They had an idea of what was a reasonable and just way to carry on economic life, a 'moral economy', as an English scholar has called it in a different context. This was something which would have been widely understood beyond the borders of France. Most German towns in the eighteenth century, for example, forbade the hoarding of grain. Englishmen still remembered old laws against 'forestalling' and on many occasions rioted violently against prices felt to be unfair and seized stocks as did the French in the 'flour war'. In an age still religious, men could find a guide in the pages of scripture: 'He that withholdeth Corn', said the book of Proverbs (xi, 26), 'the People shall curse him.' The flour war reveals a whole universe of assumptions embedded in the economy of the *ancien régime*, as well as the material situation of Frenchmen at a particular moment.

None the less, Turgot and his supporters among the 'enlightened' continued to believe that his policies had suffered an attempted sabotage by agitators who had whipped up crowds with the aim of disrupting the food supply of Paris and so producing a great disturbance there to overthrow the ministry. The government took up this comforting explanation, held to its free trade policy and turned the best engine of public relations it had to use by ordering the parish clergy of France to preach in support of free trade. Divine authority as well as deductive logic was marshalled in the support of economic theory.

It did not at first seem that Turgot's position was weakened. The free trade policy had been successfully maintained. The minister had stood firm when others had flinched, and this was impressive. His support among his colleagues was believed to have been reinforced. Yet there was a measure of illusion in such an analysis. The politics of *anciens régimes* were above all court politics: they were personal, since the ultimate mechanism which had to be set in motion was the king's will. The composition and views of his entourage were therefore of the first importance. In that of Louis XVI there had always been opponents of Turgot, or sympathizers with those whom he kept from office. After the *guerre de farines* they had a new argument in the danger of alienating the sympathy of the people from the monarchy. Young rulers were likely to appreciate this danger. Marie Antoinette, the Austrian-born queen, certainly felt it and spoke of it, and she had other grievances against Turgot, too, over failures to obtain appointments for favourites and over the wish of the Controller to reduce expenses at court – a wish rendered no more palatable to a princess whose own mother found her over-frivolous and flighty by the somewhat moralizing tone in which he phrased such aims. It would have mattered less what the queen thought had her views remained unknown, but this was impossible in the intense and gossipy atmosphere of the court. Once it was known that she disapproved of him, it became inevitable that others would cease to second him or support him loyally.

Whatever praise is due to Turgot's statesmanlike vision, it is impossible to credit him with great political sagacity. A more prudent man would not at this juncture have added to his enemies by asking for toleration for Protestants and thus raising clerical animosity against him. He seems none the less to have tried to go ahead with prudence in his next and final great step, the introduction of a programme of six reform edicts. Four of them concerned minor matters; two were much more far-reaching. One abolished the guilds which regulated the commerce and manufactures of Paris. These were corporations controlling entry to trades and protecting their members by restrictive practices and the measure was not only a step towards the liberation of the economy for the operation of market forces like the freeing of the grain trade, but an attack on legal privilege. The second important edict abolished the system by which public works were financed, the royal *corvées*, or rights to exact forced labour, usually commuted by those who owed this service to a money payment of a tax like any other. They were replaced by a tax upon landowners.

Turgot improved the occasion – and it is perhaps characteristic of his political lack of touch – by including in the preamble to the edict on the *corvées* a general condemnation of privilege. It may have been this which prompted the *Parlement* of Paris to refuse to register the edict, which stopped it coming into effect. The magistrates went further, and began to allege that in the ministerial plans was concealed a whole system of subversion of the traditional order – a notion of which much more was to be heard and which had already made its appearance in an earlier row with a reforming minister. In so far as 'plotting' was involved, there was nothing in this; in so far as Turgot stood for the ideas of a new age, on the other hand, there was something to it.

As in the flour war, Turgot won the battle, though he was to lose the war. On 12 March 1776, the king enforced the registration of the six edicts by the *Parlement* of Paris. Yet exactly two months later, Turgot was dismissed. The king had been unable to resist the pressure on him. It did not help that Turgot's financial policies had been very successful, that credit had revived and the deficit had been reduced, for his enemies had a possible replacement, the Swiss financier Necker, waiting in the wings to demonstrate his financial wizardry. In the end, the personal politics of the French monarchy proved fatal to the great reformer.

Turgot was not to be the last of Louis XVI's ministers abandoned by the monarch he sought to serve. Ironically, only shortly before his dismissal, Turgot warned his master that weakness had led to the fall of another king – Charles I of England. A parallel between his fate and that of Louis was later to be drawn in more tragic circumstances. In the setting of the court a more supple minister than Turgot and a more independent and self-confident king than Louis XVI were needed if the animosities stirred up by even moderate retrenchment and economy were to be overcome. It had been pointed out that the expenses of the civil side of the royal household of France alone absorbed a greater revenue than the king of Prussia enjoyed from all his lands at his accession. There was a formidable vested interest here.

But more than this was involved. Turgot was a modern man in a society not ready for him. Behind the specific measures with which he is associated, there is a vision of a new sort of world, where economic law and the reasonableness of men would operate untrammelled by institutions which had outlived their purpose and merely cloaked private interest. France in the 1770s was not ready for the changes this implied. Neither peasant, nor guildsman, nor magistrate nor courtier could separate themselves from the assumptions of their day. In the context of little economic elasticity and a highly personalized politics they could resist successfully. Turgot's failure showed that French society was too weighed down by inertia, prejudice and vested interest for fundamental improvement until a far worse crisis occurred.

After Turgot's fall his work was destroyed. The *corvées* were reimposed, free trade in grain was ended and the guilds of Paris were revived. But nothing was done to break the power of a vice in which France was increasingly squeezed as the years went by, whose two sides were population and food-supply. Further hard times were to follow and would provoke another attempt to overhaul the whole régime and set it on a new course – the last one, as it turned out. By then there would be a disastrous worsening of the financial situation, too. Turgot had urged that the monarchy should not engage in the American war, fearing both the cost and the international complications which would follow. Two years after his fall, the French alliance with the Americans opened the way to the piling up of state debts to unmanageable levels and the final breakdown of the *ancien régime*.

By then, the route to a modernized society such as Turgot dreamed of had been prescribed with astonishing intellectual authority in a book which, more than any other, gave the progressive thought of the next half-century a point of departure. 1776 was something of a vintage year for the British intellect. It brought the publication of the first volume of Gibbon's great history and of Bentham's scathing reply to Blackstone, *The Fragment on Government*. Yet neither of these books had been awaited with such excitement as *The Wealth of Nations* by Adam Smith, a Scotch professor already well-known for his writings and lecturing on moral philosophy. His book went into five editions in his own lifetime. It was to be complimented in the House of Commons by the Prime Minister. It made its mark almost at once among a wide public, something which owed much to the lucidity and ease with which Adam Smith took his readers through economic theory; he had an expository skill which amounted to genius. Though it was soon attacked, and young economists have ever since cut their teeth by pointing out its fundamental ambiguities and inadequacies, it is not too much to say that *The Wealth of Nations* founded the science of economics. But it did more than that, for it crystallized the social outlook of a civilization and gave definitive expression to some of its master-ideas. *The Wealth of Nations* is one of the great sources of liberalism and its only literary masterpiece after Hobbes.

Though they are by no means always original, the book abounds in striking ideas. Often, they are embodied in good phrases, too. The 'invisible hand' became a cliché, and Smith anticipated Napoleon with 'a nation of shopkeepers'. But the greatness of the book lies less in the penetration of its individual ideas than in the plausibility of the whole to which they contributed. It is as a great synthesis, the first in its field, that *The Wealth of Nations* defined a field of study, the whole society of man in its economic aspect. 'Political Oeconomy' existed before Smith wrote, but he first gave it a classical context; he left a new subject behind him. This was in a sense a by-product; *The Wealth of Nations* was meant to be a tract for the times, a denunciation of abuses. Yet this denunciation rested upon general statements about the regularities observable in a vast range of subject-matter. This combination of empirical and deductive methods was to remain a characteristic of the science as Adam Smith left it.

The Wealth of Nations rested upon two postulates and a paradox. Adam Smith took it for granted first that men were roughly equal in capacity and uniform in psychology and second that their economic relationships could form a harmonious and ordered whole (an idea he took from French thinkers). The paradox was that this harmony was to be best realized by the disregarding of collective economic goals and the single-hearted pursuit by individual men of their selfish ends.

The idea of an underlying harmony in society and that it might be comprehensible was not, of course, new. Yet such a notion had hitherto usually been the concern of philosophers or theologians: with Adam Smith it became the basis of the thinking of practical men. In an earlier moral treatise he had invoked a beneficent deity as the ground of the essential harmonies of the uncontaminated social order; in *The Wealth of Nations*, the agency of God is muted, and the reader is presented with the idea that the equilibrium to which economic forces tend is natural. They move with something of the majesty of the Newtonian planets to a God-given end. Even if the harmony was not likely to be perfect, thought Smith, it was nevertheless general and only slight interferences were required to assure its continuation or to assure the achievement of ends which lay outside this system. There emerges in the end from Smith the beneficent and optimistic assumption that economic life is not just a matter of squabbling over the division of a cake of limited size and that a general interest is not only conceivable but demonstrable. This general interest lay in the increase of wealth to which the natural harmony tended: hence the full title of his book, *An Inquiry into the Nature and Causes of the Wealth of Nations.*

Wealth required co-operation. But the practical way to it lay through competition. 'Man has almost constant occasion for the help of his brethren,' said Smith. 'It is in vain for him to expect it from their benevolence only. ... It is not from the benevolence of the butcher, the brewer or the baker that we expect our dinner, but from their regard for their own interest.' The containment of personal greed in economic life had often been attempted, sometimes in the name of Christian charity, sometimes in the name of the good of the community or of part of it. This was the aim of the traditional 'moral economy' in every country. Smith implied that it was folly. The operation of untrammelled competition which traditional and popular moralists deplored was, he sought to demonstrate, just the agency which did most to produce the economic equilibrium which made possible the growth of wealth. Antagonism thus became productive. Master was fundamentally opposed to man over wages, merchants, traders and apprentices strove to hamstring the consumer with restrictive practices, and high profits were bound to be at the expense of the customer. Yet, said Smith, the individual's pursuit of gain would serve society as a whole. 'The natural effort of every individual to better his own condition, when suffered to exert itself with freedom and security, is so powerful a principle that it is alone, and without any assistance ... capable of carrying on the society to wealth and prosperity.'

This was the voice of a new age of social thought. Smith's demonstration that the best spur to improvements of method and economics of working was individual ambition was a revolutionary upturning of priorities which were accepted over most of Europe in his day. A year before he published, a royal official in France, grappling with the rumpus of the *guerre de farines* had worriedly asked whether it would not turn out that the government's unlimited protection for the producer of grain who wanted to sell at the best price was not a kind of moral authorization of greed? This exposes assumptions diametrically opposed to those expressed in Smith's comment about the butcher, the baker and the brewer.

Although it is the doctrine with which Adam Smith's name was always to be linked, he did not invent the phrase *laissez-faire* – leave things alone – nor was he the first person to think that, in default of specific grounds for the contrary, economic life should be free from interference by government. Moreover he saw that it was not only governments which might distort the natural flow of economic life and he hedged his warnings about with qualifications. He was not the dogmatic doctrinaire some later depicted. What he did was to provide a more massive and thorough application of the principle of non-intervention than any of his predecessors. Although a current towards freer trade was already flowing before he wrote (as Turgot showed), Adam Smith gave a more comprehensive account of economic life and a more radical application of economic liberalism than it had ever had before. He implanted on the received economic doctrine of the day the conviction that to interfere with the self-adjusting economic equilibrium to which the market tended would produce not merely inefficiency (that is, less wealth) but also inequality of effort and, therefore, injustice. If his thinking liberated economics from one set moral presupposition, that is to say, it tied it no less decisively to certain others.

The background against which he wrote was practical rather than theoretical and it was the practice of interference with the economy followed by every government of his age. It had contributed to the outbreak of the colonial rebellion in America and its application by the monarchies of Europe did not always suggest that it could promote economic growth. But direct government policy was not the only artificial restraint upon the economy which Smith identified. There were other institutions, sanctioned by law and therefore lifted above the healthy operation of the market, such as the chartered companies whose privileges amounted to the removal of competition, apprentice-ship which distorted labour-supply by preventing it from commanding its natural price, entails settlements, and the practice of primo-geniture, which made impossible a proper market in land, endowments which protected schools and universities from the need to satisfy public demand in education, the monopoly power of rapacious professions such as the doctors, and many more. Even informal associations were dangerous, for 'people of the same trade seldom meet together, even for merriment or diversion, but the conversation ends in a conspiracy against the public, or some contrivance to raise prices.' Today Smith's targets would be such bodies as Trades Unions or the American Medical Association as well as governments.

In advocating the removal of all restraints on competition which could not specifically be justified by some non-economic value, Smith was, of course, accepting some premises that were questionable, some illegitimate. An optimistic view of human nature gave him a comforting belief that all men were basically equal in the ability to compete. When a man found his right economic role, Smith thought he would be as able to succeed in it as any other man in his. He could recognize the real differences in bargaining power between masters and men, without recognizing that there might be also more fundamental inequalities which would distort his perfect market even when the distortions were not sanctified by law. Yet the institutionalized distortions of the market preoccupied him. They got in the way of the great engine of progress and indeed of the social good, the production of wealth. In the priority which he gave to this Adam Smith was a great intellectual innovator. He was the initiator of the worship of growth.

Smith's most influential contemporaries and predecessors were preoccupied with a measure of wealth, money, which he thought inadequate. Smith transferred the emphasis to goods. The production of goods for consumption constituted income, and in that income, and not in treasure, lay a country's wealth. The same was true of the individual. It was not in gold under his bed that a man was rich, but in his power to buy goods for his consumption and enjoyment. 'Consumption is the sole end and purpose of all production,' Smith had said. This was the beginning of what Karl Marx, a later economic thinker of comparable stature, was to term the 'fetish of commodities'.

Scepticism about growth is now fashionable but Smith's doctrine was liberating in its day. On it was built the productive effort which means that our own notion of a fitting standard of life is further removed from that of Smith's day than was his from that of Henry viii's. He did not confine the benefits he saw to the better-off. 'No society', he said, 'can surely be flourishing and happy, of which the far greater part of the members are poor and miserable,' and he was possibly the first man to insist that high wages might mean high productivity. In the last lay the possibility of a greater diffusion of well-being and in that lay much more, for in wealth lay the road to civilization, and through civilization could be sought justice. Here Smith's economics joined hands with his moral views. From this was to flow the liberal conviction of the next century that more was involved in the liberal economy than materialism. Men came in the end to feel that free trade was an almost religious cause because it could promote – or its absence could hinder – the coming of a better moral order.

Another doctrine with a considerable future was to be found in Smith's view of the role of labour in the production of wealth. There had already been hints in Locke, but the *Wealth of Nations* is explicit: real wealth, said Smith, consisted of 'the annual produce of the land and labour of society'. 'The annual labour of every nation is the fund which originally supplies it with all the necessaries and conveniences of life which it annually consumes, and which consist always either in the immediate produce of that labour, or in what is purchased with that labour from other nations.' The measurement of value was a matter of the time, hardship and ingenuity which were the components of labour, arrived at 'by the higglings and bargaining of the market, according to that rough sort of equality which, though not exact, is sufficient for carrying on the basis of common life'. 'The real price of everything . . . is the toil and trouble of acquiring it.' On the labour theory of value was to be erected a denunciation of the exploitation of labour by capital, but the kernel of the idea of exploitation had been already stated by Smith: 'The property which every man has in his own labour, as it is the original foundation of all other property, so it is the most sacred and inviolable.'

No great thinker has his thought conveyed to later generations so exactly as he would have wished. To interpret is to change, and Smith's teaching soon came sometimes to stand for a doctrine whose unqualified dogmatism he would have disliked. This was less the work of professional economists who consciously modified Smith's views when they believed them mistaken than of those who vulgarized and popularized the ideas of *laissez-faire*, and by no means all the channels by which this happened are known to us. The result, nevertheless, was that by the middle of the nineteenth century the prevailing social philosophy in England, industrially the most advanced country in the world, was one which believed it owed its wealth and civilization to non-interference with the economy and unbridled individual competition. Even if he had formally abandoned a belief in God, the liberal behaved at least as if the self-equilibrating market was God-given: this was the heart of the *bourgeois* world outlook. But it shared also Smith's deep conviction of the equivalence of progress in commerce and in civilization. Wealth was visible evidence of a superiority that was moral as well as material. If competition increased prosperity, it therefore had a cosmic significance. Freedom from interference with the economy became the overriding good because it could make possible all other goods. Smith's ideas, crudely distorted though they sometimes were, thus lay at the heart of the whole ideology of what only later came to be called liberalism.

The coincidence of the man and the epoch still seems extraordinary.

Industrialization had barely begun in England when Smith wrote – he does not mention steam – yet the analysis of society and the economy which he set out proved better fitted to the society which emerged in the early nineteenth century than did any alternative, whether for explanatory or normative purposes. The bad effects of this were easy enough to discern and have been frequently denounced. Of course it was a pity that the authority of so great a thinker should have been used as a cloak for cupidity, and that his dislike of restrictions which did not operate to the common benefit should have been used to demolish restraints on individual gain at the expense of the community. Such things should be noted, but they do not obliterate the huge creative importance of Smith's ideas, whose impact reverberated far beyond the economy. *The Wealth of Nations* was the book of a new age. Like the Declaration of Independence, it remains a landmark in the history of thought. In it can be found the lineaments of a new civilization, the liberal world glimpsed by Turgot. Yet 'liberal' and 'liberalism' did not exist as words with an ideological content in 1776.

2 The Western World

The revolution in America, the failure of reform in the most important of European monarchies and the publication of a book which laid out the social philosophy of a coming age are useful vantage points from which to take bearings on the next seventy or so years. They imply or hint at much of what is to come. Before exploring that future, though, a boundary has to be drawn around the subject other than the one provided by dates. The Western World is that part of the globe where the dominant pattern of civilization is of European origin. This is not a static entity. In the eighteenth century the countries of which it was composed were all grouped about the Atlantic Ocean or formed part of the hinterland of those that were. Between 1775 and 1847, the boundaries around them were greatly enlarged. In South America, the first part of the world to which European institutions had been transplanted since the crusading era, this was less obvious than else-where. With the exception of the relatively small areas of British, Dutch and French Guyana, the mainland had long been divided between the Portuguese and the Spanish. There was a huge unexplored region in the Amazon basin, the Brazilian Matto Grosso, and another south of the River Plate. By 1847, Spanish and Portuguese governments had gone and the whole continent was divided (still except for the Guyanas) into independent sovereign states, but the reality which lay behind this political map was still that of seventy years before: a thin and scattered population, mainly grouped in the towns of the colonial era and lacking the means to make an effective penetration of a huge and unexplored hinterland until the arrival of steamboat, railway and telegraph.

In North America a much greater change could be measured both cartographically and demographically. In 1775, the subjects of the British Crown were almost entirely confined to the thirteen colonies east of the Alleghanies, the valley of the St Lawrence and a few places on the shores of the Great Lakes. There were a few French settlements on the Mississippi and, further west, in a huge area which stretched as far as the Pacific, a scatter of Spanish missions and trading-posts. In 1784, the Russians set up their first post in Alaska. As in South America, assertions of sovereignty had an element of the fictitious about them in the northern continent. Not enough was actually known about its geographical shape to be sure exactly what was being claimed.

By 1847 there was a huge change in the North American map. Though much of the continent was still unknown and unexplored, the Canadian north, especially, being *terra incognita*, the outlines of continental geography and the major political claims were clearly defined. In the previous year, it had been settled that the boundary of the United States and Canada should run west from the Lake of the Woods along the forty-ninth parallel to the sea. The Russians had pushed further south in Alaska, though in 1841 they had sold to an American company the fort they had built thirty years earlier just north of San Francisco and soon after abandoned their Californian claims. In the south-west Mexican and United States claims had still to be settled in 1847, but by then the political geography of North America had taken what was almost its modern shape.

As in South America, such changes on the map did not adequately represent social and administrative reality and hardly define the boundaries of civilization. In 1847, some of the territory east of the Mississippi still did not enjoy statehood and there were only five states of the Union west of the river. Most of the continent was organized only on paper. It was almost empty, occupied only by a few Indians and the occasional hunter and trapper. Yet between the Mississippi and the Alleghanies a huge transformation had occurred since 1775. In 1850, the census revealed that Ohio was the third largest state in the Union, with nearly two million inhabitants out of a total of twenty-three millions or so. More than half the population (about thirteen millions) still lived in the old colonies and the later Atlantic states, but nearly eight millions lived on the other side of the mountains in the valleys of the Ohio, Tennessee, Wabash and Illinois, and the regions south of the Great Lakes, where in 1789 there had been perhaps a hundred thousand in all – about one-fortieth of the whole population that year. Just under two millions lived in the country west of the Mississippi, only about a hundred thousand of them on the Pacific coast. These figures reflected a huge displacement of the centre of gravity of the United States and a shift in the frontier of settlement of the Caucasian stocks which were by 1847 also spreading, though on a much smaller scale, into South Africa and Australasia.

Changes on the southern and eastern frontiers of the Western World between 1775 and 1847 were also considerable, but harder to pin down exactly. There were a number of blurred areas. The Islamic world continued to be the only great tradition of civilization with which Europe was directly and continuously in contact and it stretched from the Straits of Gibraltar along the African coast to the Ottoman frontier in central Europe and southern Russia. The status of some areas in this long zone of contact poses problems of definition. When France seized Algiers in 1830, for example, it was the beginning of a century of European settlement and economic influence in North Africa which would leave a profound cultural and political impact on its coastal fringe, where European cities would rise. Yet for all the revolutionary impact of the market economy and western ideas, Algeria would survive as a fundamentally Islamic society, in spite of its 'westerniza- tion' at certain levels. A different problem arises in Egypt, where the Greek pasha from Salonika, Mehemet Ali, strove in the early nineteenth century to create a modern – that is to say, westernized – state with the aid of technicians, manuals and educators imported from Europe. He was successful, to the extent that Egypt was effectively recognized as an independent nation by the Ottomans in 1833, a high watermark, for in 1841 the Turks recovered much of what they had lost, and Mehemet Ali was confined to Egypt as a hereditary possession. He had nevertheless brought about a revolutionary change, creating a society in Egypt tied more closely to the West than any other in the Islamic world except Lebanon.

Other difficulties arise in south-east Europe and the Balkans. Two new nations, Serbia and Greece, emerged from Turkish rule, and some European powers made important gains at the expense of the Ottoman Empire. The new nations quickly adopted some of the trappings of westernization, Greece more successfully than Serbia, and the new territories of the Austrian and Russian empires were, of course, submitted to their administrative systems. How much this actually changed the life of the people on the spot is debatable. Many of them were formally Christian, but they belonged for the most part to the Eastern Orthodox Church. They had been able to maintain their religious and therefore cultural distinction under Ottoman rule. They often remained as barbaric and remote from what was taken to be civilized life in western Europe or North America as they had done for centuries under Turkish domination.

To the east and north of Europe's Islamic marches lay Russia. With qualifications, she was clearly a part of the Western World and more so, perhaps, in 1775 than in 1847. Like the oceanic nations of western Europe, she had been expanding for centuries and this makes it very difficult to say where we should think the Western World finally peters out on the map. The boundaries of Islam, represented by the two weak empires of Ottoman Turkey and Persia, lay on the far side of the cultural frontier (and their condition was a powerful force drawing Russian power forward) but there is a huge ill-defined area to consider before they are reached. A decisive phase had begun in 1783, when, after a drive lasting nearly a century, with earlier brief successes, Russia was firmly established on the Black Sea. Further advances carried the Russian frontier in the south-west to the River Pruth before 1847. At the other end of the Black Sea, Georgia, much of Armenia and Daghestan were annexed, too. Further east, Russian towns had already been founded across the Urals in the sixteenth century; in the next they existed on the coast of the Sea of Okhotsk, another five thousand miles to the east. Russian trade to Irkutsk, on Lake Baikal, at the doors of Mongolia, followed a route about four thousand miles long, most of it by river. Seven different ones had to be navigated by Moscow merchants seeking tea, tobacco, drugs and luxuries from China. Along the route was a thin chain of trading-posts and small towns. There were some convict settlements, too. But beyond them stretched regions only to be likened to parts of the American and Canadian west and north-west, endless tracts of forests, tundra and desert, unoccupied by men except for a few savage tribes and entered only by hunters and the occasional merchant. Siberia was not really to be opened by better communications or settled in great numbers until the twentieth century. Nevertheless, the East was of growing interest and importance to the government in St Petersburg. A governor-general of eastern Siberia was in fact first appointed exactly in 1847 because of concern that events in China threatened a decline in Russia's capacity to protect her interests in the Far East.

The tiny settlements of Russians in North America do not really bear upon the problem of outlining the 'Western World', but one other area where delimitation presents a problem was also one which involved Russia, that of central Asia. In this huge area, a police threat was presented to settlement and trade by nomadic native peoples. The clash of interests with other powers such as occurred with Turkey and Persia here still lay in the future. Russian power did not extend even to the Aral Sea by 1847 and was then grappling with the problems of ruling Moslem peoples such as the Bashkirs with a minimum of expense and a fragmentary administrative structure. In Caucasia and Transcaucasia conditions were a little less primitive. There were survivals of Christian cultures with centuries of history behind them and a brief occupation of the southern shores of the Caspian had taken place as early as the 1720s, though followed by withdrawal.

The rest of the globe still presented fairly clearly defined areas which were clearly not a part of the communities of Western civilizations. Africa was still a very dark continent, and decrepit though they might be, the great traditions of Arabic Islam, of Persia, India, China, Japan and the world of South-East Asia were clearly distinct from the Western World, though some of them were already incorporated by force or economics into the global system it dominated. The most important of these was India, almost all of which came under British rule in these years, a fact of huge importance for world history as well as for Western.

The one great area where it is inappropriate to speak of a delimiting of Western influence was the Pacific. Right at the start of this era, Captain Cook's third and last of his great voyages of exploration opened forty years in which the Pacific was finally mapped and, because of the absence of powerful indigenous states and cultures, was incorporated in the Western system as mainland Asia and Africa never were. In part this was a matter of trade and economic exploitation, but it was in part also a repeat performance of what Europeans had done in America, for by 1847 Australia and New Zealand were both firmly planted with European stocks. The native peoples sometimes suffered – as they did in Australia – in ways in which other peoples had suffered earlier from contact with Europe in the Americas. Others among them hung on to their independence, but were increasingly under pressure, as were the peoples of what Cook called the Sandwich islands and a later generation Hawaii.

The globe was thus tied together by a growing Western dominance which took many forms. That of knowledge of its surface was the foundation. On this rested political rule, the subtler authority conveyed by superior power and a growing network of commerce. All of them churned up peoples and mixed their affairs more and more together in a process irreversible by 1847. This was not wholly sinister; by that date there were already Asians anxious to take from the Western World the cultural advantages it seemed to possess. Nor was it a process incapable of humanization; though slavery still existed in the Western World in 1847, the Atlantic slave trade so important to Western commerce for two and a half centuries was outlawed by then and this was done because of economic and moral forces within the Western World, not under pressure from the outside.

The anti-slavery movement had originated in Europe which, though no longer itself the whole Western World, as it had once been, was still in 1847 its centre of gravity. Considered as a source of civilization, one great division within Europe was then almost as remarkable as it is today, that between East and West. Its origins lay deep in the past, even before Europe existed. The first great frontier of its civilization had been the *limes* of the Roman Empire; beyond it lay the paganism and barbarism of primitive northern and eastern Europe. A racial distinction added new contrasts when the Slav peoples successfully established themselves and spread over eastern Europe during and after the big displacements of the Teutonic peoples towards the West. The Slavs, of whom the greatest branch was the Russian people, forged a distinctive destiny in a long struggle to survive Teutonic pressure from the West and Asian onslaught from the East. They were different from the former not only in race but in religion. They were Christian, but belonged to the Eastern Church, not that of Rome which so profoundly marked the West. Another historical experience which marked off some of the East was Ottoman conquest and its later slow retreat. Still another was isolation, or near-isolation, from the oceanic forces which transformed economies and societies in the West in the sixteenth and seventeenth centuries and re-oriented the destinies of Western nations across the seas. The difference in historical phase between two Europes was already visible by the eighteenth century; in the West could be seen the crumbling of the medieval rural order of feudal society, the growth of towns, a new cultural and religious pluralism, the coming of organized science, while the huge spaces of the East were characterized by the growing imposition of serfdom, the absence of cities and cultural differentiation and a lack of intellectual speculation. The landlord looked out from his estate – sometimes one of vast size – upon a society barren of much that was taken for granted in France, Italy or the Netherlands – let alone Great Britain or North America – in 1775. Sometimes he knew what he lacked and sought to import it. In 1847, the view was little changed and the contrast with the West was all the more violent, for there had played much more decisively upon the West than upon the East the forces of revolution and improvement. The political boundaries reached by the armies of the French Revolution redefined the two zones of sociability, and the economic changes of industrialization and the coming of a market society produced even more rapid changes to push them apart.

The Europe which looked out on the rest of the world, assessed its reactions to it and set about exploiting it had been that of the Western nations. Russia was the only great state in the East and she took virtually no part in the great expansion of European influence in the eighteenth and nineteenth centuries except by advancing her own land frontiers along traditional lines. In the exploration, commerce, colonizing and missionary work which were the conduits of European influence to the rest of the world, she played virtually no part.

No doubt because of this, nothing like the importance that was attached in the West to the consideration of Europe's relations with other parts of the globe was to be seen in Russia. In the eighteenth century, an important psychological moment in European culture was passed, probably before 1775. This was the movement at which wonder and admiration for the achievements of other civilizations, those of Asia in particular, gave way to a confident assurance that Europe – and therefore the Western World – knew better. An important symptom was the way in which the worship of things Chinese which characterized much of the eighteenth century gave way in the next to contempt and arrogance towards China's backwardness. The attitude was new in 1775 but had deep origins. Perhaps there was always at the back of the European mind the unconscious inheritance and example of Christianity, the awareness of possession of a truth which should be spread (and the eighteenth century began the greatest age of missionary enterprise since the first centuries of Christianity). To technical achievement there was added the arrogance of material pride. 'The accommodation of a European prince,' remarked Adam Smith, 'does not always so much exceed that of an industrious and frugal peasant, as the accommodation of the latter exceeds that of many an African king, the absolute master of the lives and liberties of ten thousand naked savages.' The observation may be thought complacent, but hardly unjust. It is interesting, too, that it linked material well-being with moral superiority, for in the reference to absolute power lay disapproval for a despotism which was increasingly associated with the backward, primitive and unprogressive. For all the material advantage they enjoyed in dealing with other traditions, the greatest advantage of men of the Western World lay in their mental attitude, a confidence in their superiority, moral and intellectual. It was to excuse and mask much brutality, but for both good and ill it was in the end to transform the globe so that a 'Western World' in the sense of this book became worldwide. But that was long after 1847, when the peoples of the Western World were still approaching the peak of their sense of their own distinctiveness.

Book II

Ancien Régime:
Ideals and Realities

3 Going concerns

The great majority of the inhabitants of the Western World lived in 1775 in continental Europe. Just as Molière's Monsieur Jourdain had been speaking prose all his life without knowing it, so most people in the Western World lived under the *ancien régime* without being aware of it. There is no easy way of translating into English the sense of this French phrase. The 'old set-up' is too colloquial not to be misleading, and 'the way things used to be' is too clumsy. For the most part, therefore, writers in English (and in other languages) have found it convenient to use the French; it has become a part of other languages, a fact which is worth a moment's consideration.

When the phrase was first used, Frenchmen meant by it only something like 'under the last king', or 'under the old management'. This indicates an important point at the outset: people were never conscious of living under the *ancien régime* while they did so, because the phrase always referred to the past and distinguished it from what came next. An *ancien régime* can be seen only in retrospect; at the time, it is experienced but can hardly be recognized or noticed.

At one moment in French history, the phrase changed its meaning. It came to stand not just for the past, for what had happened in a vague, temporal way, but for a complete society which could now be seen to have existed in the past and was felt to do so no longer. It came, in short, to stand for a whole order of things, that which had existed before the great French Revolution of the end of the eighteenth century. This change in usage was caused by that revolution. When we find the phrase being used in a letter by the Queen of France in 1792, its bearing is still much the traditional one; it still means only 'the previous state of affairs'. In the next twenty years, this was to change. The Revolution came to be seen as having so transformed France that when men looked at the institutions under which they had lived before it, they felt they could see them as a whole. It became a phrase connoting not merely a past time but, above all, social institutions and principles and (as we have said) a generous measure of moral approval or condemnation of them. The *Ancien Régime* (capitals were common by 1815) pilloried by the revolutionaries was static, irrational, immoral in principle and corrupt in practice, perversely pitting itself against the dynamic force of beneficial change. Conversely, their opponents saw it as moral and practical order, the natural structures of society and the family, the authority of history and tradition, refinement and civilization.

Both usages were in principle sound. Societies are wholes, not aggregates. The phrase was soon applied to countries other than France, though the things it connoted were not everywhere the same. Some countries exemplified them much more cleverly than others. The idea of an *ancien régime* must not be used too rigidly, but it draws attention to social, political and ideological principles taken for granted pretty generally in continental Europe in the eighteenth century. Societies very different from one another can none the less share assumptions which characterize an epoch or a civilization.

What would be taken for granted by most continental Europeans in the eighteenth century and, to some extent, by Englishmen and English settlers abroad, would be assumptions which can be sketched briefly in such propositions as these: God made the world and gave it a moral and social structure; His revelation in Jesus Christ imposes a duty upon society to protect the Church, Christian truth and moral principles in a positive way by promoting sound behaviour and belief and harrying bad; Christianity teaches that the existing structure of society is in principle good and should be upheld; this structure is organized hierarchically and for the most part its hierarchies are hereditary, their apex usually being found in a monarch; privileges and duties are distributed in a manner which can be justified by reference to this hierarchy. It is also true (our list of assumptions could continue) that while the organization of society around hereditary units was a fundamental datum of society under the *ancien régime*, it took for granted respect for other groups in which men came together for religious, professional, economic or social purposes; corporations with these ends were thought the proper regulators of much of daily life – the practice of trade or the enjoyment of legal rights, for example – and the interests of individuals belonging to them came emphatically second to those of these legal persons. Many of these corporations were very local in their effectiveness and recruitment, but they were none the less important; they were not to be overridden lightly by the state, since the state was itself an agglomeration of corporations in equilibrium. The local nature of the concern they usually reflected was in a way a recognition of the hindrances to central power in an age when transport was rudimentary and the techniques of social control at the disposal of government very weak.

It was also then assumed that much more of personal behaviour should be regulated by law and traditional practice than today. A man's rights to his own might be very safe from legal interference, but this did not mean he could do what he liked with his own. Thus there was something of a paradox to be observed: governments were supposed to be restrained in ways which would now seem strange, while much more interference with a man's private affairs than is now thought tolerable was taken for granted.

Social restraint reflected the pervasive anti-individualism of the *ancien régime*. Moreover, moral and ideological truth were thought indivisible and this left little room in theory for the vagaries of the individual. In spite of the fragmented appearance given to society by the corporate principle, there was no pluralism in its values, unless it had been grudgingly accepted at some time in the past as the price which had to be paid for the survival of society at all in face of the challenge of religious division. In such a case, religious minorities might be hemmed in with legal restrictions but defined as corporations which, for particular purposes, enjoyed narrow rights in the regulations of their own affairs.

Across all these assumptions ran an overriding mental conservatism. One of the deepest differences between our own age and the *ancien régime* is the pervading conviction of those times that it was innovation which needed to be justified, not the past. A huge inertia generated by usage, tradition, prescription and the brutal fact of simple ignorance, lay heavily upon the institutions of the eighteenth century. As there had been for centuries, there was a self-evident justification for the ways of our fathers, for the forms and laws they had evolved and set down. One way in which this expressed itself was in an intense legalism, a fascination with old documents, judgments, lineage and inheritance. The higher classes were preoccupied with questions of blood, ancestry and family honour. Yet none of this preoccupation with the past was true historical-mindedness. Men were obsessed with the past as guidance, as precedent, even as spectacle, but not for its own sake. Few men had much sense that they were not looking at the same world as their ancestors – indeed, it was still in many places true that they were – or that they looked at it with different eyes.

At the heart of the *ancien régime* lay religion, physically obvious in huge numbers of churches, chapels, monasteries and convents dominating an emptier countryside and smaller towns than today's. It was obvious too in clerical dress; besides the religious of the enclosed orders who never emerged beyond the walls and grilles of their houses, there were shoals of clergy, above all in Roman Catholic countries, moving about the streets. Besides the cassocks of the parish priests, there were the habits of the teaching, preaching and charitable orders, the black suits of *abbés* and unbeneficed churchmen who were to be found in the *salons* of the great as supplicants, almoners and pedagogues. Others formed part of educational corporations. In Protestant as well as Roman Catholic countries the clergy still ran most of the educational apparatus; Oxford and Cambridge were as much clerical corporations as was the Sorbonne.

The result was an interpenetration of religion and ordinary life so close as to make it hard to divide them. It does not seem that the clergy could often afford to be complacent about the actual religious practice of many of their flock, but in Protestant and Catholic countries alike, the Church still played a part in individual lives which now seems inconceivable. Over the great events of men's lives – their baptism and admission to the community of the Faithful, their marriages, the christening of their children, their deathbeds – the Church presided. The rhythms of daily life, when they were not set by weather and season, were the rhythms of the Christian calendar. Though they were fewer in Protestant than in Catholic countries, almost the only holidays were religious festivals, some of them celebrated by special Masses, processions, feastings and games. From the pulpit came the only systematic teaching that most people ever received and it was used to relay the pronouncements of civil authority, too: preaching was the only vehicle of mass-communication and had a long and dramatic history of political involvement.

At the level of popular mentality, religion was often superstition. Miracles occurred; visions were seen. Men still believed in the devil, ghosts and witches. Of course the story was different among the educated. But kings were still obeyed because God, men believed, had brought them to their thrones. Louis xvi went to Rheims for his coronation and, above all, for his annointing with the sacral oil whose operation placed him in a long line of kings which stretched back far before Clovis to the young David whom Samuel annointed.

At his coronation Louis xvi swore, like his predecessors, to punish heresy in his dominions. True, the implacable fury shown towards this crime in earlier times had abated: Protestants could live in France. Yet they had no legal status and no prospect of advancement except by their own efforts outside the official hierarchies, or in the lower ranks of the army. They were not legally married unless before a Catholic priest, and Protestant children might well be legal bastards, incapable – for example – of inheriting property. Alarmed when Turgot asked for toleration for the Reformed Church, the clergy of France published a remonstrance to the king urging him to zealous execution of his coronation promise. 'It is reserved for you', they said, 'to give the death-blow to Calvinism in your kingdom.' At the other end of Europe, Russian law had until 1773 prescribed burning at the stake as the punishment for proselytizing on behalf of Islam (and Russia had many Moslem subjects) and an office of 'New Converts' set up in 1740 had been known to accept the baptism at gunpoint of entire villages of Moslems on the Volga. This had changed only when the Empress Catherine, convinced that it would be prudent to integrate her Islamic subjects with her régime, promulgated in 1773 an edict establishing toleration for all faiths: it did not, of course, mean the Russian authorities would not later connive at anti-Jewish pogroms. Even in tolerant England, seventeenth-century penal laws imposed social and legal handicaps on Roman Catholics. What is more, proposals to remove them led to popular resistance which produced the worst disturbances of the century, the 'Gordon Riots' of 1780 in London; they caused more damage and loss of life than anything which happened in Paris during the French Revolution. Neither Catholics nor Protestant dissenters, moreover, legally attended English universities. This situation did not mirror that in France or most Catholic countries; in England religious discrimination had been based on political distrust, not on horror of heresy. Yet even in England, Protestant dissenters were only exempted from pains and penalties by the 'Toleration Act' and certain legal fictions; they were not, that is to say, seen as subjects the equal of members of the Established Church. What was common to all such expressions of intolerance was the assumption that Church and State were and ought to be inseparably interdependent and intertwined.

Voices were beginning to be heard criticizing some aspects of this connection. But most people still lived in a theocentric universe and it appeared natural to many – even in the pluralistic religious world of North America – that the authority of the magistrate should uphold religion and the moral code it taught. As social regulators, Church and State supplemented one another in many countries. Blasphemy was a crime as well as a sin, and religion and the law went hand in hand in the condemnation of unnatural crimes. For historical reasons, great areas of law, mainly affecting marital, family and testamentory matters, were actually handled not by lay but by ecclesiastical courts. Parsons of the Church of England sat on the bench as Justices of the Peace, and all over Europe there were bishops exercising lay jurisdiction. The earthly head of the Catholic Church, the Pope, was not just a priest but a temporal ruler too. More practically, most of the apparatus of charity and poor-relief was in the hands of churchmen in Catholic countries.

At first sight, the *ancien régime* thus embodied a formidable concentration of authority. The next century, convinced of the necessary autonomy of the economic sphere, was appalled by laws on usury and price-controls, for example, and saw them as improper intrusions upon an area in which the individual ought to operate almost free from restraint. The corrosion of an ideal system had already gone some way, as Turgot's efforts and those of like-minded reformers showed. There were many who condemned the censorship of speech and print. Yet many of the targets of such criticism were pretty much illusory. The apparent scope of public authority in the eighteenth century had as much aspiration as reality to it.

The state itself, for all its apparent importance, was limited in power in many ways which would now seem surprising. To begin with, it was often entangled with other social regulators of which the most important was the Church. Interdependence and co-operation required respect for their spheres of action and their legal immunity. There were also practical and mechanical considerations. The general prevalence of monarchical forms gives an impression of coherence and efficacy to authority which must be qualified in a thousand ways. Even in Great Britain, the disentanglement of the personal finances of the monarch from those of the State had barely been achieved; everywhere else this rudimentary step towards the rationalization of administrative structures had yet to appear. The bureaucracies of eighteenth-century states, too, were only occasionally capable of working with a regularity now taken for granted and certainly could not undertake tasks on anything like the modern scale. Elementary statistical information was often lacking and everywhere administration was complicated and confused by the need to find ways of carrying it out which would actually work. Hence the use of officials of the personal household of a ruler, the farming of taxes, the delegation of authority to local notables, the granting of privileges in return for local government, the reliance upon the sense of position and self-esteem of great nobles for diplomatic duties and much more. Nor did such public employees (in the modern sense) as existed usually form part of a coherent and unified system of bureaucracy except in some of the smaller German states; no equivalent of a modern civil service existed in any eighteenth-century great power.

Such facts confused the structure of authority and combined with others to make the scope of government much more limited than would now be acceptable. Even the strongest governments of the *ancien régime* were weak in modern terms. Frederick the Great of Prussia was thought a model for rulers who sought the centralized control of their dominions. He also inherited a tradition of unquestioned service to his dynasty. Nevertheless, he could not bring about the abolition of serfdom which he desired because his administration rested on the service of the serf-owning Prussian squirearchy. Poor communications, the scarcity of competent and trained officials and the scarcity of accurate information (about landholding, for example) made it very hard to devise effective taxation or tap military resources except in the crudest ways, by indirect taxation which fell heaviest on the poor or by indiscriminate levies. Direct taxation was always hard to impose in a form which would not be passed on to the worse-off by the better-off, and wealth other than in real property was hard to tax at all.

Such considerations, arising from the weakness of fundamental practice and possibilities in government, in turn threw back the authorities upon other devices. They left functions of government in the hands of private corporations or persons, sold them to contractors or simply left them unperformed. Even law and order was in some countries largely abandoned to chance in country districts. Effective, continuous government was expensive and the resources were not there.

Social forms and attitudes also checked the powers of government. Society was seen as a collection of groups and individuals with privileges and rights which required continuous assertion and defence. Government was not necessarily in anybody's interest except that of the ruler. When the French *parlements* spoke of the dangers of 'despotism', they were not merely indulging in abuse but calling attention to precise threats to individual legal rights. When, in the much more progressive society of Great Britain, the government proposed to reform the structure of the East India Company, grave doubts were voiced not only because people believed that the rights granted to individuals under the company's charter should not be tampered with but also because the proposed changes were seen as evidence of a dangerous tendency to increase the powers of the Crown – that is, of government.

Respect for rights was the basis of all constitutional and political thinking under the *ancien régime*. The rights concerned were particular and personal, not general, and they explain the importance attached to rank and status. Who you were defined your rights. Though voices were beginning to be heard by 1775 which denied that all existing privileges could be justified, there was a tenacious respect for privilege as a principle, if it rested on legality. Needless to say, distinctions of rank, anomalous as they would later seem, did not appear in need of justification in the eyes of those who enjoyed the privileges they conferred. But many of those who did not enjoy them would none the less

39

think them defensible too, because the definition and defence of personal rights was the exemplary mode of political activity in the *ancien régime*. *Ius suum cuique* – to each, his own; on respect for privilege and liberties rested the whole of society. If justice is the satisfaction of reasonable expectations, then the *ancien régime* was long felt to be just because its authorities sought to provide and safeguard a structure of individual privileges, rather than (as did those of later *régimes*) the operation of general rules equally applied.

Such privileges fell usually into a hierarchical structure. Although there were a few individuals who already looked beyond generally received ideas and dreamed of a hierarchy of talent instead of birth, even they rarely questioned the basic principle of social subordination and hierarchy which ran right through the *ancien régime*, whatever they might think of its particular expressions. Even monarchies had a pecking-order. The hierarchical principle ran right down into society in hereditary forms, but was supplemented also by distinctions which did not arise from birth. These sometimes matched differences of wealth, but by no means as they do today, when few legal, social or cultural marks of status outweigh the gradation imposed by wealth. In the eighteenth century, legal status mattered more and even if it roughly corresponded to the economic one, it did not depend on it. A poor nobleman was still a nobleman; because he was poor, his nobility was all the more important. Sometimes there were formal obstacles to the assimilation of different hierarchies. Many countries, for example, forbade noblemen to practise trade or reserved to them the ownership of certain classes of land. Other laws preserved among commoners the gradations between master, journeyman and apprentice. Such distinctions were increasingly criticized because they hindered the economic advance of individuals; by and large the original functional aspect of legal distinctions of status had long crumbled and they rested on prescription and usage. Distinctions were therefore harder and harder to justify. The roots of the large degree of exemption from personal taxation enjoyed by noblemen in most countries might, for example, lie in the old military role of the noble order, but by the eighteenth century exemption was simply a legal fact. Distinctions among non-nobles were sometimes criticized, too. While France had two non-noble 'estates', the clergy and the Third Estate of commoners who comprised everybody else, Sweden had three: clergy, burghers and peasants. Many Swedes were left outside these classifications and the privilege of representation in the *Riksdag* which they conveyed. Burghers, for example, meant mainly retailers and artisans; bankers and iron-masters were not in this class. Nor were all those who tilled their own or rented homesteads and looked and worked like peasants members of the peasant Estate, which was comprised only of those who held certain categories of land.

Such complications (and there are many more bizarre than these) defy generalization, but one can be relied upon: by and large, the *ancien régime* was so set up that the class which benefited most from it was the landed nobility. Often its members enjoyed important fiscal and judicial privileges, as in France. Sometimes they dominated the civil administration, as in Sweden or Russia, and always they exercised a virtual monopoly of command in the armed services. As a rule, they were the largest individual landowners and, given their numbers, owned a quite disproportionate share of this primary source of economic and social power even in countries where there were many commoner proprietors or where ecclesiastical corporations owned much of it. Even in Great Britain, socially and legally very unlike most continental European countries, great noblemen were the usual leaders of the political connections which fought over the spoils of office and restricted the freedom of government, though their power was exercised in ways very different from those of their counterparts elsewhere, through their electoral influence. They enjoyed a prestige certainly as great as their European equivalents, even if it was defined not by legal status but by ownership of property.

The fundamental importance of rank explains the attention paid in the eighteenth century to the symbols of status which now seems so striking a feature of the *ancien régime*. Upon the right definition of a man's status turned important questions about rights possessed and duties incumbent. Hence the seemingly exaggerated concern with nice points of precedence and etiquette, the 'cascade of snobbishness' which one hostile observer discerned as the animating fact of French social life, the elaborate legal devices of primogeniture, entails and *fidei-commessi* for preserving a family's status. Here again Great Britain was sharply different from continental countries. In most of Europe, noble status was shared by all children of a nobleman. In England, no formal legal distinction of nobility existed except the peerage, and the peer's distinction descended only to his eldest son. England was conscious enough of status, but had in large measure disconnected it from legal distinctions and thus escapes classification as a typical society of the *ancien régime*. The unique English contribution to social categorization already existed, the 'gentleman', and he was distinguished socially, morally and culturally, but not legally. Though the English landowning classes, like their equivalents elsewhere, provided the top of the social hierarchy, they did not enjoy the legal privilege which elsewhere buttressed and defined such a position.

In most countries legal forms provided the framework in which most people thought about society, and legal questions played a great part in its regulation. This was connected with the absence of a later invention, true politics. Under the *ancien régime*, politics had in theory no place, except, possibly, at the level of the royal court, where aspirants to influence would struggle for the ear of king or favourite. This is more properly called intrigue. Of the modern notion of fighting out by peaceful means of struggles for power before an audience which is in some sense a judge, the *ancien régime* had little idea. Only Great Britain among the great powers had politics. The United Provinces and some Swiss cantons also had them; those of the first turned on a division between 'Orangists' who, by and large, sought to accentuate the authority of the quasi-monarchical Stadholder, and 'Patriots' who were more radical. In Geneva, what was at stake was the possession of full civic rights. It is striking that the British, Dutch and Genevan politics were all, in reality, oligarchic, the mass of the people taking no part in them except by rioting when a faction among the oligarchs encouraged or inflamed them to do so. (Food riots were a different matter.) In other countries issues which would now be regarded as political were fought out in legal terms, because it was only when legal doubts arose about policies that there were theoretical grounds for debating them at all at any level other than that of the ruler's council.

In some places, it still seemed natural to use feudal terminology to explain the relations between rulers and subjects and these too left no place for politics. In almost every continental European country rural life was strongly marked by a feudal structure and theory. Lawyers dealt with questions of property in a context of feudal law. This was not to say that there existed a 'feudalism' such as a medieval historian would consider typical. It was rather that land-holding was dominated by legal concepts which were feudal in origin. In every European country there existed alongside the fact of landownership the fact of legal lordship, sometimes meaning something important in practice, sometimes not. Lordships were originally delegations of sovereignty, made in virtue of some function which was discharged by the lord. This utilitarian justification had long since ceased to be a reality and the lordship had become hereditary and alienable property, more and more exploited solely with regard to its economic potential. The feudal estate or seigneury was from one point of view a bundle of legal rights entitling the lord to certain dues, on the other it was concretely the land over which these rights ran. They almost always included jurisdiction and a great variety of obligations owed by the tenants to the lord in kind and labour, many of which were commuted for money charges.

In the most startling examples of the feudal rural order, there were very heavy labour services. In virtually every country except England there were serfs in the eighteenth century, but this might mean very different things. Broadly speaking, the burden it laid on those bound to the soil grew heavier and their powerlessness at law greater as one went eastwards. In the 1770s in Bohemia it was not unusual for serfs to have to work from three to six days a week on their lords' land before being free to till their own. The power of the Polish landlords over their serfs was enormous and it was only on lands whose ultimate lord was the king that the peasants had access to a tribunal before which they could bring their masters.

Increasingly, the feudal framework of society was criticized during the eighteenth century for its irrationality, its tyrannies and its economic failure. Even the lord did not always find that it suited him. Almost everywhere it caused and exacerbated social conflict and litigation. Some steps were taken in western Europe to deal with its more monstrous features; in 1779, for example, serfdom was abolished on the royal domains in France. But it lay like a great blight across the economy as well as encumbering the path towards the rationalization of government under the *ancien régime*, irritating men by its forms, long after the life had gone out of them.

The other great obstacles to effective government in the *ancien régime* were also medieval survivals, the corporatism and localism which gave society a cellular rather than pyramidal structure. The most conspicuous example of the first was the division of society into social Orders, 'Estates' or *stände*, each legally insulated from the others. Often these distinctions came to a head in permanent representative institutions: the United Kingdom could provide an example in the hereditary membership of the House of Lords, the deliberative assembly of the peerage, through which it still took a share in law-making. Apart from this, though, the English example was only a relic; the distinction at law of an English peer was virtually restricted to his right to a writ of summons to a parliament. Of the idea of a self-contained noble corporation no reality remained since an abortive attempt to close the peerage to newcomers early in the century and its numbers were greatly added to at the end of it. England was unique in this respect; almost every aspect of its society had evolved far beyond the categories of the continental *ancien régime*.

Elsewhere, Estates and Orders were very important. Where they had representative institutions, as in Sweden, they were political forces of great importance. In France, the Estates-General which assembled deputies of all three Estates had not met since 1614; for Frenchmen it was the status they derived from membership of one or other order which mattered, not legislative power. Poland was an extreme case, a country consisting legally of only one class, the nobles. They made up the 'Polish Nation', while peasants and townsmen did not have any legal corporate existence at all. Among continental states, only Russia, where nobility was based in principle on service and all were subject to autocracy, did not have corporate privilege as the basis of its social life and its absence appalled subjects of other rulers.

Locality divided men legally, too. The Habsburgs had different powers in their duchies of Milan and Brabant. Frenchmen were governed differently according to whether they lived in a *pays d'état* with its own representative institutions, or a *pays d'élection* where royal government had to contend with no such cushion. When Frenchmen came in 1789 to write down their grievances for the king's consideration, some of them thought it worthwhile to insist that the king of France should be known in their region only as count of Provence; the distinction of title registered an important difference of legal powers in their eyes. Any French law court would have agreed with them. Corporatism and localism – and towns, counties, provinces were all seen as corporations – had great importance because of the idea that status was defined by privileges enforceable at law. Liberty, under the *ancien régime*, meant the maintenance of legal rights. These often belonged to groups as well as to individuals. Besides provinces, towns and cities, professional and occupational groups, such as guilds, universities and confraternities, had them, too. In Roman Catholic and some Protestant countries, the Church was the greatest corporation of all, possessing greater privileges and immunities than any other and able to buttress them by great acquisitions of wealth because it never died.

Such institutions and the weakness they imposed on government go a long way to explain the difficulty of reform in the *ancien régime* if by reform is meant increased governmental efficiency or progress towards equality of legal status. Behind them there lay also a pervasive and fundamental conservatism very important in inhibiting conscious change, the assumption of stability: things would remain as they were. Political change was for most men only the possibility of righting things that had gone wrong, restoring a disturbed balance – or a threat that men might seek to take what was not rightfully theirs and thus disturb the balanced order. 'Revolution' was a word used by Englishmen and Frenchmen, but only in the limited sense of replacing one ruler or set of rul   by another. It did not imply a total overthrow of a social order. Rebellions and *jacqueries* might take place, but their aim, when justifiable, was the righting of known wrong; if they were not justifiable in these terms, they were to be deplored and punished. There was no sense that alternative models of society ought to shape conscious social change.

Thus although Europe could display many varieties within the *ancien régime*, most of the principles on which society was built would have been respected in all of them. Even in the up-to-date, commercially minded Netherlands, there were still legal serfs in 1775 – though they could be, in fact, prosperous smallholders in all but law and name. The only major country in which the principles of the *ancien régime* did not dominate social thinking and practice was England, already equipped with a legislative sovereign irresistible by any immunity or privilege, already having discarded her feudal past, already conceiving society as an assemblage of individuals minding their own business over a much wider area of their lives than would have been thought possible, let alone proper, in most continental states. Even in England, though, while the assumption of hierarchy was not completely matched by legal distinction as it was on the Continent, eighteenth-century society was dominated by an aristocratic landowning class. Its members recognized one another by breeding and habits, more open though it was to recruitment from outside than most continental nobilities.

4 States and nations

Two basic ideas underlie the political structure of the modern world. One is that its land surface should be divided into areas unified under independent authorities with the last word about what goes on inside their well-defined boundaries. The other is that such areas should be lived in when possible by people possessing a sense of community which constitutes nationhood or nationality. Neither of these assumptions was current in the Europe of the *ancien régime*. The ideas of state and nation were by no means what they are today and one result was a map much less tidy than ours.

Inside France, for example, there were towns immune from royal decrees which ran outside their walls. The king of France ruled them, but could not treat them as he treated his other lands. German princes, living on the other side of the Rhine, held certain lands on the French side as his feudal vassals and subordinates, though at home they were independent of any subjection except the duty they owed to the shadowy authority of the emperor. He reigned over the Holy Roman Empire, being elected to its crown by a college which comprised the greatest princes of Germany – yet since the sixteenth century, the emperors had with one exception (Charles VII) come from the same Austrian family, the Habsburgs. Their hereditary grip had, indeed, become so strong that it had even overcome prejudice – and, some said, law – in promoting to the imperial throne in 1745 (when her husband was elected emperor) a woman, the empress Maria Theresia, still reigning in 1775. She was not only empress, for she had other dominions, too, which fell outside the Empire. She was, for example, queen of Hungary, where different laws and institutions obtained from those of Austria, let alone from those of the jumble of kingdoms, dukedoms, archbishoprics and bishoprics, imperial towns and lands of imperial knights of Germany over which her authority was, in effect, only a matter of diplomatic influence and a lingering respect for her office. One of the princes who ruled over an important German state was the Elector of Hanover; he has appeared already in these pages in his better-known role of king of England, George III. Many Englishmen had resented that their country should be (they suspected) towed in the wake of the 'cockle-boat' Hanover but they had to endure the fact of the unquestionable legality of the attachment. The House of Hanover had not given up its historic rights when one of its sons ascended the English throne. Another prince was the Elector of Brandenburg, also king of Prussia. A large part of his possessions, too, in east and west Prussia, lay beyond the imperial frontier and there he was theoretically as well as actually an independent sovereign; Brandenburg and Pomerania were inside it.

Enclaves were another complicating factor. In the heart of the Rhone valley, surrounded by French territory, lay the papal possessions of Avignon and Orange. Another papal enclave lay inside the kingdom of the Two Sicilies, at Benevento, a little town of small importance but a constant irritant to royal ministers anxious to assert their master's authority, and a hostage to fortune of papal policy. The Papal States were an astonishing anomaly in a category by themselves: a jumble of acquisitions around the original Patrimony of St Peter made the head of Christendom a major Italian prince, with all the practical and moral disadvantages that implied.

It is very difficult to represent such tangled relationships, jurisdictions and loyalties on a map. Eighteenth-century Europe was not only a political patchwork but within individual patches there were delicate and subtle shadings. This diversity was the result of the working-out over centuries of two principles which lay at the heart of relations between rulers in the *ancien régime*, the proprietorial principle and respect for traditional rights.

The first explains why it is still convenient to think of eighteenth-century diplomacy in terms of relations between persons rather than relations between states. If the great king of France Louis XIV actually *did* say '*L'Etat c'est moi*', he was from a legal point of view expressing a truism, for legally he was the only tie between millions of men whom we now call French but who might then have thought of themselves as Languedociens, Béarnais, Bretons or Strasbourgeois. The primacy of the ruler was reflected in the diplomatic conventions of the day; ambassadors were the representatives of one king in the presence of another, and a vestige of this remains in the fact that foreign ambassadors in London are still formally accredited to the court of St James. There were, of course, many important qualifications in practice on this personal interpretation of relations which, for want of a better word, we must call by the anachronistic word 'international'. A British embassy might go to China in the name of king George, but the ministers thinking that closer relations might promote better trade had the East India Company in mind, not George III's private purse, and could be displaced by the House of Commons as well as by their royal master. Nevertheless, elsewhere the personal and proprietorial model of government was much more real and expressed itself in the *insouciance* with which the rulers of eastern Europe carved up territories without regard to the wishes of their inhabitants. It was his own subjects that Frederick the Great once engagingly referred to as herds of deer, a simple expression of the view of monarchy as a superior exercise of a landlord's rights.

Respect for rights was the other pole of thinking about political organization. These were not natural but legal, historic, chartered, prescriptive rights, defensible in courts of law. We have already met them in considering the internal organization of societies during the *ancien régime* and they were important also in shaping the relations of different societies to one another. Respect for rights gave a very legalistic flavour to much eighteenth-century diplomacy. It reflected – for example in the assertion of the historic right of the Estates of Brabant or Hungary against their Austrian ruler – and intensified the complication and fragmentation of the exercise of power. It was expressed in the enduring complications introduced into international life by the vagaries of inheritance and disputes over legacies and claims. It was another expression of the fragile and tentative hold which the *ancien régime* had upon the notion of sovereignty. This was true even of Great Britain, the state which expressed the idea of legislative sovereignty most clearly in its practice, for no one denied the power of an Act of Parliament, though some still disliked admitting it openly.

Against the background of such assumptions, the relations of rulers and states were bound to be significantly differentiated from those of later periods. It would not be true to say that religion counted for nothing in determining alignments and conflicts in 1775, but it counted for little, and for far, far less than a century before, while of future ideological divisions there was no trace. Overwhelmingly, the more important political units were organized as monarchies. There was not because of that any abstract hostility to republics. The few which existed in Europe seemed crazy, worm-eaten baroque survivals; Venice and Genoa illustrated the supposed propensity of the form to decadence and oligarchy, while the history of the semi-monarchical United Provinces was regarded as a confirmation of the potential instability and faction of the form. The new confederation of states which emerged in North America from the War of Independence hardly changed these attitudes. Only a few recognized a new principle of organization in the claim of popular sovereignty and many of those hoped or feared that the new republics of the West would soon crumble under the strains of internecine strife and geographical extension. Diplomats argued and soldiers fought not about ideology or political forms but about dynastic interest (here the proprietorial theme was strongly evident), commercial advantage, territorial and demographic gains and simple power.

Though such concerns were sometimes traversed by currents of popular sentiment and patriotism, modern nationalism did not exist. One thinker, Rousseau, who admired national sentiment and saw in it a possible foundation for a state, had sadly commented that in a cosmopolitan age 'there are no longer Frenchmen, Germans or Italians'. This was hardly true, but it was of course true that whereas Frenchmen could focus their feelings in institutions evolved by centuries of struggle and consolidation, Germans and Italians had only the fading myths of Empire and Papacy on which to build. Some stateless peoples, it should none the less be remarked, had a sense of nationality (or were evolving one) because of oppression. This had been true of the Catalans in the seventeenth century and was soon to become much more clear in south-eastern Europe, in lands under Ottoman or Habsburg rule. Here, social oppression, maladministration and sometimes religion sharpened the sense of identity latent in so ethnically diverse a region. The Romanians of Transylvania, for example, gradually began to acquire a sense of grievance against their Germanic and Magyar overlords; it burst out in bloody rebellion in the 1780s, and a new phase of national development began with the invoking of arguments based on natural rights. A different sort of national consciousness, meanwhile, was hardening among the English colonial settlers of Ireland, cut off by wealth, law and religion from the Catholic Irish, but increasingly aware, too, of the irksomeness of government from Westminster.

Yet eighteenth-century statesmen moved in a world shaped by older ideas and prejudices than those of nationality, in spite of these straws in the wind. They were concerned with the relationships of rulers great and small in the setting of the prevailing assumptions of the *ancien régime*. The most important of these relationships were those between a relatively small number of great powers which then, as now, were distinguished by their superior wealth and war-making capacity.

Indisputably the leading power among these was France. She had centuries of national definition behind her and was one of the wealthiest and most populous states in the world. Under Louis xiv her armies had given her a long hegemony in western Europe and she was to enjoy another, briefer but even wider, at the beginning of the nineteenth century. A diplomatic service (largely the foundation of Louis xiv) of unrivalled size and experience protected French interests.

To these important assets were added the impalpable influences of prestige. French culture in all its manifestations, from furniture and fashion to philosophy, was admired everywhere by the leaders of society and culture, and the French language was the *lingua franca* of Western civilization. Even spectacle played its part, for the pace-setter of monarchical style for all Europe was still to be found at Versailles, where the glitter of a court which in 1789 found room for six thousand civil officers and eight thousand military dazzled the eyes of Europe.

The filaments of Bourbon family connections stretched out from its senior branch to cadet houses in other countries. The other great Bourbon power was Spain, where a branch of the family had ruled since the death of the last Habsburg king of Spain without an heir. Spain had once been indisputably the supreme power of Europe and, indeed, of the world. By 1775 she was no longer that, but neither was she the wreck the Bourbons had inherited. Their rule had checked and partially reversed the course to decline. They had rebuilt Spanish naval power and launched policies to reinvigorate the economy. Charles III, king from 1759 to 1788, was a particularly successful selector of able ministers who brought about a real economic and cultural revival, interrupted only by the financial setbacks which followed Spanish entry to the American war of independence in 1779. But this war, too, brought its successes; Spain was to regain Florida and Minorca in it. Although an attempt to recover Gibraltar failed, Spain was, at the death of Charles III, still an important colonial and naval power.

Bourbon rulers had also established themselves in Italy, at Naples (where Charles III had been king before he migrated to Spain) and Parma. Co-operation between the Bourbon states was a reality. France and Spain, even before the alliance of 1779, had been linked by 'Family Compacts' and the Bourbon Courts had acted in concert to force the Pope to consent to the dissolution of the Society of Jesus in 1773. But the Bourbon states of Italy were only two among that peninsula's jumble of old republics (Venice, Genoa, Lucca and San Marino) and monarchies (Sardinia and the Two Sicilies, the grand duchy of Tuscany, the duchies of Parma, Modena, Milan and Mantua, and the Papal States) which provided its political framework. Sardinia and the Papacy were the most important of the truly independent Italian states. Among the others, some fell within a Habsburg system which balanced the Bourbon. An Austrian governor ruled the duchies of Mantua and Milan for Vienna. A son of Maria Theresia was grand duke of Tuscany, and a daughter wife to the Bourbon king of the Two Sicilies.

The centre and main weight of Habsburg power was in central

Europe. Vienna was the capital of dominions whose only unity lay in their common submission to the dynasty. The Austrian Netherlands, covering most of modern Belgium, and the Lombard duchies were the most important disconnected and outlying Habsburg territories; both were acquired in the eighteenth century. The Habsburg heartland was the belt of territories within the Holy Roman Empire which ran south from Bohemia and Moravia, through Austria, Styria and Carinthia to the narrow bridgehead on the Adriatic at Trieste. In the west, this central block stretched out to the Tyrol. Beyond its eastern and south-eastern frontiers were the formerly Polish lands of Galicia, acquired only in 1772, and, most important, the sprawling kingdom of Hungary, with its separate crown and independently minded nobility.

Much of Hungary had been won back from the Turks only in 1699. As even this brief account suggests, therefore, there was a curious paradox in the Habsburg achievement. Though the Habsburgs were an ancient house, their empire was really a very recent creation. The family's great era had begun with their fifteenth-century acquisition of the crown of the Holy Roman Empire which they still held in 1775. It is very difficult to say exactly what its real significance was by then. The Empire (as it was usually called) was, roughly, the old Burgundian Netherlands, Germany and Austria. Its boundaries ran from the Baltic coast about half-way between the Vistula and Oder down round Austria to the Adriatic, then north from there, round Switzerland, roughly following the Rhine until it turned westwards to run along the French frontier with the Netherlands.

The Empire was an extraordinary political fact. It contained some three hundred political units for the most part independent of one another, formally subordinated to the emperor, and linked in various ways to him. There were a few powerful states, some dignified as 'electorates' – their rulers, that is to say, took part in the choice of the emperor, who, formally speaking, was elected. The most powerful of these was Brandenburg, or Prussia. Saxony, Bavaria, the Palatinate and Hanover provided the lay electoral princes; the others were clerics. The map was made still more untidy because even the big states were not always made up of continuous tracts of land. Within the Empire the king of Prussia ruled Cleves, straddling the Rhine nearly 150 miles from the frontier of the Mark of Brandenburg and itself in two pieces, East Frisia (clustered about Emden on the Dutch border and the North Sea coast), Lingen, Minden and Ravensburg which were isolated units in north-western Germany, and Baireuth and Anspach (the second of them itself containing enclaves of other rulers' territories) down in the south. There was, finally, far away to the south-west the little Swiss canton of Neufchatel which belonged to him. The Habsburgs were, possibly, even worse off if the tiny size of some of their German territories is taken into account as well as their fragmentation. 'Further Austria' was a scatter of bits and pieces on the upper Danube and upper Rhine; between them and Austria proper lay the important electorate of Bavaria and the bishopric of Salzburg, one of the many imperial states ruled by a prince-bishop.

Certainly the Habsburgs did not rule Germany. Yet they were great German princes, and the authority of the Empire counted for something. They had sought to strengthen their position in Germany during the eighteenth century, but without success, and had actually lost one important territory, Silesia, to the king of Prussia. Their efforts to regain it pressed Habsburg government forward upon the road to financial reform, but this brought out into the light the problems of government which were inherent in the variety of the Habsburg possessions. The Habsburg monarchy may be regarded as the classical expression of the difficulties of *ancien régime* government. Essentially the problem which faced the emperors, and which came out much more clearly under Joseph II than during the rule of his more cautious mother, was that of sovereignty. The Habsburg Empire was not a state; there was no common centre of sovereignty, if by that is meant a recognized source of legislative authority. The emperor ruled Austria directly, but in the Netherlands his officers had to negotiate with the Estates of Brabant, in Prague with those of Bohemia. The Diet of Hungary was so powerful that it dealt with Maria Theresia as 'Queen of Hungary', and her son avoided coronation with the crown of St Stephen so that he should not have to make the traditional coronation promises to uphold Hungarian liberties and privileges.

The constitutional problems presented by so odd a collection of dependencies linked by personal union are half the story of the origin of 'enlightened despotism' in the Habsburg dominions. The other half is the story of the rivalry with Prussia.

Prussia and Russia were the two new important cards added to the European pack since the end of the Thirty Years' War. Both had a long history but rose to eminence only in the decline of Sweden in the second half of the seventeenth century. Frederick II, king of Prussia for thirty-five years already in 1775, had carried his state to an astonishing peak of power and prestige. The resources with which he began had not been large (the well-filled war-chest of his father was soon spent) and there had been terrible setbacks, but during his reign he more than doubled the population of his state, to nearly six millions. Some of these were immigrants, more were the reflection of military or diplomatic aggrandizement. After 1763 Frederick was almost continuously at peace, and a substantial number of them were the Poles of the lower Vistula whose acquisition in the first Partition linked Pomerania territorially to East Prussia and gave Prussia control of the main artery by which Polish trade reached the Baltic. Frederick's other great acquisition had been Silesia, which he had wrested from the young Maria Theresia. It was the foundation of later Prussian economic predominance in Germany. From this seizure stemmed a Habsburg-Hohenzollern rivalry which, though at times muted or masked, was to be a major theme of European international politics until 1866, when Austria ceased to be a German power.

Frederick's success was based on inherited advantages. His predecessors left him a state about a third of which was royal domain, the actual possession of the royal landlord. This much simplified the revenue problems which faced all eighteenth-century states and had usually to be solved in a context of what an eighteenth-century writer had called 'intermediary powers' – the local representative bodies, corporations and estates whose privileges and liberties stood in the way of governments seeking to mobilize the wealth of their societies. Prussia also had a service tradition among her nobles; the King of Prussia was their employer and although this meant that they could be sure that his policies would not cut at the roots of the social system, they accepted a discipline and an austerity of administrative practice not to be found elsewhere in Europe.

Frederick's foreign policy rested in the 1770s on alliance with Russia; he did not forget that his capital, Berlin, had been occupied by Russian soldiers. After 1780, when the alliance lapsed, he relied more upon his prestige and attractiveness to other German princes as a counterbalance to Austria inside Germany. His diplomatic and military success, none the less, is not the only reason why he was to be called 'Frederick the Great'. He was a ruler much admired abroad for other reasons. A few English public houses to this day commemorate in their names and signs the 'Protestant hero' who had been the ally of Great Britain in the Seven Years' War (though his later distrust of English policy is forgotten). Advanced thinkers in the West had been enchanted by the spectacle of a king whose rule seemed progressive, who liked French conversation and wrote French verses, and who was anti-clerical or at least sceptical. The Prussian tradition in religion was tolerant; this had made possible the attraction of immigrants to people the wide tracts of Brandenburg.

Though there was much illusion in admiration of Frederick (that of foreign writers and thinkers did not always survive close acquaintance with the Court), he deserves his place at the head of the list of Prussia's kings. Though he made mistakes, he was supple and could learn from

53

failure. He was tenacious of purpose and ruthless. Above all, he was tireless, his own best civil servant, running his country like a great private estate. His nephew and successor, Frederick William II, who came to the throne in 1786, was soon to show how Frederick's greatness was rooted in character. He had been an extemporizer of genius, who could run things well and Frederick William could not. There would be ill-judged policies, owing much to favourites, and when a great challenge which should also have been an opportunity came along in the French Revolution, Prussia would drift into a position Frederick the Great would never have allowed, that of playing second fiddle to Austria.

Unquestionably, the greatest of the powers of eastern Europe in 1775 was Russia, a giant which had in a century made giant strides. In the west, the first partition of Poland carried her frontier beyond the upper Dvina and Dnieper and there were even greater gains to come. The treaty of Kutchuk Kainardji, two years later, had given her a south-western frontier on the lower Bug. This territorial expansion had been matched by economic growth. At the summit of the imperial structure was the glittering court of Catherine II, another ruler whose proposals for reforming legislation convinced progressive observers in Western countries that she was a child of 'enlightenment', as the catch-phrase of the age had it. Like Frederick she courted the approval of foreign men of letters and she, too, upheld religious toleration. In a way, she was enlightened. But she had to govern Russia, and the country was already very distinct in its social structure and cultural formation. Most Russian subjects were serfs whose legal status and economic condition worsened during the eighteenth century. Although they long gave Russia great military power because of the advantage deriving from numbers, the serfs also presented a threat. A large population was spread over a land surface which made effective, close supervision by central government impossible. Misery and oppression always threatened a revolt. In 1774, the greatest of all peasant rebellions, that of Pugachev, was so dangerous that it drew off at a crucial moment military forces needed against the Turks and thus obliged Russia to accept a less favourable peace than had been hoped. The scale of government in this vast land, together with a growing social problem, tended to put the authority of the ministers at St Petersburg more and more behind the gentry and nobility whose estates and manors provided the primary governmental and administrative structure. Thus, for all the autocratic power enjoyed by the Tsars (whose very title proclaimed them inheritors of the Roman Empire), the monarchy was dependent upon its nobility and tied to its interests.

In the eighteenth century, the Habsburg, the Hohenzollern and the

Romanov dynasties presided over the almost continuous expansion of their territories. The two losers, from whose bulk they carried off huge fragments of territory, were the ancient republic of Poland and the Ottoman Empire. Poland had for decades been visibly in decline, her internal politics (which largely revolved about the election of puppet kings) being dominated by Russian intrigue and pressure and the rivalries of great families. The first partition took away a quarter of her territory and about four million of her 11,500,000 inhabitants. The shock was great; one consequence was an unprecedented and in part spontaneous drive for reform and intellectual improvement among the 'Polish nation'. This consisted of the noble class, which made up about eight per cent of the total population (as against, say, about one per cent in France). Below them were the peasants – Polish towns were few and small, agriculture and a transit trade sustaining the country's economy – whose condition was such that when an English writer wished to bring home to his country the gravity of the oppression suffered by French peasants, he described them as 'almost on a level with Polish slaves'. This population was also unusual in that Poland was the only country in Europe where there were large numbers of Jews in the countryside, an additional complication in a population divided between Poles, Ukrainians and Russians. This discontented mass was a poor foundation for political reform of what has been described as 'anarchical oligarchy'. To make matters worse, Poland also suffered from religious divisions. The eighteenth-century story of the Ottoman Empire in Europe had been one of almost unbroken retreat, the main beneficiaries of which had been the Habsburg and Russian emperors. 1775 is not a date of any significance in this process. The treaty which had ended one war with Russia the previous year did not win Catherine the possession of Constantinople she perhaps envisaged but gave the Crimean Tartars independence from Turkey (followed in 1783 by their annexation by Russia), free transit for Russian merchant ships to the Mediterranean and Turkish recognition of Russia's special position and privilege as protector of Turkey's Christian subjects. The loss of the first Moslem part of the Ottoman Empire, even though one only loosely subordinate to the suzerainty of the Sultan, was a landmark. But the treaty had marked more than this. The concession over Greek Christians was enormously significant; judiciously used, it gave Russia a means to intervene in Turkey's internal affairs by prising open any question involving the 'Greeks'.

Thus, the Ottomans had long since ceased to be a menace to Europe and had become instead a temptation to European predators. With Kutchuk Kainardji they began also to be a problem: Turkish decline, seemingly not to be checked by the to and fro of conservative and modernizing forces at Istanbul, revealed inescapable conflicts of interest between her neighbours. As Russia advanced towards the mouth of the Danube, Habsburg fears for their interests in the valley and the Balkans became inflamed; as Russian ships sailed into the Mediterranean, British and French interests in the Levant acquired a new significance. The 'Eastern Question' which worried nineteenth-century statesmen had begun.

5 The minds of men

The history of mentality cannot be separated from the history of politics, society, economics or, for that matter, from most of the rest of human experience. But it does not usually fit itself into the same discernible phases as other kinds of history, and it is sometimes contrasted strongly with them. These things are emphatically true of the eighteenth century, or have seemed to be when its mental history is looked at from the point of view which has become almost classical. That point of view both drew an exaggeratedly sharp line round the topic and set it off very deliberately against its political and social context. This was because the men of the eighteenth century themselves saw much of their age in this way. We have inherited from them, some of whom approved and some of whom deplored it, the stereotype of an intellectual epoch characterized above all by a critical stance and innovatory vigour. From these stem also a certain evaluation of its intellectual achievement; again, for good or evil, it was an age conscious of its own intellectual importance. The labels in the history books drive home this impression: *siècle des lumières, Aufklärung*, the Age of Reason. The dominant impression left by it is one of upheaval and novelty. Sometimes this was and is judged to be a progressive and liberating thing – thus, for example, Shelley saw the ideas of the age before his own – sometimes it was thought poisonous and corrupting, as de Maistre saw them. But both the good conceit of themselves shown by eighteenth-century writers and the violence of their critics testify to the importance they thought the age to have in intellectual history, and both located this importance in innovation.

Such views are none the less misleading. They complicate further still the problem of sketching, however lightly, the contours of what was most important in the history of Western mentality between 1775 and 1847. For the last quarter of the eighteenth century, it would be very inadequate to assume that the word 'Enlightenment' effectively summed up the age. Thirty years before the end of the century, Enlightenment had already reached its climax; other currents of thought (some antagonistic to it) were already operating. Twenty years earlier still, the intellectual foundations of the whole structure of Enlightenment had been demolished by Hume (admittedly an Enlightenment thinker). Even more important qualifications are required if we consider behaviour. The century of Voltaire was one in which fashionable people bid heavily for seats from which to witness the appalling torments inflicted on a would-be assassin of Louis xv, one in which, in 1783, horrified French peasants set upon a balloon fallen within a few miles of Paris and destroyed it under the belief that it was the moon, and a century which would close with revolutionaries having visions of angels with tricoloured wings. France was not unique; thousands of examples could be found in other countries – England, for example, where the nineteenth century opened with the flowering of the crazy cult of Joanna Southcott's Box. Purely statistically, the salient fact about eighteenth-century mentality is that the minds of most Europeans in 1800 were very little different from those of their predecessors a hundred years earlier.

This background is not much lightened by the undoubted evidence of growing literacy in some countries as the century went on. In its last quarter, the period which particularly concerns us, there was another striking phenomenon which may have been linked to this, the first real growth of a newspaper Press. Yet the ability to read by no means meant access to the works of advanced speculation which are now remembered as the major literary embodiments of 'Enlightenment', nor was it likely, once away from one or two major centres, that most people wanted to read that sort of book in any case. In the 1770s, as in 1600, the stock-in-trade of the purveyors of the cheap books which were the most popular reading in France remained consistent. Frenchmen wanted to read about the lives of saints, unhappy and happy love affairs, the derring-do of the paladins of chivalry, and the wonders and prodigies contained in almanacks and books of magic. The same was probably true in other countries where a popular reading public existed; much popular literacy in Protestant countries, too, went into reading the Bible. Newspapers were unlikely to reach many people, and if they did, they contained little that would be thought provocative. Moreover, though newspapers were widespread – almost every German city had one – circulations were very small outside England. It is not unreasonable to say that the contents of popular mentality in continental Europe and even of that of much of the directing classes changed hardly at all between 1700 and 1789.

This has been obscured because there are some striking exceptions, but also because it is natural, in the Western World, to treat the history of mentality as the history of formal culture and of that small part of the literate elite which has given every age whatever intellectual cutting-edge it possesses. Those who belong to this small class have been so important that this emphasis is wholly justifiable, providing the limitation of the influence of such elites on the minds of the great mass of their contemporaries is not forgotten. Only a few intellectuals had important access to and influence over the masses. These were the clergy, who, in spite of notable exceptions and frequent examples of private explorations in 'advanced' books, did not as a whole busy themselves much with intellectual or moral innovation. Most men in 1800, as in 1700, had some sort of dim theocentric view of the world and their lives which, with custom and tradition, provided a settled framework for a mentality whose inertia was enormous. Ideas which an intellectual historian thinks of as typical of 1775 were not shared by most men until many decades had passed – if then.

Religion also still had great power among the leaders of society. Many members of the literate and cultural elites themselves did not share the leading ideas of the age, and those many were a majority in some countries – in Spain, say, or Russia. Even where infidelity had made great inroads into belief, as it seems to have done among the French aristocracy and educated classes, this often made little difference to such observances as church-going and it was impossible to marry except in a religious ceremony. Only very rarely did a strong-minded man refuse the sacrament on his deathbed or a nobleman openly flout the observances enjoined by his Church. The strange eighteenth-century craze for freemasonry and similar activities, though condemned by the Catholic Church, often expressed itself in ostentatious religious practices. The formal framework of the lives of *all* men was still religion; the social assumptions by which the ruling classes lived (whatever they said) were traditional ones.

Finally, there is also one commonsense point to be borne in mind; ideas no more move in linear progression than do other aspects of human development. The reasonableness and optimism which some have seen as characteristic of the eighteenth century were no longer the only intellectual fashions in 1775 and to that extent the moment which some have seen as the most characteristic phase of eighteenth-century thought was passing. The philosophical basis of rational optimism had been formally terribly damaged by Hume and morally slighted by Rousseau. Men were beginning to seek in mysticism and mumbo-jumbo satisfaction which formal religion and scepticism both failed to provide. Europe was at the beginning of a movement later termed by some scholars 'pre-romanticism' when they wished to separate it both from what preceded it and from what followed.

If these reservations are borne in mind, then it is a little safer to turn back towards the guiding idea that the age had none the less a certain intellectual unity. There was a personal as well as a theoretical basis for this. Since the later seventeenth century a new phenomenon had appeared in Europe, that of an international intelligentsia, all of whose members, whatever the issues separating them one from another, shared a common sense of direction and, more loosely, common values. One scholar speaks of 'a family of intellectuals united by a single style of thinking'; 'sect' was a word used at the time, often in an unfriendly way, and certainly there is a feeling of the *coterie* about much of the intellectual correspondence of the era.

Language united them, too. The French component and flavour was predominant in the intellectual life of the Western World by 1775. The original impulse to much of the speculation and writing of the age which now seems most typical of it was to be sought in England, but in the second half of the eighteenth century the word *philosophe* was commonly used to describe a certain style of intellectual activity; the word was, of course, French. 'Formerly,' wrote an Italian nobleman in 1776 'everything was Roman; nowadays, everything is French.' 'Broadly speaking, every European is a Frenchman,' he went on (and called his book *L'Europe française*). French comfort and clothes led fashion throughout Europe. French art and architecture was imitated in miniature reproductions of the court of Versailles all over Germany. French books and ideas were everywhere eagerly bought. Their subversive power was paid the compliment of great efforts by the Spanish Inquisition to close the frontier to them. Above all, French was the *lingua franca* of the educated. To take one country alone, among Italians, Alfieri, Goldoni and Casanova all wrote in French. Maria Theresia, her children (who numbered in their ranks four crowned heads or royal consorts), Catherine the Great and Frederick the Great all corresponded in it and spoke it. The last despised German and, as Voltaire had remarked, that was the language least heard at his court.

Within the intellectual world defined by familiarity with the French language and admiration for the books produced in it there existed a predisposition central to Enlightenment thought, that in favour of intellectual freedom. Broadly speaking, this was to remain at the heart of the tradition sometimes identified as moral and political liberalism right through the nineteenth century and beyond. The last outstanding figure among the philosophers of the Enlightenment was the German Immanuel Kant. In 1784 he identified the central nature of the issue of freedom in an essay whose title posed a great question: *What is Enlightenment?* Kant, unlike many who ask rhetorical questions, attempted to answer his. He formulated his general conclusion thus:

'Enlightenment is man's release from self-incurred tutelage. Tutelage is man's inability to make use of his understanding without directions from another.' The motto of the age, he thought, should be *sapere aude* – dare to know, and this was indeed a motto already familiar, because much quoted by thinkers earlier in the century.

Knowledge and understanding were therefore linked to the idea of freedom. The example of it was to spread from one state to another and from religious thought where the weight of authority was most marked to other fields of intellectual activity. Kant did not himself pitch the claims of his age too high, even in this restricted field of religious speculation. Significantly (from this point of view) he called his century the century of Frederick. In his king and ruler Kant saw the best embodiment of the principle of toleration which was the practical expression of his notion of enlightenment, but he recognized how far this principle had to go. 'If we are asked, "do we now live in an *enlightened age*?",' he wrote, 'The answer is "No, but we live in an *age of enlightenment*."' And he was optimistic that the principle of replacing authority by self-direction in matters of the mind would go further. Liberty, for Kant, had a contagious element in it. 'The manner of thinking of the head of a state who favours religious enlightenment goes further, as he sees that there is no danger to his lawgiving in allowing his subjects to make public use of their reason and to publish their thoughts on a better formulation of his legislation and even their open-minded criticism of the laws already made. Of this we have a shining example wherein no monarch is superior to him whom we honour.' Other monarchs were to follow this example, notably Joseph II and, in a smaller measure, Louis XVI, who conceded to his Protestant subjects in 1788 civil rights which put them on a much more equal footing with Catholics. On the other hand, the English, who already enjoyed a wide measure of toleration in practice, found it difficult to go further and agree about further relief from their legal disabilities for Protestant dissenters or Roman Catholics.

Religious toleration was central to the idea that all thought and speculation should be free from restraint, an idea still sometimes violently resisted. Kant thought that the process of undermining intellectual authority had in fact gone a long way and in his major philosophical work, *The Critique of Pure Reason*, he remarked that 'our age is, in especial degree, the age of criticism, and to criticism everything must submit.' The point could have been made with reference to the Enlightenment itself, and in Kant's ideas can be seen new currents which marked the later Enlightenment and distinguished it from what had gone before. There had always been a great practical emphasis to advanced thought in the eighteenth century; one sign of a new trend was that this became even more pronounced. Men such as Turgot belonged to a generation passionately concerned to improve material reality and rationalize behaviour. To them, freedom often seemed the right way ahead. But in Kant, as in Rousseau, there is something else, a valuing of freedom for its own sake, as a thing in itself, regardless of its practical consequences. From this was to stem the assertiveness of romantic individualism which in the end broke out in many more extreme forms than the thinkers of the mid-century Enlightenment could have approved.

Before 1789, not a great deal was to be heard about freedom in this exalted and subjective sense. The generation among whose leading figures were Turgot, Jefferson, Smith, Kant and Bentham still prized freedom in the main because its results were self-evidently or deducibly good. Yet not all of them could agree about the value of the most basic sort of freedom, that of the individual, though enlightened ideas were central to a movement for the abolition of slavery which began to attract public attention in Great Britain and France in the last quarter of the century. Arguments were drawn from the assertions that men were equal in rights, and they combined with the compassion aroused by growing awareness of the evils of slavery and, in particular, the slave trade. Christians were by no means always so quick to take up this cause as they might have been. It is interesting that the man whose name is later most closely attached to the struggle for the abolition of the slave trade, Wilberforce, acquired his convictions that the trade was wrong before he succumbed to the evangelical religion which made him so formidable an advocate of abolition.

Concern for men's rights and for their humanity was taken generally by the enlightened to be a sign of progress. An earlier pessimism was replaced in the last quarter of the century by a much greater expression of confidence in progress. Turgot was probably the first to achieve high office among those who believed in the perfectibility of man. In the 1790s, amid the turmoil and far from reassuring evidence provided by a revolution, Condorcet wrote a *Sketch for a Historical Picture of the Progress of the Human Mind* which is the purest embodiment of the faith in progress, and announced bravely in it that 'the human race still revolts the philosopher who contemplates its history; but it no longer humiliates him, and now offers him hope for the future.' Such a faith sustained the idea of Improvement, whether the faith was articulate or not. It was rooted in the assumptions of the confident phase of the Enlightenment and was long to survive.

Optimism about the malleability of man went along with confidence in progress and the ability of man to pursue his own goals once freed from external tutelage. One consequence was the first great surge of advance in educational thinking since the Renaissance. The invention of a new word marked it: pedagogy. The date 1775 matters as little here as in most other matters of intellectual history. Many currents poured into the new concern; a psychology derived ultimately from Locke, the seventeenth-century English philosopher, a new sentimental appreciation of the needs and possibilities of the child to be found in Rousseau, and the practical experience of the great Roman Catholic teaching Orders of clergy were among them. Its expressions were equally diverse, from the movement to present knowledge to a large audience through encyclopaedias to the reform of universities by the state, and attempts to confine this movement in a chronological strait-jacket are bound to fail. One other obvious characteristic of the concern of the second half of the eighteenth century over education is that its aims were ambiguous and its results therefore incoherent. On the one hand, an emphasis on individualism is discernible which suggests a re-orientation of society toward new principles. Rousseau's Emile was to be allowed no book before adolescence except *Robinson Crusoe*: this bible of the virtues of independence, adaptability and self-reliance might well be thought a very appropriate recommendation for a generation about to witness the rejection by Europe of its corporate past and its revolutionizing towards an individualism of the market. Yet much more destructive and practical achievements were soon being registered by rulers who introduced educational reforms with very different aims in view. The outstanding example, perhaps, was Joseph 11, whose utilitarian and authoritarian viewpoint, and concern for state power, led him not only into conflict with the Church but into such details as the regulation of the wearing of stays by girls in convents.

One point is fairly clear: faith in education fed faith in progress. This had already led by 1775 to a change in attitudes to the past which spread into every aspect of cultural and social life. There was a huge eighteenth-century effort to write history, an effort which has been said to have resulted in the most important intellectual achievement of the age. But a way of looking at the past can also have an influence beyond the traditional formal boundaries of historiography, and the eighteenth century in fact opened an age when men who were not scholars would learn to think about themselves differently, because they would see themselves against different backgrounds from their predecessors.

Broadly speaking, in 1700 the 'past' had meant only what was contained in sacred scripture together with Roman Antiquity. Between it and modern times there stretched a pretty undifferentiated continuum. In the first half of the century Voltaire distinguished the Renaissance as a great age of civilization; men accepted the view that a discovery of learning had led to science and other good things which characterized an advanced civilization beginning to move forward rapidly once more. But between Renaissance and Antiquity stretched the Middle Ages, a period thought hardly worthy of serious cultural consideration, whatever the importance of its institutional obscurities to legists and controversialists. By and large, this attitude animated Gibbon, the greatest of Englightenment historians. It was reflected too in an excessive enthusiasm for Rome among the cultured which was expressed nostalgically in the theatrical prints of Piranesi, who depicted a Rome in ruins, but ruins none the less dwarfing the modern men who wandered among them and lived in their crevices.

A change in this attitude came from several sources. One was the rediscovery of Greece, the missing half of classical antiquity. It had never, of course, been wholly forgotten, but it was not until the middle of the eighteenth century that the idealization of Greece began which was so to transform men's view of the past. Soon Goethe and Flaxman were to express disappointment that Rome did not come up to Piranesi's images, and the neo-classical vogue which was to dominate art from 1770 to 1820 was launched.

But there was more than scene-shifting in the background to the remaking of men's view of their past. One contribution to it came from the growing relativism which characterized eighteenth-century writing on moral, theological and social topics. This was in a measure a function of better information about other cultures as more and more of the world was penetrated by Europeans. It was logical that exploration should be extended in time as well as space. The distinctiveness of historic cultures was well-known; it could perhaps be accepted as readily as that of the Chinese had been. A new interest in the pagan past and admiration for its supposed virtues confirmed the anti-Christian stance of some publicists. It is important not to exaggerate this or to think of it as more general than it was. It was a matter of a few, though an important few, who have left a huge mark in the documentation; Gibbon confessed that he had been unaware of the degree of attachment of so many men to formal Christianity and was therefore startled by the criticism which his mocking and sceptical tone provoked. Even Voltaire never said that he was himself an atheist.

None the less, although many people continued to live and write as though the assumptions of traditional Christianity and those of unfettered criticism were compatible, it is undeniable that there began to show itself in the 1770s and 1780s – well before the French Revolution – a new fear of the danger Enlightenment presented to organized religion. It was in the early 1770s that the French clergy, long obsessed, if they were conservatively inclined, with the struggle against Jansenism, began to give more attention to the *philosophes* as their most dangerous enemy. Yet this theme, too, gives little respect to artificial periodization. The great era of anti-clericalism in Enlightenment thought had been the first half of the century, and its main battleground had been the issue of toleration. This was not over by 1775, but by then there were plenty of signs that the ideas of the Enlightenment had made headway even among the clergy themselves. Possibly it was just this, together with the shock produced by the dissolution of the Society of Jesus, which led to a new violence in clerical polemic in France against 'philosophy' in the 1770s and 1780s.

Whatever the root causes, one result was the creation of a new mythology, that of Enlightenment as an essentially corrupting, negative, irreligious and malevolently inspired force. Such a view existed before 1789 and can hardly have failed to flatter the self-esteem of anti-clerical writers. Rousseau had quarrelled with the *philosophes* but shared many assumptions and goals with them. None the less, his attack on artificiality and the fetish of reason in the name of the moral guidance available in the emotions blurred easily into the religious counterattack on impiety and immorality. Already in Kant, the climax of Enlightenment thought, there are present considerations which made it impossible any longer to recognize the world of the Encyclopaedia.

Many of these expressed themselves in literature, and this has led to a convenient label for them and the general influence underlying them: pre-romanticism. One identifying characteristic was a change in the idea of nature, one of the master-ideas of the whole century. From being predominantly associated with rational order or conceived as the expression of a reasonable creator's will, nature came to be recognized as something embodying incoherences and contrasts, something expressed, above all, as much in the emotions as in the reasoning faculties. Such intuitions went back a long way. Before 1750 Rousseau wrote the essay in which he argued the corrupting effects of civilization upon man's natural dispositions, and he was perhaps chiefly remarkable rather for the vigour with which he pursued the teachings of sentiment in his writings and for the beauty of the French in which he expressed them, than in his awareness of this theme.

Yet the appeal to sentiment for authority in morals, politics and aesthetics was one of the forces making for the fragmentation of a formerly coherent intellectual world in the last quarter of the century. It expressed itself in a multitude of forms, from a new taste for solitary and dramatic landscapes, dwarfing the once proud lords of creation who gazed upon them, to the appearance of the *Lyrical Ballads* of 1789 in which Wordsworth and Coleridge sought to present poetic insights in a selection of the speech of everyday. The most fundamental effects were moral: the consultation of the uncorrupted conscience within instead of convention, standing law, public opinion, the teachings of the Church or any other objective – that is, external – guide. This was as truly a revolutionary seed as had been the inner light of Puritanism in earlier ages. It was to be enthroned at the heart of formal philosophy by Kant's conception of the categorical imperative, the moral legislator in the breast of each man. That this was also a doctrine at once democratic – because the uneducated and poor had access to the promptings of conscience as readily as the instructed and rich – and individualist was to appear only as the early nineteenth century brought romanticism's most dramatic expressions in public action, but anarchic individualism, the assertion that genius knows no rules, was present already in the German literary movement which won for itself the label of *Sturm und Drang*.

More people saw the plays of Klinger or Schiller, where the principles of this movement were given expression, than read the works of Kant. This is a consideration which must affect judgments of pre-romanticism as it affects judgments on Enlightenment. No doubt, too, very few people read the works of the Marquis de Sade though both Kant and Rousseau would have found little acceptable in what they said. For all their rejection of some enlightened assumptions, the pre-romantics were as firmly anchored in the assumption of a harmonious order which must entail a rational order as were those whom they criticized. They distinguished themselves by their means of perceiving this order, rather than by any rejection of it in principle.

A reminder of these complexities is the point at which to return to the monolithic and powerful, but misleading, myth of the eighteenth century on the Age of Enlightenment with which we began. In it, the men of the Enlightenment seem a much more united body holding a more coherent body of ideas than was in fact the case. Anti-Enlightenment fostered this myth. It thus gave critics of the *status quo* a standard about which to rally. In the nineteenth century the reprinting of the works of the *philosophes* became one of the indices of liberalism. Yet the *philosophes* – who were ready enough, it must be said, in their own day to exaggerate the intensity and coherence of criticism directed against them – were, for the most part, socially completely acceptable to the elites of the societies in which they moved. They gave these societies much of their tone and often had allies in high places. Christian culture itself, to judge by its official guardians, seemed to be able to accommodate much of their teaching. They almost always shunned radical social change of a kind which would have sapped the hierarchies of which they were themselves a part. Much of what now seems most characteristic of eighteenth-century thought was given unity and emphasis only by its opponents, after the shock of the Revolution had appeared to justify their fears. Yet the heart of Enlightenment was not really doctrine or even a set of goals but a common manner in intellectual activity which gave greatest value among intellectual qualities to reasonableness, scepticism and freedom of speculation. This was the secret of its great liberating power.

6 Political change

The most conscious agency at work to undermine and transform the *ancien régime* was the State itself. It was for a long time the most important, too, expressing itself in different countries in activities which have seemed to have enough in common to be summed up in a contemporary phrase: enlightened despotism. The heart of this was to be found in attempts to centralize power in absolute monarchy. They went a long way before absolutism itself began to be undermined by social and economic changes which were to sweep it away in most countries in the next century. In the eighteenth century these were less powerful. Monarchical authority was the main source of change before 1789.

Though the enlightened despots had to act with means which were crude and feeble by comparison with the later powers of the state, they yet showed a vigour which startled contemporaries. They caused surprise first by the seeming lack of respect for historic rights and institutions which they showed in the pursuit of centralization and rationalization of government, and secondly by the enthusiasm they sometimes professed for advanced ideas. Some of them carried on long flirtations with the *philosophes* – as did Frederick the Great and Catherine of Russia – while others, themselves more orthodox, employed ministers (such as Turgot) who were deeply sympathetic to the enlightened tradition. These aspects of enlightened despotism reflected its double nature. It was in part negative, an attempted response by new means to the weakness of the state, in part positive, a desire to reform and to look well to contemporaries. The public relations side of this was on the whole successful. Though there were some disconcerting personal encounters, *philosophes* were usually flattered by royal notice and patronage. It was easy for them to accept it because they were for the most part less interested in liberty and the wishes of the majority (which was likely to be bigoted and brutal) than in certain specific reforms, among which religious toleration and freedom of expression of opinion usually took the first place; these were less difficult to grant than many other benefits.

In many ways, Frederick the Great was the most successful of enlightened despots. The growth of the number of his subjects and the extent of his domains were measurable achievements. The Prussian economy, too, prospered during his reign. The State was a model of religious toleration, and humane reforms were made in the law. Many of these successes, on the other hand, had little to do with enlightenment. They were the traditional policies of a Prussian government which had always had advantages which were not available to other states. Though geographically scattered, Frederick's lands contained no local representative estates or corporations capable of standing up to royal authority. That authority, too, could be exercised very directly and effectively in that part of Prussia which was actually royal domain, the outright property of the royal landlord. Much, finally, depended on the king himself. Good government was not ineradicably institutionalized in Prussia, as the faltering of its powers after Frederick's death was to show. It depended on the will-power and industry of one man, not upon a system.

Limitations upon the achievements of enlightened despotism in Prussia also arose from the assumptions behind Frederick's policies. Mercantilism, for example, though a doctrine shared with other states, hampered economic development. Another consequence of Frederick's essential conservatism was his indulgence of nobility. For all their lack of representative institutions, the Prussian nobles were powerful because they were the backbone of the Prussian bureaucracy and army. They could not be lightly offended – not that Frederick wished to offend them. He would not give commissions in the army to non-nobles except in wartime emergencies and though a businessman might get important privileges – and even a portrait of the king himself – from his royal patron, he was not given noble rank. Because of this respect for his nobles and their privileges, there were things which even a serjeant-major king could not order them to do. Characteristically, even under his successor, the aristocracy of service which was represented by the growing number of non-noble civil servants was rewarded in 1794 not by giving its members access to nobility but by constituting them legally as a new corporate body, the *Beamtenstand*. This was far from a step forward from *ancien régime* ideas; to constitute a new estate of the realm was a dramatic confirmation that they continued.

The restrictions upon Catherine II of Russia were in some ways the strongest of all those acting upon 'enlightened despots'. To begin with, she seems herself to have accepted much more willingly than some of her fellow-rulers restraints suggested by prudence: 'You write only on paper,' she once told the *philosophe* Diderot, 'I have to write on human skin.' The practical problems of government in Russia, whatever

69

policies were considered desirable, were in themselves an encouragement to caution. Over its huge area, communications were poor. The
literate population was probably a smaller proportion of the whole than
in any other European state. Only a feeble bureaucracy existed to
provide an alternative to the nobility as an instrument of government.
The result was confusion about the purposes of government, gaps and
irregularities in the application of legislation, inefficiency and waste-
fulness.

The weakness of the government does much to explain the concessions of Catherine to her nobility, who were released from the obligations
to service which had been increasingly heavy from their introduction in
the sixteenth century and became heaviest during the reign of Peter the
Great. The view long held that she also gave the nobility – who were
most of the landlord class – an even stronger grip on their peasants has,
on the other hand, been criticized. In 1775 an imperial manifesto
actually forbade the re-enserfment of a serf once freed, while ways of
enserfing peasants which had grown up earlier in the century had
already by then been made illegal, and at the end of the century the
first limitations were imposed upon the landlord's exploitation of his
serf labour as he would. It has been calculated that although there
were provinces which did not reflect the trend, the proportion of the
serf population to the whole population of Russia began to go down
from the decade 1772–82.

This is by no means an easy question to unravel and what is clearer
is that Catherine disappointed some who had hoped to see her do more
in the way of reform. From a distance, Western admirers praised her
for religious tolerance, yet her coadjutor Potemkin was a bigoted
Orthodox churchman, she did not scruple to impose force against the
Old Believers and she imprisoned Radischev, the first Russian radical.

Catherine had clothed the traditional reality of Russian autocracy,
of which she was an assiduous and worthy upholder, with the glitter
of the superficial civilization of St Petersburg and crowned it with an
aura of success. This was more noticeable in her foreign than in her
domestic government, where she acted very traditionally. The role of
the autocracy in Russia had always been actually to *make* a state in a
huge space without natural frontiers. This imposed the need to incorporate new territory within its boundaries and then to weld it to the
Russian state by strong government. Given the background of cultural
backwardness, this could only mean harsh government. Military
methods were often employed, for example in a brutal imposition of
Russian settlement and government in the Crimea after 1783. Potemkin
used his authority and powers as a military commander to obtain
results not available from the crude civil administrative machine. The

local results were almost always at the expense of non-Russian peoples, and this may, in the long run, be thought to have been a source of weakness to the Tsarist state. Non-Russians had played a conspicuous part in Pugachev's rising and there were to be many revolutionary movements among them in the nineteenth century. The most important subject people was the Polish: while the first Partition had given Russia many former Polish subjects who were not themselves Poles but Ukrainians and Little Russians and so alienated from their Polish masters, the next two Partitions (and, in the next century, further acquisitions) gave Russia what was to prove the most troublesome subject people in Europe.

Some of the obstacles to reform which were respected by Frederick and Catherine were internal; in the case of Joseph II they were almost exclusively external. In the first place came the conservatism of his mother, the Empress Maria Theresia, who shared in the government of the Empire and dominated it until her death in 1780. Others lay in the structure of the Empire, whose shape was defined by historic and entrenched rights and privileges. Joseph himself felt few inhibitions. His brother, Leopold of Tuscany, expressed uneasiness at the radicalism with which he took up and attempted to put into practice ideas which, if not new, were now given striking emphasis. Among them was a pervasive anti-clericalism whose practical roots may be sought in the obstacle which the corporate privilege of the church put in the way of reform of the state. Resources for taxation were bitten into by mortmain. A clerical monopoly of education stood in the way of its use as an instrument of social engineering. Canon Law and sanctuary encumbered legal reform. The climate of opinion in which Joseph wished to deploy his reform was set, moreover, by the commentary provided by pulpit confessional and classroom.

Struggles with the Church therefore took up much of his time and energy. On the whole he had his way until, towards the end of his reign, they became entangled in other struggles, those with local privileged and representative bodies such as the Estates of Brabant and Hungary. This ended with his Belgian provinces in full revolt and royal policy in retreat in Hungary. Soon, men would begin to look back to Joseph as a ruler who had anticipated the anti-social and anti-religious policies which they discerned in the French Revolution.

In retrospect, this theme was to loom large in much later discussion of 'enlightened despotism' but it is too simple to say that the phenomenon simply gave a foretaste of the great Revolution. What was in common between the work of later Frenchmen and the servants of the enlightened despots was a common will to assert the sovereignty of the State. They derived this sovereignty from different sources, inherited absolutism in the one case, and the people in the other, but its supremacy was common ground. On the other hand, the enlightened despots were monarchs: their own position was justified by the same arguments as those sustaining the hierarchies over which they presided and they could not reject birth, nobility and history as could the men of 1789.

The similarities in religious policies were misleading, too. Much of Joseph's quarrel with ecclesiastics was over straightforward issues of jurisdiction and immunity which were the familiar stock-in-trade of centuries of Church and State dispute. Historical quarrels with the Papacy over regalian rights had been going on all through the eighteenth century in Spain and Naples, for instance. But no eighteenth-century monarch could or wanted to dispense with religion; there was only a tiny element of pure anti-religious feeling in their policies at most. What they expressed was rather an anti-ecclesiastical and anti-clerical bias. Economically, reformers were antagonized because they thought there were too many clergy for society to support and because too much property was in clerical hands which were not stimulated to make the best of it by commercial pressures Fiscal and judicial immunities offended lay lawyers. Humanity was outraged by the continued intolerance of churchmen towards heretics and Jews and Enlightenment by their use of a near-monopoly of the cultural and educational apparatus to stifle thought. But nothing was heard at the level of government of outright and essential criticism of Christianity or the Church. In the eighteenth century, political debate on religious questions still fell well within the confines of the assumption that religion was to be respected and upheld.

This was, for example, true of the debate in several countries on Jansenism, an ill-defined notion, many of whose manifestations came by the end of the eighteenth century to seem very remote from the theology of Jansen, the seventeenth-century Dutch divine whose name it commemorated. Though doctrinal in origin, Jansenism became a political issue in many countries. Usually it favoured reforming monarchs, providing a foothold among the clergy and faithful for anti-clerical policies. This was because ecclesiastical authority focussed at Rome; Jansenists tended to favour the authority of local bishops against that of the Pope, whose authority they thought subject to that of a general council. Moreover, they took a narrow view of the privileges the church required; 'My kingdom is not of this world' was one of their favourite texts. Providing the church were left by the state to get on with its essential tasks of preaching the Word and making available the sacraments, Jansenists were not disposed to quarrel with legislation which cut into ecclesiastical privilege. Jansenism in Italy, Febronianism in Germany and regalianism in Spain had therefore all much the same tendency to support the work of the enlightened despots.

The support of Jansenists for Leopold of Tuscany or Joseph certified the concern of such monarchs for the true interests of religion; what they did could be seen as ecclesiastical reform. Anti-clerical they might be, but anti-Christian the monarchs were sure they were not. They accepted fundamental religious limits to their freedom as they did fundamental social restraints; they did not contest the principle of rank and wealth. Nor did even radical thinkers in the eighteenth century make the mistake of thinking there was a necessary connection between Enlightenment and democracy. It was Condorcet who remarked that 'a monarch can act in accordance with the principles of enlightened men without being held up by popular opinion.'

As the example of Turgot showed, France was not untouched by the aspiration to reform of the state which was the heart of enlightened despotism. Yet although France was in many ways culturally the most advanced of continental great powers, her institutions for a long time cushioned her from fundamental change and did so until it was too late for change which was not revolutionary. The 1770s and 1780s were crucial decades because the problems of France then became insoluble within the inherited framework. A crushing burden was added to them by the American war which carried the debts of the state to unprecedented heights. The financial problem of the French *ancien régime* now took its final shape: how could France be given back the freedom to pursue an independent foreign policy – which meant an expensive one – while avoiding a bankruptcy which would destroy confidence in the credit of the monarchy and alienate large numbers of investors?

This problem had to be solved in the 1780s in a context triply poisoned and encumbered. Partly because of the unwillingness of the Crown to press forward ruthlessly and partly because of the strength of the institutions with which the privileged classes defended themselves, enlightened despotism did not work in France. All that it seemed able to do was to provide the Church, the *parlements* and the local provincial Estates which spoke for conservatism with a plausible claim to be resisting a 'despotism' which threatened the historic French constitution. Many of those using such arguments undoubtedly believed them. As the decade began to draw to a close, the political battle was more and more polarized into the issue of whether the Crown could find a way forward to reform acceptable to Frenchmen which would not be blocked by the legal opposition of the *parlements*.

The second blight settling upon French affairs from 1786 onwards was that of growing economic hardship. The long-term price and population rise which always produced acute hardship in bad times now reached its climax after two bad harvests in 1787 and 1788. A trade recession which they made inevitable was accentuated by political uneasiness about public credit and a disturbed international situation. Early in 1789 some Frenchmen were spending nine-tenths of their earnings on bread. An economic balance always fragile was approaching breaking-point, and new attempts to liberate the internal grain trade only made things worse.

The third factor operating to make a solution harder was a growing expectancy of reform. Intolerance of governmental failure was shown in the rising volume of published criticism which was at work upon public opinion in Paris, whence it was disseminated through private individuals, reading-rooms, cultural societies and masonic lodges to the provinces. The censorship was by the 1780s very ineffective, and a huge volume of publication, including the beginnings of a periodical press, began to exercise a dominant effect upon opinion. Broadly speaking, it drove home a series of simple lessons, some of them mutually contradictory but still effective in spite of this. Privilege of all sorts was more and more called in question as inimical to the general welfare. So, at the same time, were the theoretically absolute powers of the monarchy which contended with privilege. There was widespread clamour for constitutional liberties, and a mounting demand for something for which the *parlements* had asked in the exactly opposite interest of staving off reform, the summoning of the only body representative of all Frenchmen under the *ancien régime*, the States-General, last assembled in 1614.

In these troubles, the Crown's position was dangerously exposed. Libels had done much to associate the monachy, through the indiscretions of the Austrian queen, with a picture of an extravagant life lived by the privileged at the expense of the mass of Frenchmen. But though this weakened the Crown's popularity, it was not a mortal danger. Such a danger lay, rather, in the subtle change taking place in the position of the monarchy in the last years of the *ancien régime*. From being thought to stand above and apart from all other interests, holding them in balance with impartiality, it was coming to be seen as actually inimical to all other interests and actually damaging to them. Yet there were few republicans in France in 1789. There was, on the contrary, still a huge faith in the monarchy, based on a great residue of habitual respect for all historic institutions. Almost all those Frenchmen who in 1789 were asking for a constitution did so, for example, because they thought that France had indeed had one, but that it had become overlaid in misuse.

The historic remedy was in the end the one to which the monarchy reached out in 1788. Baffled in its search for reform by other roots, the only recourse was to the States-General, a body whose constitutionality was unimpeachable. What was not clear was what its powers were, but the king asked his people to send deputies to it equipped with *cahiers* of grievances whose drawing-up provoked the widest hopes. By the time that happened, the royal government had at last out-flanked the *parlementaire* lawyers by ignoring their demand that the States-General should meet in the same form as in 1614, and ordered instead that they should contain twice as many deputies of the un-privileged as of the privileged orders. But this still left open the question whether the two privileged estates could veto reforms demanded by the Third.

From the other side of the Channel, the English watched with interest the politics of their victorious rival of 1783 slipping into disarray. British politics in the eighteenth century had been marked by great stability since the settling of the dynastic questions. After George III's accession to the throne there had been political storms but their effects were safely contained within the traditional class. What was essentially at stake in these quarrels was the degree of independence of the major politicians which the Crown possessed in the choice of its ministers. Language sometimes ran high, especially during the dark days of the American War, and the king was as willing to paint the picture in strong colours as any, being of a temperament easily excited and depressed. In the end, he demonstrated that in the absence of a great national issue, the Crown could maintain its choice of a minister even when he had no command of a majority in the House of Commons, but also that the minister would have to seek as soon as he could safely do so the endorsement of his position by an election to provide a majority for him. This happened in 1784, when the youngest prime minister in British history, William Pitt, managed a successful general election which gave him a more unassailable grasp on office. Yet if this was a victory for the king, who had been able to stick to the minister he had chosen, it was a hollow one, for it rubbed home the ultimate political authority of the House of Commons.

Essentially, British politics in the eighteenth century were about access to patronage, and they would long continue to be so. Between the great constitutional statutes of the Revolution and Queen Anne at one end, and the reforms whose flood began to sweep in from the 1820s, there stretched a legislative desert, a sure sign of the essential stability of the system. There were plenty of statutes, of course, but the over-whelming mass of legislation took the form of private acts of parliament affecting particular and local questions – many of them Acts of Enclosure – with a few measures from time to time on particular and

75

extraordinary public matters: India and Ireland loomed significantly large here. For constitutional legislation such as that of the seventeenth century, the United Kingdom would have to wait until economic and social change had so much effect that legislative consequences could not be shirked.

This did not mean that there were not already those who questioned the going concern. Quarrels over the parliamentary influence of the king during the American war led to demands for parliamentary reform. Usually, they were still couched in conservative terms; men asked for more seats in the House of Commons for the counties, because it was part of the prevailing political mythology that MPs who sat for counties were less venal, more independent of pressure and promise, than those who sat for boroughs. Only a few people went further than this and asked for a change of principle in the constitution, by widening the electorate. Some other demands also began to be heard. England had long had religious toleration, but non-Anglicans suffered disabilities at law. An attempt to promote legislation to remove those of Roman Catholics provoked a volcanic eruption of popular fury in 1780, when the Gordon Riots (so called after the distracted Protestant peer who led the opposition to Catholic relief) delivered London to a week's rioting and uproar worse by far than anything Paris was to see in the Revolution. Those who sought to relieve Protestant dissent did not meet opposition on this scale, but neither did they get very far with the politicians.

The United Kingdom thus presented a paradox. Though in the process of a double revolution, towards world power and towards a new kind of society based on industry, and although enjoying a civic and cultural life very open in texture and enormously advanced by comparison with continental countries, she none the less had a political stability which was soon to be the envy of all Europe. With a population about two-fifths of that of France, England was wealthy enough to be a great power because she had discovered ways of tapping her wealth without giving government despotic power over its subjects. Englishmen knew they were free men when they looked at Europe, and if they did not, their masters told them so.

Americans, of course, also knew after 1783 that they were free men, but this was when they looked at England; they lived neither under kings, encumbered by hereditary grandees, nor under the restraints of a land long occupied and divided. Nor, they knew, did they have masters. Blacks had masters, but in the eyes of most whites they were no more Americans than were the savage Indian: an American was a white man. Some Americans were in fact worried that there were no obvious masters. From the moment of independence, the major political and ideological issue which hung over the first decades of the young republic was that of democracy. 'The distinction of classes begins to disappear,' wrote Washington sorrowfully in 1788. 'Your people, sir – your people, is a great *beast*!', Hamilton is supposed to have said. Restrictive franchises in several states long gave expression to such fears.

Broadly speaking, the place where you lived and your feelings about democracy determined political allegiance in the young republic. Two parties appeared. Federalists were those who had struggled to buttress the authority of the national government in the constitutional debates. They had the support of commercial and financial interests in New England and on the seaboard which looked for advantages in the regulation of tariff and commercial questions with an eye to protection and in the establishment of sound national credit. Washington's sympathies moved towards the Federalists in his second term of office. The Constitution had said little about the positive powers of the President and did much to establish their far-reaching nature. When Washington retired, the national credit was sound, the machinery of national government had been organized and manned, the entire administrative and diplomatic services were responsible to the President and not to Congress and a rebellion had been put down. These were great steps in consolidation. Moreover, an open party struggle had been delayed.

It could not be prevented for ever. Already, some felt warmly that the hero of Independence had made a bad president. 'This day ought to be a jubilee in the United States,' wrote a Philadelphia newspaper as Washington stepped down. 'The man who is the source of all the misfortunes of our country is this day reduced to a level with his fellow citizens.' This was because, in the eyes of those who thought like this, the achievements of the Federalists were not in the interests of the majority, nor of the most typical, of Americans, and Washington's use of his presidential powers appalled many who thought such behaviour smacked of despotism. Those who felt like this looked to the Republicans for political leadership.

Republicans stood for distrust of central government, for the upholding of agrarian interests and the voice of the common man, if he lived in the West and South. Their most notable leader was Thomas Jefferson, the Virginian author of the Declaration of Independence, an aristocrat if America had such a thing, whose father had farmed four thousand acres. He was himself to be twice President of the United States and had a mind so interesting that his conversation has been considered one of the controlling influences of American history. A man of great creative power, he designed not only his own lovely house at Monticello but the equally striking campus of the University of

Virginia (which he founded). He is one of the tiny band of intellectuals who have held high political office and still seem attractive, in many ways the perfect man of the Enlightenment. Jefferson was a deist and a firm believer in progress. He had all the faults of his type and century, for he was prone to generalize from slight evidence, had a craving for omniscience which opened the way to charges of superficiality and was dogmatic and unfair to opponents. But he was a great man.

Jefferson's political ideas are well-known because he often set them out in vigorous prose; their expression was not confined to the Declaration of Independence. 'I am never a friend to energetic government,' he said, 'It is always oppressive.' For him, the pursuit of happiness meant access to the moral progress which a man could seek if he had the freedom to cultivate his own garden in peace. Aristocrat though he was, Jefferson was an egalitarian, but one whose egalitarian ideas were firmly rooted in the rural, freeholding America which was characteristic of his day. The democracy he envisaged was a democracy of yeomen – some of them, no doubt, slave-owners, as he was.

Given the enthusiasm of some Federalists for active intervention by the national government in the economy, and their distrust of the small farmers who had sought to liquidate their debts by inflation at the expense of their creditors, their dislike of Jefferson and the Republicans is understandable. But there was more than this to divide the two parties. One was that distinctions between parties in the young republic already dimly prefigured a future sectional clash. There is already present in the 1790s a contrast between New England, led by Massachusetts, and the South, led by Virginia. This was at one level a matter of economics, of maritime and commercial interests as against planting and farming. It was in part a matter of debtor and creditor, of a section whose farmers had sold their depreciated government paper for cash in hard times and another section where most of those who invested in such government paper were to be found. There was an ideological level to the division, too, for Virginia was suspicious of England while New England, once the war was over, was constantly aware of the common ties binding America to her former masters. Finally, there was a class question; except for the patrician Virginian leaders, the South contained most of those who had done least well out of the war, while in the North wealth had continued to accumulate in the hands which already held it. Buried in these distinctions were themes which would run through and control American history down to 1865. That they should also have become the basis of political parties was largely due to one man, Alexander Hamilton.

Washington made Hamilton Secretary to the Treasury. He pressed forward with a series of far-sighted measures which sought, through the establishment of a sound currency, a banking system and a protective tariff, to ensure for the United States the wealthy industrial future which Hamilton discerned for her in his most persuasive state paper, his *Report on Manufactures* of 1791. In this prophetic document, Hamilton recognized – though he tried to argue away – the sectional distrusts which rested on economic differentiation. But the whole of his policy aggravated them, benefiting the North. The states with the heaviest war debts, which Hamilton succeeded in transferring to the national government, were in the North. The paper now redeemed at face value by the Federal government was held mainly in the North – after much of it had been bought at low prices in the South. The new bank of the United States would help financiers and merchants, not those whose capital was tied up in land and slaves. A tariff would protect nascent manufactures but put up prices for the agrarian consumer.

Allegations of corruption and hypocrisy soon embittered debate. Then came the impact of a revolution in France in 1789. At the start, Americans tended to see it with approval and could hardly deplore the later appearance there of a new republic. There were also sentiments still alive which gave importance to the Franco-American alliance, undermined though that connection had been even before 1789 by the strong revival and development of economic and commercial ties with Great Britain. Only war between France and other European states brought a decisive change. Though formally an ally of France, the United States would not risk undertaking the protection of French Caribbean colonies. A neutrality proclamation which Washington issued on his own initiative in 1793 made this clear. Soon, too, the activity of French diplomatic agents who sought to dabble in American policy began to frighten some conservatively inclined Americans. This gave a further dimension to the party conflict. The war and its consequences pushed the Federalists more and more into hostility to France. Ship-owners and those who sought to consolidate the improvement in national credit tended to be pro-British. The ministers of religion of New England, an influential force, detested what they saw as French 'atheism'. Meanwhile, the planter interest tended to become pro-French. Deism, the revolutionary tradition and sentiment towards their ally pulled Jefferson and his friends into support of the French Revolution.

That event also turned relations between states upside down as they had not been turned upside down since the Protestant Reformation. Yet the eighteenth-century international scene was by no means stable even before 1789. The American war burst into a world full of diplomatic tension. The international competition which produced this was no longer rooted in ideology as it had sometimes been in the era of religious wars, nor was it quite so uncompromisingly dynastic as hitherto. Instead, the matter of diplomacy was more and more about the relations towards one another of governments increasingly ruling well-defined areas and increasingly the custodians of important social and even national interests. Competition to protect these was, of course, the fundamental source of the eighteenth-century urge to reform the state, because of the growing costs it imposed. It was expensive to be a great power and this put traditional institutions under strain as states-men sought for more money to pay the soldiers and build the ships which international competition required.

Roughly speaking, eighteenth-century diplomacy focussed on four great questions or bundles of questions. One was settled by mid-century; this was the shape of the dynastic and political geography of western Europe. So far as Great Britain, Spain and Portugal, Italy and France were concerned, this provided a structure maintained with only minor or temporary modification until well after 1847. The other three questions were much more alive. One was worldwide, a great colonial competition which had begun in the seventeenth century and which, by 1775, was reduced to a struggle between two states, Great Britain and France. Spain, Portugal and the United Provinces, the first great colonial powers, were no longer competitors. Habsburg attempts to get into the business of extra-European commerce and colonialism had in the end come to naught on the rock of implacable British hostility. Prussia, too, had made efforts to get into the Far Eastern trade which came to little. It was really only Great Britain and France which were in the running. In 1775 the contest seemed to have been decided in Great Britain's favour, too. France had by then surrendered Canada to her, and had virtually given up any serious forward effort in India. Nevertheless, France was still a colonial and naval power.

The other two major issues which ran though international affairs in the later half of the eighteenth century were both of them European, or almost wholly European. One was the Habsburg-Hohenzollern rivalry which had flared up in the 1740s with Frederick's seizure of Silesia, a prize which he still held in 1775. This was a quarrel which was to be interrupted and masked, after his death. Later it would be resumed and not settled until after 1847. It took various forms, but the essential question was whether the Habsburg monarchy should maintain its traditional ascendancy in Germany, or whether Germany should be a zone of influence from which Austria was excluded and in which, therefore, it was likely that the influence of Prussia, most powerful of the purely German states, should prevail.

The last major issue which concerned statesmen more or less continuously was the Eastern Question, somewhat misleadingly named because there was usually more than one 'Eastern Question', though there were common elements running through them. The most important of these was the growing power and importance of Russia. First fully evident in the Seven Years' War (1756–63), it was by 1775 unmistakable. The growth of Russian power continued across two phases of the Eastern Question. The first was one in which the crucial issue was the balancing of the interests of Russia, Prussia and the Habsburgs in eastern Europe, where a truncated and weakened Poland still survived between them in 1775 (Swedish power, once so influential in the area, was by then no longer of primary importance). The next phase, which may be called the nineteenth-century one, may begin according to choice either in 1774, when Russia imposed a victorious peace on Turkey, or in 1783, when she annexed the territories of the khanate of the Crimean Tatars. Each of these events announces the same fact: the Eastern Question was henceforth about the future of the Ottoman Empire, about its possible successors, about the balance of power in the Black Sea, the Danube valley, the Balkans and eventually the eastern Mediterranean, a vast area whose future was to take far longer than that of western Europe, Poland or Germany to settle.

Twenty years after the Peace of Paris, it looked as if the French had successfully played their return match in the colonial competition. The British had lost the Thirteen Colonies, and this was in the eyes of every European statesman and many Britons a colossal humiliation and a real loss of power. Apart from this, the peace was by no means so unfavourable to the United Kingdom. The fortress of Gibraltar, which the Spanish had hoped to recapture, was not given up even if Minorca had to be, and Great Britain had obtained the Bahamas and an assortment of West Indian islands to balance the French recovery of some of hers and the recognition of French rights to trade in the East Indies and India. Other changes, too, were by no means unfavourable, though this would take some time to appear. American colonies might be independent, but their former economic ties with England remained and were soon to be reinforced and increased. The appearance of the new Union, too, did not necessarily militate only against the interest of Great Britain. Though some Americans coveted Canada and discovered plentiful causes for irritation with Great Britain over boundary questions and the slow fulfilment of British obligations to evacuate western posts, the British recognition of the Mississippi as the western boundary of the United States was a blow to France and Spain. Both of these states had plans for expansion in that area and on the northern rim of the Caribbean. More serious still, the actual financial cost of victory to France had been very heavy; the cost of humiliating her enemy, winning limited (if real) territorial and commercial gains for herself and Spain and the possible goodwill of the Americans was the crippling of her finances.

This posed important questions at home; abroad, it was even more damaging. It began to be clear that France might not again be able to act as a great power, if the price was so high. This would be fatal to the traditional position of France in Europe, for she had interests in other parts of Europe which had to be maintained by diplomacy and, if necessary, by arms. Anglo-French rivalry had European as well as colonial dimensions. It involved the affairs of Germany; an Austrian princess was queen of France and France the ally of the Emperor.

France and Austria were always concerned about the Netherlands, the southern part being Austrian, the northern being the independent Dutch United Provinces. This was an area in which British policy was traditionally interested and traditionally deeply suspicious of French intentions from the days of Louis xiv to the 1830s. In the 1780s, diplomacy was stirred up by the attempts of Joseph ii both to open the Scheldt to international trade (which should have pleased his Belgian subjects and displeased the Dutch) and to get rid of the Belgian provinces to someone else. At the same time came internal troubles in the United Provinces which led by 1787 to the French supporting one party, the revolutionists, and the British and Prussians joining in an alliance with the Dutch, which clearly indicated that French influence would preponderate in Holland only at the cost of war. It was to be a matter of another six years before this happened; meanwhile, the powerlessness of France which resulted from her internal weakness was very obvious; it inflamed anti-British feeling in France. The victor of 1783 could not enforce her will on her own borders.

The affairs of the Netherlands also complicated the Habsburg-Hohenzollern rivalry. In 1775, Prussia was in the lead; she retained Silesia and had gained more than Austria from the first Partition of Poland. Within a few years, Prussia and Austria were again at war – though not, it was to prove, very bloodily – over a German issue, that of Bavaria. The quarrel blew up out of a disputed claim of succession in the old style, complicated by feudal and dynastic claims, which led to the occupation of parts of the electorate by Austrian forces in 1778. Frederick hastily put himself behind a rival claimant, posed as the protector of the German princes against a grasping emperor and invaded Habsburg Bohemia to support his assertion. The Austrian army which marched to oppose him did not fight, but difficulties of obtaining supplies led to the commemoration of the campaign as the 'Potato War'; after a dismal winter the armies went home, France and Russia having interposed their mediatory efforts to impose a settlement which gave Austria about a sixth of her claims in Bavaria. It was generally agreed that Frederick had been the winner. His influence and prestige in Germany grew at the cost of Joseph II.

Frederick died in 1786 and before then had scored once more in the long duel, when Joseph had to give up a scheme to exchange Bavaria for the Austrian Netherlands, and Frederick appeared for the last time as leader of Germany in the *Furstenbund*, a league of princes to maintain their rights and prevent the union of Bavaria and Austria. The pendulum was about to swing the other way. His successor, Frederick William II, continued his hostility towards Austria, but with much less success, though he was supported by the British in Holland against Austria's ally, France, in the Triple Alliance of 1788 which brought Prussia's standing to its greatest height. A decline then began almost at once. Prussian policy overreached itself in attempting to use an Austrian entanglement with the Turks to make unacceptable demands, and Great Britain and Holland refused support. The result was that Prussia had to settle by herself with Austria in 1790. The first half-century of Prusso-Austrian conflict was ended. Austria, liberated from the threat of war with Prussia, turned to defeat the Turks.

In the background to the Habsburg-Hohenzollern story lies the shadow of Russia. She was to be pace-maker in the Eastern Question for over a century. Since the sixteenth century Europe's relations with the Ottoman Empire had usually been regarded as primarily the concern of the Habsburgs and the Catholic kingdom of Poland. When Ottoman power was at last clearly seen to be on the defensive, these two powers began to pick up territorial rewards. By 1718 the Austro-Turkish frontier was already across the Danube in northern Serbia and Bosnia, and across the Transylvanian Alps to include western Wallachia. But by this time, too, a great new fact which changed the Eastern Question had appeared in the shape of the expanding Russia of Peter the Great. The nineteenth-century Eastern Question was from this time already discernible: who was to have the spoils if Turkey continued to give ground and how were all the interested parties to be satisfied that the balance of power which followed the eclipse of Turkey was acceptable?

This question was not settled by 1800, nor by 1847; it became enlarged at last to take in the Asian and African territories of the Ottoman succession – the whole Middle East – and, indeed, in this respect is with us still. None the less, important new developments had occurred by 1800: the Polish State had by then disappeared, its fragmented remains providing the fulcrum on which a new balance of power in eastern Europe was to rest for over a century, Turkish power had lost the battle to keep Russia off the Black Sea and (after a recovery against Austria in the middle of the century) further ground in the Danube valley, and the extra-European stage of the Ottoman succession problem had opened in Egypt.

Almost all of these were consequences of the continuing rise of Russian power. What this power could do in central Europe if provoked to interfere there was already clear in the Seven Years' War and the first Partition of Poland. After it, the Russian drive to the south preoccupied statesmen for the next twenty years. The mouths of all Russia's great rivers ran to the Black Sea, whose northern coasts were important to Russian trade, and the Ottoman Empire was temptingly distracted by internal debates over the degree to which Western influences should be allowed to compromise her Islamic culture in the interests of modernization. By and large, only the French did much to befriend the Turks, and they soon had their hands full with the American war. Austria was distracted by German affairs and was always likely to be as much attracted by the prospect of gains which would balance Russia's as in preventing those.

By and large, therefore, Russian policy made the running in the Eastern Question. It was especially active under Catherine. There was talk of her having a 'Grand Design' of a Greek Empire with its capital at Constantinople. She had encouraged rebellion among the Greek subjects of the Porte before Kutchuk Kainardji gave her the right to intervene in Ottoman affairs on their behalf. One of her grandsons had been given the name of Constantine, the evocative name of the first Christian Emperor of Rome and the name also of the last emperor of Byzantium. On some of her coins Catherine stamped the image of Constantinople's St Sophia, once the greatest church of Christendom.

The first step after Kainardji was to settle the fate of the Crimean Tatars. Their khanate stretched much further than their name suggests, even though the Crimea was its centre. At its height it ran from the Caucasus to Transylvania; thus a great stretch of territory was nominally ruled by the khan who was really titular head of an oligarchy of Tatar aristocrats. Since the fifteenth century the khans had acknowledged the suzerainty of the Turkish sultan and had come to rely on Ottoman money for the upkeep of their state. They were an important buffer between Russia and the main Turkish power and when Kainardji brought to an end their acknowledgment of Ottoman suzerainty, an era ended: this was the first dependent Moslem area to be lost by the Ottoman Empire, and Russia could now establish herself formally on the Black Sea. For a few years, Catherine was content to maintain an independent Crimean state, but its internal troubles led to the abandonment of this idea. In 1783 the Crimean Tatars were annexed to Russia. It could now be only a matter of time before there was a Russian fleet based on the Crimean ports. Meanwhile, in the same year, the extension of Russian protection to a Georgian prince further alarmed the Turks. They had hung on grimly in 1774 to the fortress of Oczakov, which controlled the mouths of the Bug and Dnieper. This was the key base from which they launched a war against Russia in 1787. The Turks felt that the sands were running out when earlier in that year Catherine, accompanied by Joseph II, had made a journey to the Crimea, where she had inspected a new naval base at Sevastopol. They feared – groundlessly – that a partition of the Ottoman Empire was in prospect, and the activity of newly appointed Russian consuls in the Danubian provinces of Moldavia and Wallachia increased their alarm.

A decision to go to war turned out badly for Turkey. The French, Prussian and British governments were all too preoccupied with Holland to help, however great their misgivings about the spread of Russian power; the Austrians, on the other hand, joined in against Turkey in 1788. A Swedish declaration of war against her distracted Russia only for a time, though Austria was forced out of the war in 1790 by troubles in her Belgian provinces. Russia none the less won victory after victory. By the treaty of peace signed at Jassy in 1792, the Dniester became the Russo-Turkish frontier. Oczakov went to Russia in spite of the protests of the British government which now began to show a steadily augmenting concern over the Russian threat to the Turks and, therefore, to British Mediterranean interests. Inside the Empire, the defeats leading up to Jassy produced under the Sultan Selim III the first major impetus towards reform, but it was not for this reason that the focus of the Eastern Question ceased for the few remaining years of the century to be the Russian threat to Constantinople, but because events in France and Poland once more preoccupied the powers.

Revolution in France sealed Poland's fate by paralysing the major land power of western Europe. The patriotic party among the Polish nobility had tried to take advantage of the distrust of other powers (notably Prussia) for Russian ambitions to push ahead with constitutional and educational reform. This excited Russian hostility. When, in 1792, Catherine's Polish puppets staged a rebellion which gave Russian armies an excuse to invade the country, the Austrians were distracted because a revolutionary government in France had declared war on the Emperor and invaded the Netherlands, while the King of Prussia, hoping for territorial gain, refused to help the Poles. In the upshot, he too invaded Poland under the pretext of crushing revolutionary doctrines spread there from France and in 1793 joined Catherine in a Second Partition of Poland. To Russia went White Russia, the western Ukraine and Podolia. The Prussians did not do so well as this, but carried off

Poznan. All the reforms were annulled by the Polish Diet, where the influence of Russia was now blatant.

The end of independent Poland was now close. A rising against the Russians the following year precipitated it. A Prussian invasion followed the defeat of Russian armies, and the Austrians also made a virtually bloodless invasion into Poland, but it was the Russians who finally took Warsaw and suppressed the rising. A division of the spoil followed and Poland ceased to exist. Once more Russia received the lion's share, but Warsaw went to Prussia. With the Partition of 1795, eastern Europe assumed more or less the shape it was to retain for over a century.

Meanwhile, crucial stages were being passed almost unnoticed in the political geography of what would one day be the first superpower. From the birth of the Union there had been Americans who saw the future in terms of expansion and glory. In 1776 an enthusiastic South Carolina pamphleteer assured his countrymen that 'The Almighty ... has made choice of the present generation to erect the American Empire, ... a new Empire, styled the United States of America. An Empire that as soon as started into Existence, attracts the Attention of the Rest of the Universe; and bids fair, by the blessing of God, to be the most glorious of any upon Record.' This was somewhat inflated language, if the circumstances of the United States at that moment were properly considered, but it found a ready audience. Only a few years later Washington spoke of his country as a 'rising empire' and Jefferson of it as 'the nest from which all America, North and South, is to be peopled'. No one then knew how wide the Continent was, but as was observable in American eagerness to accept the British proposal that the western frontier move forward to the Mississippi in 1783, American nationalist sentiment had from the start an important expansionist and aggressive component.

None the less, dreams of empire were long disproportionate to American resources. Hopes of conquering Canada and Nova Scotia during the war had been thwarted in spite of the French alliance. The new republic still had great powers for neighbours, and could not lightly contemplate conflict with them single-handed in the aftermath of the revolutionary war. Changes in the shape of the country were not in any important degree before 1800 a matter of changes in the frontiers the United States shared with other powers, though these were much disputed. The longest shared boundary was with Spain, still in the last year of the eighteenth century ruler of the Floridas (the Gulf coast as far west as the Mississippi) and, in theory, of the whole trans-Mississippi west, the land called Louisiana. In the north, an often uncertain boundary separated the Canadian subjects of George III from the United States along a line from the Lake of the Woods eastward through the Great Lakes and along rivers to the St Lawrence, and the frontier of Maine. In the empty country below this line and between the Alleghanies and the Mississippi there was no other great power involved, and it was here that the most important developments in the history of the new republic went forward in the 1780s and 1790s.

Government had little to do with it. The Federalists, who were interested in strong and assertive policies of nation-building, were not in control until 1789 and even then their resources were small. What was decisive was the transformation of the area by the decisions of thousands of Americans and new Americans to go west in search of fortune or freedom in the first stage of the most important folk-migration of modern times. Even the area's limits were uncertain. As far west as the Mississippi the Peace of Paris left boundaries with British claims vague. They would take nearly sixty years to define, and the first step was the removal in the 1790s of British occupancy of posts in territory which had been part of the United States since 1783. The removal of this irritation by Jay's treaty of 1794 was another nail in the coffin of the old Franco-American alliance.

Meanwhile, the vast area in which the royal government had tried to protect the rights of the Indian aborigines invited occupation. Several of the colonies had large claims to western lands defined by simply extending their own northern and southern boundaries to the west. A crucial step in regulating this area was the North-West Ordinance which Congress authorized in 1787 in a session with representatives of only eight states present. This laid down organizing principles for the subsequent continental expansion of the United States; it is thus a document almost as fundamental as the Constitution in shaping the country's destiny. It organized the territory north-west of the Ohio (the states' claims to which had been ceded beforehand to the Union) in such a way that it was to proceed eventually to statehood, as the population grew, in units which would eventually stand on an equal footing with all other states in the Union. The continent was not, therefore, to be ruled as a dependency for longer than was necessary to establish independent units of self-government. Almost incidentally, too, slavery was excluded by law from the North-West Territory.

This gave a framework of government to the area into which immigrants were already pouring. By 1790 there were already 120,000 Transappalachian Americans. Though the first state to join the Union after Independence was Vermont (in 1791), the future Kentucky and Tennessee were then being settled and in the following year Kentucky became the fifteenth state. This was the beginning of a revolution in American domestic history and, in the end, in her international standing. Though American politics were dominated by debate on the forms of a new constitution and its later evolution in practice, it was recognized as early as the constitutional debates themselves that a new political force had already to be reckoned with because of the growth of the country. This was sectionalism, the propensity of groups of states distinguished by regional and economic characteristics to act politically in similar ways and form political alliances. One worried easterner put it bluntly soon after Independence had been won: 'If the Western people get the power into their hands,' said Gouverneur Morris, 'they will ruin the Atlantic states.'

The international consequences appeared only very slowly. The British had running diplomatic battles with the Americans over non-compliance with the peace terms and there were tentative French and Spanish dabblings with potential recessionists in the south and west. But this was all that brought to the notice of diplomats the first stirrings of a future great power. Nor were the rulers of the United States unwilling that this should be so. Washington crowned his contribution to American foreign policy by delivering a 'Farewell Address' to his fellow countrymen on laying down his office which argued the wisdom of non-entanglement in Europe's affairs so persuasively that it became a classic reference for future American isolationists.

Relativities of scale also made it by no means unreasonable that Europe should be unimpressed by the importance of America. Even in 1800, when the United States occupied an area equal to the British Isles, France, Germany, Spain and Italy together – about half Europe – there were scattered in this area only a little more than five million people; that is, about the population of England and Wales. At the end of the eighteenth century, after more than a century and a half of settlement, it was only in southern New England and the middle states that cultivated land exceeded in acreage the primeval forest.

From Washington, the federal capital, to Natchez, the military post on the Mississippi which was the most remote, was approximately the same distance as that between Paris and Constantinople. Within this vast expanse lay formidable physical and climatic hindrances to movement. Little existed to overcome them for, if anything, American communications were even worse than those of Europe, where centuries of work had provided a network of water-routes for the transport of heavy goods and even a few decent roads. America, though rich in waterways, had none which helped to tie the United States together. Indeed, the most important of them promised disunity. Once out of the eastern coastal plain and over the mountains the traveller found himself in a great basin where all rivers flowed down to the Mississippi, away from the populated east. The new communities in the west were bound to think of their future in terms of a Gulf outlet rather than of one to the Atlantic; the Mississippi would be their centre of gravity rather than the cities of the east. Here was the bedrock of more sectional differentiation.

Distance also provided a simpler threat to government in the frictional waste of energy it imposed. This was bound to reduce the effectiveness of administration and national leadership and accentuate the tendencies to local organization built into the constitution. Republics, especially federal republics, were constitutional devices which, in European experience, did not suit the government of large areas. Whatever the consequences might be for the freedom of Americans this boded ill for national power.

Meanwhile international events affected American domestic politics. Fear of French revolutionary doctrine and methods and consciousness of the weakness of the national government under the constitution led in 1798 and 1799 to laws to strengthen the government's hand. This was not displeasing to the Federalists, and those who feared democracy but it called forth protests that such laws were unconstitutional and void. This was the first appearance in the politics of the United States of the doctrine that the states could not be bound by unconstitutional legislation by Congress, the doctrine of 'States' Rights' which all parties were in the next century to take up at some time or another. Suspicion of central government was readily provoked and confirmed the fragility of national power; it was to become a national tradition. It was offset only slowly by the operation of the constitution, the ascendancy of the presidency and Federalist conduct of foreign policy.

Book III

Revolutions and Restorations

7 A New Age?

Significance depends on your point of view. An excellent illustration of this can be found in a declaration of pregnancy made to the Paris police in 1794 by a country girl, Marguerite Barrois. The document was buried in the archives until recovered by an English historian in the course of his researches and it reveals a not very surprising story; unhappy creature, Marguerite had been seduced by a boy from her own part of the world a couple of days after she arrived in Paris. Even the rapidity with which she succumbed is probably not very unusual. There is only one striking fact about the story: the night of the seduction was that of the overthrow of Robespierre, the tyrant or saviour (according to your point of view) who had dominated politics all that year and had been overturned by a *coup* the previous day. Politicians and historians have long seen the day as a turning-point. No doubt Marguerite did, too, but, as struck Professor Cobb, probably for quite different reasons.

Important though 1789 was for their country, in the lives of many Frenchmen it probably mattered most because of some event of family history, the death of a parent, or the birth of a child. Yet the year has come to be treated as one of the delimiting epochs of world history. Not only did something important happen then but (and perhaps this counts for more) people soon believed that something uniquely important happened then. But before accepting it as a good point at which to lop a story in two, it is worthwhile to remember briefly how much is obscured or distorted by insisting overmuch on such a date. Many of what were to be seen as master-ideas of the French Revolution, for example, were already at work before 1789 through reforming ministers. Men saw this at the time and sometimes accused revolutionary politicians of wishing to continue subversive programmes launched by royal ministers such as Choiseul or Turgot. The most popular politician in 1789, indeed, was a royal minister, the Swiss Necker, back for his second spell of office after a first in the early 1780s. Then, as in 1789, he was preoccupied by the reform of the State, starting with its finances.

93

A great French sociologist of the following century drew attention to the paradox that revolution came to France just when its king was at last setting seriously about the business of reform. He could have pointed to other monarchs who ran into trouble on this score. The Austrian government pursued reform vigorously under Joseph II; one example was an invasion of privilege in the Netherlands, culminating in the abolition of Estates of Brabant in June 1789. This appeared to the churchmen and nobles of Belgium a grave threat; a revolt ensued in which, incidentally, there first appeared the tricolour, later to be the symbol of revolution throughout Europe (the one carried by the Belgians was red, yellow and black, the colours of Brabant). This led to the collapse of Austrian rule by Christmas, a revolution which owed nothing to what happened in France. Joseph II's measures elsewhere, too, had been widely (and rightly) seen by his subjects to subvert the existing order; like many eighteenth-century rulers, he was opposed by the legally privileged orders in almost all his dominions. Further, the religious policy later pursued by the first Assembly of the French Revolution would have made perfect sense to Joseph's civil servants.

Such coincidences of aim are less surprising if we remember the continuity of personnel in government and administration during this period. Revolution, even when imposed most blatantly and arbitrarily from above by French arms, could not make a clean sweep of the official classes and experts, nor did it have to; it found plenty of men willing to work for it. Reforms imposed by French armies in neighbouring countries within a few years of 1789 were often welcomed by local bureaucrats; sometimes they saw in them (attacks on feudal institutions, for example) projects they had long cherished. In such cases, revolution brought a change of degree, rather than of principle; changes were already under way before the great era of political upheaval began in 1789 and we should not be hypnotized by the imaginary line which cuts across history in that year.

None the less, there *was* a real revolutionary break in history which was more than one of degree. What began in 1789 was very different from the stirrings of resentment over the American disaster which appeared in the 1780s in England, the ineffectual attempts to reform the Polish commonwealth and other rumblings which have led to talk of a general 'democratic' revolution of which what happened in France was only a part. Such a view blurs too much and is anachronistic. Certainly a mild and generalized radicalism can be discerned in England, mixed up with the campaigns against unpopular ministers. There was agitation there for the removal of civic disabilities still resting on Protestant dissenters and some talk of electoral reform. Yet, significantly, few arguments of democratic principle were put forward for such changes. Electoral reformers sought, rather, to increase the number of what was supposedly the most independent kind of MP, those who sat for the counties, traditionally the men who stood up to ministerial oratory and on their own feet against 'influence'. This, for all its attractiveness, was a conservative demand, not a progressive one. Little more was heard of it after a general election in 1784 which was the first for over half a century to be recognised as a clear expression of public opinion and gave a new ministry assured support in Parliament. Similarly, the 'patriotic' stirrings of Belgians in 1789 were a counter-attack by the forces of privilege and particularism against the enlightened reform of Joseph II which they saw as a menace – just as the summoning of the States-General in France in the same year also menaced privilege, legal and customary rights. Here is another paradox: the beneficiaries of such rights, it is proper to remark, were above all the great aristocrats, yet it was among them that the greatest enthusiasm for 'enlightened' ideas and the most enthusiastic patronage for the writers of the Enlightenment could be found before 1789.

These complications ought to prevent us from falling into a cosmic Whig view of history in looking at 1789. Slogans and catch-words later to become deeply invested with progressive significance did not then always carry the overtones we attribute to them. Long before the States-General met, there were demands in France for the protection of a written constitution against 'ministerial despotism', but this phrase meant interference with the traditional structure of rights, privileges and values not the menace of an illiberal repression. Such language was often used. Even the supine traditional elites of Lombardy feebly exerted themselves at the death of Joseph II, when a relaxation of the reforming pressure of his ministers led to talk of the grant of a constitution by his successor, Leopold. Even American politics was not without its ambiguities. Some Germans had been enthusiastic about the American Revolution not because they saw in it a universal cause but because the charter of Massachusetts seemed to them as worthy of defence as their own municipal privileges – and no more worthy. Americans gave themselves a constitution, some of them thought, to avoid falling under the sway of a strong government which might be democratic in tendency. In England, meanwhile, though some of their members might look ahead to piecemeal improvement of the law, the 'Revolution' societies formed in 1788 were celebrating a revolution which had already for a hundred years given them rights which would be under increasing attack elsewhere in the next fifty.

Of course, new and progressive forces were in play. Undoubtedly, the Enlightenment heritage was important in creating a new atmosphere within which politics would unroll. As a coherent political fact, on the other hand, the Enlightenment hardly existed; it had never had any precise and agreed political content once it moved away from anti-clericalism. Its most obvious effect in politics apart from this was in popularizing new methods of criticism of the past – the criteria of rationality, utility and material prosperity – and the assumption that the achievement of happiness was inseparably linked to progressive government and was a matter of giving expression to natural rights. In the end this was to suffuse political thinking in the Western World and produce an era of modernizing and individualizing whose first climax came in France – when, however, it did not appear as a simple clash of progress and reaction but as a jumbled *mêlée*.

This first climax still gives 1789 its mythical power. In May there met at Versailles the States-General of France, assembled for the first time since 1614 and the result of indirect elections which approached as nearly to a consultation of the whole people as any country could then achieve. This ancient and respected institution (so respected, indeed, that no agreement was possible about the extent of its extraordinary powers) had been wheeled out of the storehouse of France's history to be a battering-ram against the forces which were believed to block the road to practical reforms on which all Frenchmen could largely agree. Their wishes were expressed in the *cahiers de doléances*, or bills of grievance, which their deputies in the States-General took with them to guide their conduct and instruct the royal government. These *cahiers* themselves were the distillation of thousands of others drawn up by parish-meetings and occupational or social groups, all of which provide the richest evidence for a nation's state of mind that there has ever been. Many of their demands, too, were conservative: that the Catholic religion should be protected and strengthened, that drinking should be discouraged, that the importing of foreign machinery should be banned, for example. Nothing could have been more respectable. Other *cahiers* demanded an end to fiscal privilege (and almost all envisaged it), better provision for the poor, and a more humane and efficient judicial system. As the popularity of the States-General showed, Frenchmen were constitutionalists at heart, even if some *cahiers* wanted a new constitution to be drawn up and others simply presumed an existing one which could be written down.

Like everything else in the *ancien régime*, the evidence of the *cahiers* is of contradiction, confusion, ambiguity, of all the variety, in fact, of a living society. Of any idea that a radical break with historical France was imminent or desirable, the Frenchmen who wrote them were almost wholly innocent. It was their almost universal conviction that a good king would once more succour his subjects, this time, as before, with the help of their views. But the special circumstances of the setting in which this expression of grievance and hope took place meant that things would in fact turn out very differently. This was why, in 1789, though the Belgians might have kicked off, it was the game played in France which gripped the world's attention.

8 The Great Revolution

14 July 1789 has a better claim than any other day to be the beginning of modern history. Two days of rioting and disorder in Paris preceded an attack that morning on a royal fortress in Paris, the Bastille. After some hours of fighting, its governor surrendered to the mob. Even these simple statements blur the extraordinary disproportion between the events and their subsequent idealization. The previous twenty years had seen far worse disturbance in other capitals. The Bastille was a fortress certainly, but one disused and poorly armed, defended by only a hundred or so pensioners and Swiss Guards. Its demolition had been considered by the government and, in the spring of 1789, had been asked for in many of the *cahiers*. Meanwhile, it had survived, functioning as a state prison, though only seven miserable wretches were found in its cells by its conquerors. Their freedom hardly justified the bloodshed. Human nature soon detracted still further from any dignity the proceedings might have had, for the governor and some of his aged garrison were butchered after their surrender, an inauguration of a tradition of mob vengeance to be nourished a few days later by further lynchings.

Altogether, its significance does not spring easily to the eye from what actually happened, yet 14 July was quickly recognized as a great turning-point. In France itself, to have been a *vainqueur de la Bastille* was in later years to be assured of respect (and perhaps even of personal survival): many who had not been present on the day appropriated to themselves the honour of membership of that ill-defined company. The storming of the Winter Palace, an act equally dramatic in the history of another revolution, displays a similar disparity between legend and reality. The crucial importance of such events lies not in what they were but in what they implied. Their role was symbolic; they shaped other events by forcing men to recognize far-reaching truths. The fall of the Bastille gave badly needed confidence to the men assembled at Versailles for the States-General. A majority of them had already turned that historic institution into a new body, which they named the National Assembly. This was a defiance of the crown. It was followed by fears that they had gone too far and might now be mastered if the royal ministers turned to force.

To blow away the chance of this happening was the great practical achievement of the mob who stormed the Bastille. It destroyed any chance that the king would support ministers who urged a simple confrontation of force by force. After 14 July he would at least have to think twice before using armed force to overawe the deputies at Versailles. The National Assembly lost its inhibitions and gained confidence as the monarchy swung round to conciliation. Necker, who had just been discharged, against the Assembly's wishes, was recalled amid popular acclamation; this seemed to clinch the point. In a longer perspective, still more was implied. Absolutism was now seen to be thwarted and the despotism so often criticized in its specific embodiments by advanced thinkers was overturned; at the time it may have been royal despotism, but the event came in the end to stand for the overthrow of a whole order, whose crumbling, destruction and transformation were in fact to take years of legislation and warfare. The fall of the Bastille remains properly the major symbol of the French Revolution because it was recognized at the time as such.

It is, of course, a symbol which distorts and simplifies, but so does the apparently simple phrase 'French Revolution' itself. Even in a restricted sense, these words may connote a process stretching from the French people's choice of deputies to the States-General in early 1789 to the final overthrow in 1815 of a French Empire which had consolidated many of the changes of the intervening years and done much to diffuse the revolution outside France. Some would wish to go further back, beyond 1789, and some (as we shall see) to trace the French Revolution on far beyond 1815. It remained well into the twentieth century the most important single inspiration of political radicalism in the western world since the Bible had been translated into the vernacular.

All this puts grave difficulties in the way of its historical – let alone ideological – assessment. Even the terms in which we talk about it cause trouble; the revolutionary generation quickly evolved a terminology to deal with its problems, and we still have to use much of it though its words often have changed their meaning. They have the partially compensating advantage that they at least direct our attention to what was essential in the revolution: it was political change. However much Frenchmen might seek economic or social ends, the crucial struggles of the Revolution were between political forces striving to effect, resist or control changes in political institutions.

Between the opening of the sessions of the States-General on 5 May and the fall of the Bastille there had been growing evidence of impatience among the politicians (as we may call the deputies who constituted the first modern political class to appear in France). First the behaviour of the legally privileged seemed to stand in their way and then, more and more, royal policy. The leaders of the Third Estate, the commoners, were increasingly aware that something *had* to be done: there had been an inflammation of popular expectation when the elections took place and it was producing increasing disorder as it played, unsatisfied, upon a hungrier and hungrier France. The self-constitution of a National Assembly by the Third Estate and some of the clergy was a revolutionary step to meet a need to show that something would be done. Moreover, it was something that most commoners and many noblemen in the Assembly were happy to do, for if the electoral education of France early in 1789 had brought about one thing, it was a spreading of the conviction that the privilege of the nobility stood in the way of any important change and ought to be removed. This was by no means out-and-out egalitarianism; as Professor Hampson has well said, the aim of those who in 1789 attacked what they saw as the artificial society based on privilege was 'to open it to those who were gentlemen in the British sense without being *gentils-hommes* in the French one'.

On 23 June Louis xvi came in person to present the programme of his ministers to what he still thought of as and called the States-General. What he proposed was common ground in most of the *cahiers*. There was to be a constitution, the nobles were to give up their fiscal privileges and taxation was to be voted by the States-General. Internal free trade, an ending of *lettres de cachet* and legal reform were to follow. This was a true reformer's programme by the test of even the most determined adherent of Enlightenment. Yet it was not acceptable. Opinion had moved a long way since May. What was proposed might well have much to be said for it, but it left legal distinction between the Orders (that is, noble privilege) intact, and was in the eyes of many deputies now vitiated by the fact that it was put forward as a unilateral legislative act of the Crown. They discussed a new issue, the question of the sovereignty of the nation.

The June–July crisis clarified this. First the Crown gave way. The king's own safety was thought threatened by popular excitement. He therefore abandoned his programme and registered this by ordering the nobles in the States-General who had not done so now to join the new National Assembly, thus tacitly recognizing its pretensions. At the same time, preparations were made to gather armed forces so that there would be no need for a further surrender. The end of the crisis came in sight when Necker – the leading proponent of reform in the ministry, at least in popular eyes – was dismissed. From the uproar which followed came the troubles which led to the fall of the Bastille and royal surrender.

This opened a great institutional revolution. The instrument of change, the National Assembly, had already been created. The next phase was the greatest destructive and constructive period of the Revolution. Within a few months most of the institutional framework of the *ancien régime* was swept away. Absolute monarchy came to an end. The 'feudal system' was declared abolished (though what this meant was not easy to say exactly); so were the ancient provinces and territorial divisions, the sovereign courts of which the *parlements* were the most famous, the right of primogeniture, the privilege of nobility and all personal legal privilege inherited from the past. The corporate structure of old France was pulled down and the ideas of Enlightenment created a new society on the same site. A new structure of local government, a new judicial system, legal equality, declared individual rights, an unrestricted liberty of the Press, religious toleration and much more were inaugurated. The centrepiece of all this was the Constitution, whose fundamentals were laid out in the autumn of 1789, but which was not put into its final form or into operation as a whole until two years later, when the National Assembly finally wound up its work and went home. It left behind a constitutional monarchy, in which the king had certain defined powers to veto for a limited time legislation put up to him by a new representative body, a Legislative Assembly elected by voters qualified by the possession of a certain income and a standardized and representative system of local government. The king was also head of the executive branch of government, with power of appointment to all military and civil offices. At the head of the Constitution stood a Declaration of the Rights of Man and the Citizen.

No one in May 1789 had expected as much and not all these achievements were to last. Nor were many subsequent changes of the Revolution. By the time the Constitution of 1791 was put into effect, it had already deeply exacerbated divisions within France. It had also created some new ones. In the end, it failed to work and brought down monarchy and parliament alike. It operated, formally, for less than a year, being replaced by unicameral republican government. All this can give an impression that the early years of the Revolution were fruitless, but this would be to put events in a false perspective.

To begin with, the achievement of a constitution at all was a great fact. From this time forwards, it was to be a constant of French politics that in times of crisis men would turn to the idea of constitutional revision. There was never to be return to the *ancien régime* with its structure of historic and prescriptive privileges; the idea of a written fundamental law defining the rights of all Frenchmen and the attributions of the organs of their government was from this time never to be lost to sight. Furthermore, with the constitution went the idea of national sovereignty and the dogma of national unity which underlay it. This was not quite so readily accepted; when a restoration of the Bourbon line took place in 1814, some argued that the constitution under which Louis XVIII returned to his throne was not one agreed like a contract by king and people, but one granted – *octroyé* – like a charter, or as Louis XVI had intended his reforms to be. Yet this view did not prevail.

The Constitution of 1791 rested on the doctrine that the nation alone could decide its own future. At its heart lay the great legislative engine, the national sovereign embodied in the Assembly. There might be enormous scope for argument about the ways in which the nation could express its views, but the idea of national sovereignty triumphed with the work of the Constituent Assembly (as the assembly of 1789 came to be called from the primacy of constitution-making in its work). It gave expression to something which had been only an idea of a few men before the Revolution and now became one of the fundamental assumptions of modern states. As one *cahier* of the Third Estate had put it in the spring of 1789, 'no one has until now had the idea that there should only be one State, one king, one fatherland and that everything should be subordinated to their interest – or, rather, if anyone did believe this, he was held to be a dreamer, a *philosophe*.' This was the idea which underlay both the destructive work of sweeping away old divisions, privileges, rights and the constructive work of building a new France. It was to prove an idea apt for export, too.

The most important work of the Revolution came before the end of 1789. Changes which came later tended not to last. Nobility, for example, was abolished in June 1790 and with it went the use of hereditary titles, yet the recognition of nobility and their use returned within twenty years. Every French regime except one until 1870 was to create more noblemen. The legal privileges which went with noble status, on the other hand, had been abolished in 1789 and were not to be revived. The property franchise did not last, nor did liberty of the Press, and religious toleration was soon compromised. Many other examples could be cited.

Possibly the most important thing the Constituent carried out was the revolutionizing of the relations of Church and State. Both the complexity and the inevitability of this flowed from the fact that religion and society were so intimately interwoven before 1789. By then, one formal breach had already been made in the religious settlement of the *ancien régime* by the concessions to French Protestants in 1788. They were still being regretted in many of the *cahiers* written by French clergy in the following year. What laymen thought of giving civic rights to Protestants is much more difficult to say. On the one hand, religious freedom for non-Catholics was made complete by the Constituent Assembly. On the other, for years to come, Frenchmen were to show by their violence to one another that religious differences might have great importance locally as badges of traditional, social, economic and cultural antipathies, some going back a very long way. But historians are still disagreeing about the reality of religious practice before 1789, let alone about the reality of men's faith and beliefs, so that it is not easier to go much further than this.

What is certainly clear in the *cahiers* is that those whose views were expressed in them – an important qualification – often showed some or lukewarm interest in toleration and certainly no hostility to the Catholic Church as an institution or as the custodian of a faith, whatever particular reforms of its structure or administration they might think were called for. This was important; Frenchmen were within a few years to be bitterly divided by religion, but in 1789 little trace of this was visible. Rather, there was substantial agreement on much that needed to be changed and there was plenty about the necessity for change in the *cahiers* of the clergy themselves.

Religious division might not have proved fatal had not institutional reform become entangled with an issue of principle which polarized loyalties. The attempt to put the French Church on a new footing, with a clergy paid by the State and elected by the people, in itself tended to divide Catholics from non-Catholics (were Jews and Protestants to vote in the election of bishops?) and even from one another, but an oath of loyalty imposed on all churchmen by the Civil Constitution of the Clergy of 1790 was fatal. To constitutionalists this was merely a civil act required of priests as of any other state-paid functionary. To non-jurors it was an attempt to usurp the authority of Rome. Many Frenchmen hoped the Pope would release them from their dilemma by allowing them to take the oath. When he did not, the choice had to be made. Within a year a rift had opened in French society as jurors and non-jurors gathered their supporters to them. The politics of the Revolution infected the rift. Loyalty to the Church came to mean loyalty to the *ancien régime*, opposition to popular sovereignty and the Rights of Man. Perhaps this was, as many have said, the unavoidable logic of the confrontation of claims at bottom incompatible. At least it is clear that no one did much to blur the issue and soften its harshness. Within a year of the Civil Constitution there were the beginnings of violence. As the Revolution continued, there were to be pogroms, massacres, deportation, exiling, murder and sacrilege as men threw their energies and emotions behind the opposing symbols of Cross or Tricolor.

Religion did most to undermine any chance that the great institutional changes of the National Assembly might give France stability. In 1790 and 1791, this was not very apparent and disorder was not too serious a menace. Economic conditions improved once the harvest of 1789 reached the mills and there was not until 1792 a considerable groundswell of popular discontent to tempt political troublemakers. Yet troublemakers abounded. There were some who wished to press much further the social and political transformation wrought by the Revolution and some who were embittered that it had gone so far. These were sometimes men of principle. There were also those who saw the changes of the Revolution simply as a chance to express old frustrations, work off old grievances, settle an old score, wrapping up these realities meanwhile in the fog of revolutionary or counter-revolutionary rhetoric. From the factions of the politicians emerged our modern notion of Left and Right, names originally applied because of the places in which men sat in relation to the presiding officer of the Assembly. They had much to exploit. Over much of the country, the Assembly could do little to enforce its will; this bred distrust and irritation at what were increasingly seen as counter-revolutionary intrigues among local authorities or the guilty complicity of the Crown whose officers were lukewarm in upholding the new law. Here was the heart of the tragedy of constitutional monarchy in France. Louis XVI was less and less trusted by his subjects who believed him to be perverted by his Austrian wife, a woman whose influence was in fact more dangerous because of her stupidity than her cunning. When the king tried to break away to the frontier in 1791, virtually all confidence in him evaporated.

In the welter of events of these years (and more were to come), there are paradoxes and complexities which are ridiculously blurred by the notion of a single revolution with a single meaning. It was a nobleman, Chateaubriand, who pointed out that the nobles began the Revolution, and for all the sentimentality which gathered around the emigration something like nine-tenths of those of noble blood in France did *not* emigrate, remaining there even during the worst of it. Another important class, the majority of Frenchmen in 1789, is that of the peasants (however we define that misleading simple term). It is well-known that they burned the manor-houses and castles of their *seigneurs*, ransacking their archives and terrorizing their womenfolk. It is slightly less well-known that this was probably more important even than the storming of the Bastille in shaping the events of 1789, and almost totally overlooked except by professional historians that this peasantry was even

at that moment in many places seeking not social and economic progress but reaction. The peasants were to prove the most tenacious
source of conservative practice in France for the next half-century. A
final example of the complexity of what we describe simply as *the*
French Revolution is provided by the fate of the monarchy, which was
abolished in September 1792. The establishment of the republic on the
day following its abolition was a great event and has been seen to
embody the essence of the Revolution. Yet this was not why the States-
General had been summoned, nor had that body been imposed on the
Crown by the radicals. Its summoning followed the thwarting of the
Crown's efforts to carry out many of just those reforms which the revolutionary and Napoleonic governments subsequently drew from the
pigeon-holes of the *ancien régime* to put into practice in the name of the
new order.

To discuss so rich and complicated a historical 'fact' as a single process
is artificial, as any historical shorthand must be. Yet some contemporaries recognized the beginning in 1789 of something new of unique and
outstanding importance. 'Your laws will become the laws of Europe,'
the National Assembly was told by Mirabeau, its dominating politician.
We can now see this to be more than rhetoric, because the things
that happened then in France released forces crucial for Europe as a
whole. This was, as Mirabeau implied, just because they took place in
France. French culture and French ideas dominated the minds of
thinking men as far east as the Urals. The monarchy of France, for all
its weakness in the eyes of posterity and its struggles with privilege,
stood at the head of a great state; it was stronger than any other west
of Russia. France's population was the biggest in the Western World
and her rate of economic growth in the eighteenth century had matched
that of her major colonial and commercial rival, Great Britain. Whatever the losses of the eighteenth-century wars, France was still the
leading European power. What happened to her therefore decided
Europe's history as well as her own. France was so important that when
she turned over in bed everyone else was squeezed. But there was also
something else involved, the universal and general principles embedded
in the Revolution and soon discerned abroad.

Many of the leaders of the French Revolution, as well as their admirers abroad, were from the start convinced that they had a message
for the world. In this the French surpassed the Americans, some of
whom might abstractly approve of republicanism and disapprove of
hereditary monarchy but almost all of whom were, whether or not
aware of it, deeply imprisoned in the beneficent and empirical assumptions of their English cultural background. They had little crusading
urge: besides, unlike the French, they were controlled by geography,

being too far away to wish to initiate any *Gesta Dei per Americanos* except in their own West. The social and political issues of the two revolutions were different, too. For all the general statements of the Declaration of Independence, the Americans had eventually sought – and achieved – self-government for communities whose internal structures they did not much wish to change. In France, institutions were attacked and overthrown in the name of the Rights of Man. But noble birth, chartered privileges, feudal dues and traditional immunities existed everywhere; their challenge in principle in the greatest of European states was a challenge to all.

For some time only a few saw this. Other rulers were at first unalarmed and even amused by the embarrassments of Louis XVI. If there was a general response among the ruling classes of Europe, it was that of the professional diplomats: the internal troubles of France, they thought, would paralyse her as a great power and would offer opportunities for actions by other powers. The outstanding exception to this complacency was the vision of Burke: as early as 1790 he had discerned a universal force loose in France to the danger of the society of Europe.

Some Frenchmen, meanwhile, saw the universal significance of their revolution as beneficent. This was what Mirabeau meant. By 1792 the meaning of this became much clearer. It was then that Arthur Young, a liberal-minded man who saw things to approve and excuse as well as things to condemn in revolution, observed that 'there can be no doubt but the spirit which has produced it will, sooner or later, spread throughout Europe, according to the different degrees of illumination among the common people.' This was the year when Goethe observed that a new age began. If one single document expresses the reintroduction of ideology into international life, it is the decree of the Convention of 19 November 1792 declaring in the name of the French Nation that it offered 'fraternity and aid' to all peoples wishing to recover their liberty. It was an invitation to world revolution.

By that time, the two great practical transformations of the Revolution had begun. One was the outbreak of war with Austria and Prussia in the spring of 1792. The other was the overthrow of monarchy, Legislative Assembly and the idea of constitutional monarchy together on 10 August.

It is at least arguable that the most important single effect of the French Revolution was to plunge Europe into a series of wars of unparalleled scale and scope which lasted with only brief interruptions for twenty-three years. This is not only because of the millions who died and the damage that was done. Great as the toll was by the standards of eighteenth-century warfare, it shrinks to insignificant proportions besides the achievements of civilized states in our own era. It was because war is an uncontrollably revolutionary agent. Even before 1789 its effect upon economic life has been argued to have been great, blighting some of its sectors while fanning others into a blaze of activity in the forced blast of wartime demand. Nearly always, it acted as a social transformer, cutting into the cadres of the traditional sources of officer-supply as noblemen were killed off and inflating a demand for officers by larger armies which could be met only by giving more commissions to men not of noble birth. Wars brought political changes, too: the relationships of great powers were traditionally shaped by them, and the United States had emerged from a victorious war at the beginning of which she had not existed. 1792 in this respect opened an era of European revolution because it opened an era of war.

Immediately, war changed both the internal history of the French Revolution and the face it presented to the outside world. Many different interests in the country hoped for profit from a war. The royal family and their counsellors wanted one because they expected defeat and believed this must redound to the advantage of the Crown which would emerge from national crisis with refurbished and renewed authority. Many politicians wanted war because they saw party advantage in it. Some used intoxicated language at the prospect. 'A nation which has won its freedom after ten centuries of slavery needs war,' ranted one of them; 'It needs war to purge away the vices of despotism, it needs war to banish from its bosom the men who might corrupt its liberty.' Still others felt alarm at what they believed was a coalition in the making against France, engineered by *émigrés* led by the king's brothers and facilitated by the development of agreement between Austria and Prussia over their respective interests in eastern Europe. Only seven votes were cast in the Legislative Assembly against the declaration of war on Austria, which finally came on 20 April. The grounds it alleged included the charge that the Emperor had protected 'rebels' – the *émigrés* – and had begun to organize a coalition against France.

The language used in the Assembly had long before begun to focus alarm in other countries. The French declaration of war gave new force to ideological fears. It spoke of a war undertaken against not a nation but its ruler, and invited, by its assurance of protection, those who wished to rebel against their sovereign to take refuge in France. Revolutionary propaganda was now launched upon a line which would run through the revolutionary appeal of the following winter. One expression of it was the slogan with which French armies operated in Belgium: 'War to the castle; peace to the cottage.' Other things, too, were beginning to fall into place. The religious divisions of France had brought the first emigrations of clergy, non-jurors who painted a picture of the France they had left as one in which a deliberate assault on religion and Catholicism, the long-matured work of 'enlightened' plotters, was under way. Such innovations as the permission of clerical marriage and the legalization of divorce were pointed to as evidence of this. Soon, political changes in Paris also brought the constitutionalist clergy who wished to remain loyal to the Revolution under suspicion and they were increasingly exposed to official hostility, too. The alarm at first felt by foreign churchmen, especially in Protestant England, began in these circumstances to seem more justifiable to many laymen as they contemplated what had happened to the French Church, once established as securely as their own.

Piece by piece, the argument of alarm fell into place and a war not begun for ideology began to look more and more like one. Soon, the English prime minister spoke of 'a spirit' appearing in some of the manufacturing towns which required the position of troops nearby, and the Austrian police began to uncover details of revolutionary plotting in masonic circles. Every fragment contributed to a new hardening of lines and to a reciprocal development of French radicalism and foreign reaction. In England, where real politics existed already, reforming causes suffered from this. Someone as moderate as Arthur Young could still in 1791 advocate parliamentary reform as a way of avoiding the revolutionary danger in England by restoring the constitution's vigour, but such sensible sentiments soon came to be rare among the conservatively inclined. In the following year Gibbon, who had shocked readers by his advanced ideas, was qualifying his judgment that slavery was to be attacked on humane grounds with a fear that such attacks might be mingled with others grounded in the rights of man. A general patriotic hardening of resistance to innovation which smacked of French presumption was coupled with fear to produce more than twenty years during which most members of the political class felt it to be dangerous to tamper with one fibre of the settled constitution in church and state.

These new rigidities were above all the product of war, and inside France the war was even more profoundly at work. It was the biggest single factor in the acceleration of revolution. Directly and materially it produced inflation and shortages of goods and thus practical grievances for extremists to exploit. Other effects were psychological. Soon there came bad news from the battlefield which spread both a mood of patriotic exasperation leading to demands for a more revolutionary conduct of the war, and a mounting panic fear. This expressed itself in a search for scapegoats; in the royal entourage and the executive branch of government there was already plenty of suspicion of those who were either supposed to be in league with the *émigrés* or known at least to have expressed alarm at further democratization or radicalization of the Revolution.

These facts put the game into the hands of politicians some of whom had as early as 1789 thought that the Revolution was taking too conservative a tack. They were allied to true popular leaders who had always distrusted the well-off who dominated the Assembly. Concentration on parliamentary history can give a misleading impression of the state of France after the October days of 1789. For all that the Constituent had done which deserved popular acclaim, there were to be many examples in the next year or so of direct action by crowds or local authorities under popular pressure which went far beyond what had been intended and showed that unsatisfied demands existed. The 'abolition' of feudalism had been decreed on 4 August, with redemption charges to be paid in compensation for some of the lost rights of landlords: attacks on *châteaux* did not stop, however, and it was often impossible to collect the legal redemption payments.

There is also a danger of underrating this essential turbulence if attention is focussed on Paris. After the winter of 1789–90, the capital began to settle down. This was not only because the political victory of bringing king and Assembly to it was satisfying and reassuring to Parisians, it was also because the authorities took care to assure the city's food-supply, and the harvest of 1789 had been good. Prices began to fall as it reached the bakeries in the form of flour and they continued to go down in 1790 and 1791. Much less of a family's income had to be spent on bread, therefore, and there was a margin for other goods. No doubt this helps to explain the surprising quiescence of Paris when the king and his family made a dash for liberty in June 1791 and were brought back from Varennes to Paris in humiliating captivity, having revealed their deep unwillingness to accept much of what the Revolution had brought about. The war transformed this quiescence both materially and psychologically; it gave agitators and popular politicians their chance.

The hurricane broke on 10 August. On that day, the National Guard battalions of the most militant of the Sections into which Paris was divided for administration attacked the royal palace and drove the royal family in flight for safety to the Assembly which, frightened at its own powerlessness, voted the 'suspension' of the king. In so far as France had a real government at this moment, it was a self-constituted insurrectionary 'Commune', or municipal council of Paris, which controlled the sectional forces. Soon, the Legislative registered its failure and powerlessness by authorizing elections for a 'Convention' to give France a new constitution.

The Legislative Assembly had in under a year dragged down monarchy with itself. The new France was to be a Republic. The constitutional monarchists had failed because they could not dominate Paris which now reached the peak of its political supremacy. Two things would have been needed: cheap food (which the war was now again making only a memory) and the confidence of the revolutionary and radical elite of the capital that reaction would not be allowed to repossess itself of power through the exploitation of constitutional freedoms and universal suffrage. The Legislative Assembly had been able to guarantee neither.

The revolutionary elite consisted of two elements, the radical faction in the clubs and among the politicians (who took their name from the most famous of the clubs, the Jacobins) and the *sans-culottes* who made up the National Guard battalions, the decisive force in the great 'days' of the Paris Revolution. The two were to drift gradually apart under the Convention (elected in September 1792) which dominated the second revolutionary era in France until it finally gave France a new constitution which came into effect in 1795 and bowed itself off the stage. Its gradual liberation from dependence on the Paris radicals was a slow process, complicated and concealed at the political level by the self-deceiving cant of an outstanding politician, Robespierre. Somewhat unfairly, he came to embody the principle of the Revolution for friends and foes alike. It was not true (as his enemies said) that he was a dictator, but he exercised a remarkable ascendancy in 1793 and 1794 in the Committee of Public Safety which was the centre of effective government, which made it plausible to call him one. He was a man of inflexible principle, chilly rectitude and great courage. Before his fall he had helped to rebuild some of the authority which the French State had lacked since 1789. This had its irony, because it helped to deprive him of the popular support which might have saved him from his political enemies, who swept him and his friends from power and to the scaffold in July 1794. With the exception of a final, half-hearted convulsion in 1795, Parisian revolt came to an end for thirty-five years. Some also thought that there had disappeared with Robespierre the hope that the Revolution would bring about greater social equality.

Yet by then the image of the Revolution had been set for ever. In the process, the word itself changed its sense. In 1789, people still spoke of 'revolution' in a reassuringly restricted sense: it usually meant only a turn of the wheel of political fortune, a change in the hands which held power, or more general changes marking an epoch in a country's affairs, such as an invasion, or the arrival of a new dynasty. An English diplomat in Paris, writing in April 1788 about the increasing desire for changes which would relieve the French monarchy of its troubles, was using the word in what was then a very usual and recognizable sense when we wrote that 'an entire revolution in the form of government is therefore looked forward to with the greatest eagerness.' He spoke, it is true, of more than a mere change of personnel, but what is still lacking is the later sense of dynamic, eruptive, mindless force. Even the British idolization of 'The Glorious Revolution' whose centenary had been enthusiastically celebrated in 1788 emphasized the limited and conservative nature of that great deliverance: new occupants of the throne and the fiction that not only had there been no fundamental change but that a threatened subversion of an old and healthy constitution had been averted.

Events in France soon overtook this way of talking. Clearly something very fundamental and radical was taking place when a nation consciously rebuilt its whole social and political system on the foundation of legal equality, when the property of the Church was secularized and a religious settlement imposed which was unacceptable to the majority of French clergy. Such institutional changes, though, were for many people less immediate in their impact than the overturning of landmarks much nearer to them. Primogeniture, nobility, tithes, chartered rights, monastic vows, coats-of-arms on coaches, weathercocks on steeples, battlements on manor houses, family pews in parish churches and a score of other familiar things were all swept away pell-mell. The change in money, weights and measures was unsettling, too, though not, perhaps, so much as the imposition of the cant of a Revolutionary speech which insisted on the *tutoyer* and *citoyen*. There was sometimes talk of a *loi agraire* which would divide men's properties (though it has often been overlooked that the Convention ordained the death penalty for anyone proposing one).

Above all, violence loomed larger and larger in the image of Revolution. It was perhaps the most important element in the appearance of a new concept of Revolution which was to prove as important as its reality. The war was again at the root of this. The end of the monarchy had first made it obvious. The fear of defeat and the looming threat of a France divided by civil war was the ever-darkening background to the Convention's politics in 1792 and 1793. To mobilize the support it desperately needed if France were to survive, the Convention abandoned the restrictions on the franchise which had signified that property had replaced birth in 1789 as the foundation of French society and gave ground before other popular demands for the hunting-out and punishment of suspected reactionaries and controls on prices. Fear was also the fundamental explanation of the period of special emergency called 'Revolutionary Government' or, more widely, the Terror. This established an enduring image of the Revolution which lived on for half-a-century in the vision of the tumbrils hauling victims to the guillotine. This was only a superficial aspect of Terror. Historians nowadays tend rather to stress its limitations and the shortcomings of the use of force by agencies authorized by the Convention to act directly in its name to uphold the war effort; often they could do very little. Many French towns and much of the countryside were little affected by Tettor, but even perceptive observers jumbled together the spontaneous (or near-spontaneous) 'September Massacres' of 1792, when the unhappy occupants of Paris prisons, among them many priests, were lynched, with the reports of mass shootings in provincial towns and the ever-active guillotine in Paris. Intelligent foreigners were impressed by a new increase in governmental power which the Terror seemed to show. The twelve members of the Committee of Public Safety mobilized their country's resources for war as the monarchies had never done, even in Prussia.

This mobilization involved much practical and verbal violence. The eighteenth century was well aware of the formal and informal role of violence in society; what was new was its institutionalizing in the service of political change. The intimidation by local militants, the streetfighting, the guillotine, the dictatorial and ruthless committee-men who nosed out suspects and enemies of the republic were the face the Terror presented to the world and it was something new. There was, of course, a great deal of exaggerated talk, and twentieth-century experience makes the actual toll of life in the Terror seem milder than that accepted today as necessary in far less excusable circumstances. Nevertheless, the mythical dimension of the Terrorists' activity was more important in forming a new idea of Revolution than the precise number of victims of their policy. This was especially true in the matter of what came to be called 'de-Christianization', a popular phenomenon, beginning in the provinces but most obvious in Paris (where the municipal officials supported it). Its origins lay in fear and panic but it seemed to foreigners that France was formally disowning her Christian origins when Mass was interrupted, sculptures were mutilated, the sacred vessel used to anoint French kings since Clovis was smashed, when ruffians paraded on the floor of the Convention in sacred vestments and a whore was enthroned on the high altar of Notre Dame in a 'Feast of Reason'. Certainly a ritual element was involved; some Frenchmen – ex-priests among them – were exorcizing their own past by authorizing these acts. But to the hostile or the foreigner they all seemed necessary attributes of a monolithic revolutionary force.

The Terror added to the existing revulsion felt for the Revolution because of the role in it of the mob. Whatever the subsequent idealization of their contribution to working-class and revolutionary tradition, the participants in an eighteenth-century or early nineteenth-century mob were likely to be very unpleasant. Callous, brutal, rapacious and dirty, a mob, English or French, and whoever might lead it, drew into the political process the *canaille* which flowed about the gutters of eighteenth-century society. Over the slum-dwellers of the towns and the half-barbaric peasants of the countryside there stretched only a thin sheet of order and civilization, fragile enough to be easily torn to shreds. This was the fear which haunted the well-off. No doubt their alarm was exaggerated and over-dramatic; yet there was excuse for alarm because the myth of a people's revolution was assiduously fed by the revolutionaries. Far from being common men themselves, the politically conscious artisans who were the *sans-culottes* of Paris nevertheless applauded the oratory and reiterated the revolutionary cant which hammered home the lesson that Jacques was as good as his master, and they did so in an age when the image of social democracy in Europe was bound to be a terrifying one. The Revolution came quickly to connote mass violence and the tyranny of the poor. Even when this image was qualified (as it often was) by the conviction that it must end in military dictatorship, this was additional cause for alarm; the expectation of direct popular action remained terrifying in an age without effective police forces.

The new violence of the Convention period devoured its own children. The Girondins, the moderate republicans, went first, in the summer of 1793, though their death-warrants followed their removal from the Convention only after the outbreak of armed resistance to its authority in the provinces. This purge was the opening of a period of some months during which the Parisians successfully imposed on the Convention measures of urgency, but as the winter wore on, government began to recover its grip on the capital. One consequence was that popular and radical leaders began to follow the Girondins to the scaffold the following spring. It seems finally to have occurred to many members of the Convention that they were all potentially in danger from the suspicious Robespierre and his friends; they overthrew and guillotined him. After this, political persecution at the top died down. In 1795 the Convention felt strong enough at last to take on the militants in their strongholds, the sectional organization of Paris. After a last popular demonstration which intimidated the Convention only briefly, the politicians sent for the soldiers. An army at last reliable – and victorious against foreign enemies – disarmed the sections, virtually without opposition, and made possible the suppression of Parisian opposition. France again had a government controlling the apparatus of public order and willing to use it – for the first time since 1789. In November a new Constitution, which gave the executive government of France to a Directory of five men, was inaugurated.

These violent and dramatic events left few enduring changes. This was not because there was any shortage of people who wished to make all things new. But the Convention was an interim regime, called to solve a constitutional problem and remaining to navigate the rapids of an emergency. The new revolutionary calendar it introduced in October 1793 (with the year 11, because the year 1 was supposed to have begun with the Convention itself) had great programmatic importance as a demonstrative break with the Christian past not only of France, 'eldest daughter of the Church', but of all Christian Europe and therefore of the Western World, but it soon dwindled in popular use (workmen did not like its ten-day weeks, which, of course, reduced their regular rest-days in number, or the disappearance of saints' days).

The great changes which had taken place earlier were stamped indelibly into France by the survival of the republic. In the turmoil of events and torrent of rhetoric and rumour which accompanied them, it was scarcely surprising that foreign observers should find it hard to get secure footing for a balanced view. Reports of the September massacres were followed by the Convention's decrees on revolutionary warfare and the imposition of French legislation in Belgium. Outrage was felt at the execution of Louis XVI (and later, of Marie Antoinette), but also terror at what revolution might portend. It was Frenchmen, after all, who spoke of throwing down the king's head as a challenge to other kings and reiterated that changes such as their own were not only desirable but morally and logically necessary in other countries and that the republic would promote them, if necessary, by force of arms. There were reports, taken seriously by experienced observers, of a great secret organization, *La Propagande*, financed by the French government to spread subversion abroad.

There was plenty of evidence, in fact, that fears of revolutionary contamination were much exaggerated. The Austrian police energetic- ally investigated masonic and jacobinically inclined circles and indeed discovered plots, but singularly futile ones. The London Corresponding Society so much feared by English conservatives had at its peak only about eight hundred members. Yet such reassuring facts did not reassure; the Jacobin Club in Paris had not had so very many members. Governments, nevertheless, did not go to war over ideological questions. The Austrians had war declared upon them by the French. The Prussians had an alliance with the Austrians and joined in auto- matically. The British finally declared war not because of the outrage their rulers felt at the trial and execution of Louis XVI but because the French, hoping to please the Belgian merchants of Antwerp, declared the Scheldt open to commerce, a step doubly inflammatory to the British. On the one hand they had distrusted French influence in the Low Countries since the days of Louis XIV and on the other the French action was almost certain to provoke a Franco-Dutch war – and Great Britain had given a guarantee to Holland in 1788. Ironically, at the moment when the British declared war, the Girondin leaders were in fact trying to stave off conflict with them.

Once begun, though, the war turned the Revolution into an ideological crusade for supporters and opponents alike. It went almost unnoticed that the Convention was willy-nilly having to run before the wind of the popular excitement in order to mobilize France's resources to avoid defeat. What was noticed was the exaggerated language of politicians which seemed to betoken deep commitment to the spread of revolution; when Saint-Just defined monarchy as crime and the republic as virtue, he confirmed the fears of conservatives (a word not yet invented) everywhere. Institutional changes in France took on a quite new importance when it appeared that the establishment of similar regimes in other countries would be imposed by subversion and conquest. It did not really matter that, on close inspection, it would turn out after the Revolution that changes had been more temporary or more limited than feared and that after twenty years many old landmarks would still be there. At the time it seemed that anarchy was only a step away in every country, and this impression haunted the statesmen of the Restoration and would be passed by them to the generation of Bismarck. Only a few men saw through it.

Simply, and even grandly, Gentz in 1794 had termed the Revolution 'one of those events which belong to the whole human race', but few would have agreed. There was long a pervasive unwillingness to see the historical necessity of 1789, though some people at least saw it as a divine scourge and therefore not totally inexplicable and without meaning. But most people looked for an explanation in the deeds of wicked men. Only malevolence seemed a sufficient explanation for such meaningless destructiveness, and men worried over supposedly long-established conspiracies; the myth of the secret societies was another enduring creation of the revolutionary era, and best-sellers were written about it. A thin plausibility was to be lent to such fears by the survival after 1815 of embittered men whose devotion to their version of the myth of revolution made them the first examples of a new breed: the professional revolutionary. Thus myth bred myth: fear of revolution and distaste for an emerging social order led to idealization of the society that was threatened; conversely, revolutionary enthusiasm often postulated a historic unity of corruption and immorality universally to be swept away.

Any statements of ideological difference soon turn out to contain such nonsense. Fear and hope are great simplifiers, blurring complexities, and the simple choices imposed by the Revolution resolutely denied some of the great paradoxes of the age. Such cut-and-dried, red-and-black simplifications as those of the dualist Left-Right scheme of politics, for example, could make no sense of England's history in these years. Yet over the whole period from 1775 to 1847, there was in the whole world no country where real social and political change went further and faster than in the United Kingdom, not even the United States. Already by 1789, most of what was later to be tenaciously defended elsewhere had already disappeared in England, where there were institutions which revolutionaries in less happy lands were to struggle for decades to establish. Yet this was also the country which was to be the most implacable and relentless enemy of the revolutionary danger embodied in France. Such complexities are, unfortunately, usually ignored by men driven by political passion and in search of release. One unhappy result was that the mythology of revolution contaminated all aspirations to change in the 1790s, even many of those to be thought of as improvement and thus in a measure compromised it, too, in the eyes of the conservatively inclined.

9 The high tide of French power

Between 1789 and 1799 the *ancien régime* was defeated in France, the Low Countries, much of western Germany and all Italy. The defeats were not everywhere permanent, but in all these countries and some others the past was at least irreparably compromised. It lost in the eyes of many people its unquestioned moral rightness. It had to go on to the defensive. After 1800 further defeats for the *ancien régime* followed so that, in the end, the only country of importance on the European continent which emerged with its institutional and moral integrity unscathed from a quarter-century of upheaval was Russia. Much had disappeared in Europe by 1815 which could not be recovered. This is above all to be explained by the direct and indirect influence of France.

The Belgian revolt which began the story of revolution outside France in 1789 had owed nothing to French example, but it was not long before the contagion of French example and propaganda began to spread. All over Europe, there appeared little groups of social and political dissenters, soon labelled 'Jacobins' by those who feared them, who were the first feeble beginnings of the phenomenon of the international Left. Sometimes they were encouraged by demonstrations of sympathy or diplomatic support by French agents. Almost always they were able to draw to themselves some of the discontented and hopeful, particularly among the young.

None the less, the excitement of a few was not really likely to result in important political results except in special circumstances such as those at Avignon, a papal enclave in France. There, in 1790, what was virtually a civil war had broken out between partisans of the French Revolution and those sympathetic to the authorities. In the following year the Constituent Assembly voted to annex Avignon and its associated territory, the Venaissin, basing its decision on the principle of popular sovereignty: the inhabitants had declared their wish to be part of France.

This was spreading revolution by violence with window-dressing. It was, though, only the first phase of the international assault on the *ancien régime*, by propaganda, inspiration, example and subversion. In 1792 a second and far more effective phase began, that of revolution by conquest. By the end of 1795, the first coalition of France's enemies had been badly damaged; Prussia (which had declared war in June 1792), Spain and the United Provinces (on which France had declared war in 1793) all made peace in that year. The Dutch changed the form of their government and set up a 'Batavian Republic' with revolutionary institutions which became a satellite of France. Meanwhile, Belgium (the former Austrian Netherlands), Nice and Savoy (which had belonged to Sardinia) and all the former independent or German territories west of the Rhine had been annexed and in them ran the law of France. The only major powers still fighting against the Revolution at the beginning of 1796 were Austria and Great Britain.

Invasion gave new importance to 'Jacobinism' outside France. When French armies entered their neighbours' territory, the local Jacobins welcomed and collaborated with them. Soon, they took part in the governments of new satellite republics set up in Switzerland and Italy as a result of successful campaigns which forced peace on Sardinia in 1796 and Austria in 1797 and led to the defeat of Naples and the overrunning of the rest of Italy, include the Papal States. 'Helvetic', 'Cisalpine', 'Ligurian', 'Roman' and 'Parthenopean' republics appeared, while Piedmont was annexed to France. Seven years after 1792, Europe had thus already experienced a great generalization of revolutionary institutions outside France, now termed *la Grande Nation*, the protector of revolution everywhere. Constitutions in all the satellite republics invoked the Rights of Man and the Citizen and set up approximate equivalents of the French administrative and political machinery. Even the terminology of the Revolution was exported to the new daughters of the republic. From 1792, when Belgium had its first taste of French occupation, to the winter of 1799, when only a French garrison cut off in Genoa by the armies of a new coalition still represented the French presence once embodied in a chain of satellite republics, the French Revolution was a governmental and social actuality to millions of western Europeans.

The new republics, and the presence of French armies in other areas, too, increased the possibility of the contamination by revolutionary ideas of countries hitherto unscathed. Alarm was felt even in the United States. The diffusion of the French language made the ideas and rhetoric of the Revolution easily accessible to foreigners who found their own needs and problems could be interpreted in the new terms. A Greek poet, Rigas Pheraeos, was one such. He had turned bandit after killing a Turk, but in the end went into exile. In Vienna, he began to consider new political ideas and methods learned from the French

Revolution. He decided to print and smuggle into Greece revolutionary and nationalist pamphlets and went so far as to set up a press in Vienna. This soon attracted the attention of the Austrian police who, with a prudent sense of the common cause of governments everywhere, handed Rigas over to the Turkish pasha of Belgrade and that was the end of him.

Revolutionary enthusiasm and irritation were sometimes, but by no means always, welcomed and encouraged by the French government. With changing membership, the Directory ruled until 1799, troubling alike by its instability those who feared reaction and those who feared fresh popular violence. Some parts of France it never really governed at all, if the test is law enforcement, and it fell back increasingly on force. The Convention had in the end turned to the army – and turned successfully – to disarm the *sans-culottes* and fight off a right-wing insurrection: the Directory proved it would be just as impartial if necessary. Generals loomed larger and larger in its affairs, though it has sometimes been overlooked that they often did so by invitation. French soldiers were to play a big part in the politics of the next century but not until 1940 did one of them act off his own bat without invitation or assistance from civilian politicians.

The Directory was ended by civilian politicians who decided to bring into the political arena the most glamorous of all the generals of the republic, the thirty-year-old Napoleon Bonaparte, fresh from a spectacular Egyptian expedition which had enabled him to add to the laurels won in the spectacular Italian campaign of 1796. He was barely French, coming from a minor family of the Corsican nobility and retaining many of the personal characteristics of that society. Even in 1796 he was still signing his name 'Buonaparte', in the Italian style. Yet he was educated in the French culture of the Enlightenment and was to identify himself and his successors with France so closely as to rival the Bourbons and the republic in their power to attract allegiance.

The *coup d'état* of 18 *Brumaire*, the year VIII (9 November 1799) installed Bonaparte in power as 'First Consul' of the new republic. He soon shouldered into obscurity the two colleagues the new constitution gave him and within five years his inauguration of a hereditary French Empire crowned the last great transformation of the Revolution. This was a personal dictatorship, but still a revolutionary one. The changes brought by Consulate and Empire – new codes of law; a Concordat restoring the Church to France and France to the Church; an administrative system placing a Prefect at the head of each Department; a new educational structure – all these were given superb publicity and due acclaim and there has never been any danger of underrating their importance. What remains worth remark about them is that their content, important as it is, is less significant than the central reality of which they were all facets. This was the great fact that it was the rule of Bonaparte which finally settled what of the Revolution should survive and what should not. He was the greatest creative statesman of his era, not because of what he originated but because of what he established. He built on the administrative foundations laid by the assemblies of the Revolution and so stabilized them that they remain to this day. He inaugurated the legal reforms meditated by the *ancien régime* which gave expression to the jurisprudential principles of the state for a century and ensured there was no return to the old days of Gallican liberties. Napoleon also reassured men: he strove to please peasants and property-owners, excited the able young, created his own nobility and caressed that of the *ancien régime*. He took his time and did not make such symbolic changes as the reintroduction of hereditary titles lightly. One example was the preservation of the Revolutionary Calendar (which gave the name of one of its months to the *coup* which brought Bonaparte to power) until 1 January 1806. By then, Bonaparte was emperor, crowned by his own hand in the presence of the Pope. The Napoleonic years were for France a long definition of what was and what was not to remain of the Revolution.

This outcome is so explicit that it is almost paradoxical to note that a great ambiguity cloaks Napoleon himself. He has been and can be seen either as a great – revolutionary – innovator, or as a great conservative. One analogy which somewhat spans this gap is with the Enlightened Despots. Like them, Napoleon was committed to courses which were in a fundamental sense revolutionary. On the other hand, he was like them also in his authoritarianism and social conservatism. This ensured him opponents among politicians and publicists who liked neither the increasing pomp of his Court nor the realities of arbitrary arrest, detention and Press censorship. He was also, like a Frederick or a Catherine, committed to much of the past, though less to the social privileges which they respected and he used as devices of government, than to more general beliefs in order, authority, property, conventional sexual morality and the family. This is, no doubt, to say that Napoleon shared the prejudices of most Frenchmen, whose conduct long showed that they thoroughly approved of a patriarchal, male-oriented social order. When some Frenchwomen had tried to enlist revolutionary principles in support of the rights they claimed for their sex under the Convention, their *sans-culotte* menfolk gave them short shrift.

In untangling the significance of what Napoleon did, there is some danger of forgetting that he shared also with monarchs of the *ancien régime* a governmental weakness which was to disappear in the later nineteenth century. Great areas of France – the Loire is the great dividing line and the *massif central* the outstanding example – were under the Consulate still barely subject to administration, if public order or the working of conscription is used as a test. This is not to say that Napoleon did not command the support of local notables in a greater measure than any regime since 1789, nor that the Emperor did not rule the towns, but only that below the impressive façade of the prefects, the judicial apparatus and the uniformity of the Codes yawned the depths of French rural societies still as remote from government as they had been under Louis xv.

It is easy to overlook the fact that, in the end, the French did not stand by Napoleon. Economic hardship and a war-weariness whose most explicit statement was the hatred of conscription were wearing away support from 1810 onwards. Yet in spite of such qualifications, Napoleon's achievement at home still remains for his countrymen a great one, inextricably entangled with the glory won by French power abroad and unlikely to be judged unfavourably. Physically, it is commemorated in the great monuments of imperial Paris and the names of victories they bear. They are persuasive: Napoleon was one of the greatest exponents of public relations as a branch of government. The establishment of order, financial and political, the bringing to fruition of reforms such as the legal codification long derived and pondered by bureaucrats are tangled in a pageant of imperial grandeur through which it is still hard to grasp the reality of Napoleonic France.

Most Frenchmen were peasants, and great difficulties stand in the way of knowing what they thought. Their attitude to the regime must be interpreted with respect for distinctions among them and with regard to the passage of time. But there is the insurmountable evidence of their votes in three plebiscites on constitutional change which is hard to qualify. On the whole, the policies adopted by the regime were reassuring to the propertied, and that meant many among the peasants. The feeling that the uncertainties of the revolutionary era were at last over, the acceptance of the Concordat by the Papacy, which thereby abandoned any possible claim to a restoration of ecclesiastical lands sold during the Revolution and, finally, the tempering of conscription so as to suit the countryside by making exemptions easier there, all helped Napoleon's courtship of this mass of Frenchmen.

The elites presented a more complex problem, but in seeking to attach them to the regime Napoleon was helped by his own opportunist lack of scruple. He was willing to recruit civil servants and advisers from any political background, providing they accepted the régime. The Revolution had opened careers to talent, regardless of birth, and Napoleon was careful to respect this. Social ascent was perhaps easier in the army than in civilian life; sixteen of the twenty-six Napoleonic marshals had been NCOs. As the Empire settled in, it was able to tempt back to its service members of the old nobility. Side by side with a former terrorist, such as Fouché, or the renegade bishop, Talleyrand, they registered the reintegration of the French ruling class. Meanwhile, Napoleon's police harried unreconciled republicans and old Jacobins (and was often directed by ex-republicans and ex-Jacobins serving as policemen and prefects).

The most important reconciliation was that of the clergy. Here it is important to be clear about what was and what was not done. At the beginning of the Consulate, church and state in France were entirely separate and hostile to one another. The Convention had cut the last tie binding the republic to the constitutional church. From then until 1801 a grudging, hostile legalism on the part of the authorities char-acterized the religious settlement of France. The only other important country where there was no established church was the United States of America, where it was forbidden by the constitution, but the atmosphere there was very different. In France, Christians were not permitted endowments or national organization and shared with other sects the use of ecclesiastical buildings (owned by the State). Many Frenchmen thus lived bitterly beside their fellow-citizens, in a state of moral civil war, their hatred kept alive by pinpricks, abuse and occa-sional intensified persecution of their priests, if they were non-jurors. The reverse of this coin, of course, was that many also lived in regions where the cult of the republican *décadi* – the day of rest every tenth, which had replaced Sunday – could not be enforced, and non-jurors survived untroubled thanks to connivance and protection by their flocks.

Bonaparte's arrival in power was soon followed by the election of a new pope. Pius VII was a bishop who had in 1797 told his charges (who had just become citizens of the new satellite, the Cisalpine Republic), that if they were good Christians, they would then be good democrats. But more than personal goodwill on the Pope's side was needed to heal the rift between church and French Republic. What was decisive was Bonaparte's appreciation of the political realities. The open wounds in French society had to be healed and the powerful forces of Catholicism put behind the incorporation of Belgians, Germans and Italians in the French State. Finally, there was the stimulus of the counter-Revolution, 'fifty *émigré* bishops in the pay of England' as Bonaparte put it.

The result was the Concordat of 1801 which, like many great agree-ments, was a compromise. Roman Catholicism was recognized as the religion of the majority of Frenchmen, the clergy obtained stipends from the state, and the church accepted that the property lost in the Revolution was gone forever. But Catholic worship was restored in

France, and Rome resumed its altars. In return, the State won the nomination of bishops, public prayers for the government and an oath of obedience and fidelity to it by the clergy. To secure a clean start, the Pope bade the bishops of France resign: those who did not were deprived, and new bishops were appointed.

The old confessional state and belief in religion uniformity had gone: the Protestant churches were given an administration and legal connection to the government like that of the Roman Church. But the papal deprivation of bishops was an unprecedented assertion of authority over the French church. It was a real increase in papal authority. Though friction quickly arose over the interpretation of the Concordat, the new alliance benefited both sides too much for its continuation to be undoubted until the French invaded the Papal States in 1808. Before that, religion had consecrated the Empire, the Pope coming to Paris to attend the imperial coronation in 1804 and endorsing the bishops' loyal subservience to the new regime. For the ordinary Catholic this was brought home in an 'Imperial Catechism' enjoining obedience to the Emperor, and the dubious innovation of a new feast to a hastily discovered St Napoleon.

The high content of purely administrative and governmental consideration in the Napoleonic church settlement is striking, but far from exhausts its significance. Within the context of the principles of 1789, always lauded, if not always actually maintained by legal safeguards, the restoration of the authority of the state in the major European land power west of Russia and its emergence from religious strife was of enormous importance in the short run, and shaped France's destinies down to the present day.

Against this positive background must be placed the undoubted fact of political failure. In the final crunch, France did not support Napoleon. Neither the political and cultural elites nor the broad masses who on other issues had expressed their views by insurrection and pogrom stood by the Emperor in 1814. At that moment he was pressed by allied armies from almost all sides. His marshals – or at least some of them – were tired of fighting all Europe, and their war-weariness was paralleled by the popular irritation against the increasingly severe conscription needed to raise his last armies. So far, perhaps, Napoleon's loss of support was a matter of military disaster and the failure of his personal judgment which had brought this out. Certainly there was little enthusiasm for the replacement of his rule by that of the Bourbons. But nor was there any will to continue the struggle.

It is when we try to go beyond this that judgment becomes harder. Obviously the imperial regime had not been able to send down roots capable of surviving hard times and the defection of the military.

Napoleon himself had always recognized a danger here. He had striven to ensure the well-being of France by economic warfare which was not only a weapon against England but a means of exploiting his continental allies and satellites as well. Yet this did not prevent the coming of hard times in 1811, when Napoleon was even willing to resume the price-controls of 1793. But the demands of conscription, though bearing mainly on the urban poor, cut across the successful long-term appeasement of the masses. The failure to attach the elites firmly to the regime is another matter. The growth of clerical irritation is comprehensible, given Napoleon's treatment of the Pope after the foundation of the Empire, culminating, as it did, in carrying him off from Rome to France. Catholic disapproval was important; it could provide ideological coherence to opposition. Another ideologically alienated group were the intellectuals. Napoleon's utilitarian approach to intellectual activity did not provide footholds for all of them, conspicuous in the regime though some scientists and legists were. Some dissidents were members and successors of the moderate Left of the revolutionary decade, the first liberals, grouped in the current of opinion called *idéologue*. These provided principled grounds of opposition which balanced on the Left the diehard legitimism of the Right.

Finally, there was a measure of unlucky timing to be allowed for in the final Napoleonic failure. Though there was a three-year-old heir to the throne in 1814, he was too young to provide a credible successor, if Napoleon were to go – and foreign armies would decide that. Consequently, there could be no smooth dynastic transition but the prospect of the complications and troubles of a regency, and a regency, moreover, in which the Austrian whom Napoleon had married in 1810 must play an important part. Fifteen years later, the story might have been different. Nevertheless, Napoleon provoked the assault by the other European powers which overthrew him at a time when the dynastic roots were still too shallow to bear the strain.

The most obvious achievement of Napoleonic France in Europe was French hegemony. Its foundation was military; the deployment with great courage and skill of the resources of France, rejuvenated by revolution, and, increasingly, those of a French Empire too. Napoleon's first great victory after *Brumaire* was the shattering of the Second Coalition, from which he had already detached Russia. In 1801 Austria, Spain and Naples made peace. In the following year, the British agreed to terms which opened the only brief period between 1793 and 1815 in which they were not at war with France. Fourteen months later, in May 1803, Great Britain again declared war. A Third Coalition was put together in the year that followed, but it was destroyed like its predecessor when Napoleon routed the Russians and Austrians at

Austerlitz at the end of 1805. A humiliating peace for Austria followed and the Neapolitan monarchy was overthrown as a punishment for joining the coalition.

Against this background of French success it was perhaps rash of the Prussians to declare war on France in October 1806. Less than a week later came a military disaster unsurpassed in Prussian history until 1945, when Napoleon overthrew the famed Prussian army at Jena. The Prussians did not at once make peace, hoping to get better terms by falling back on their Russian allies, but by the end of the year Napoleon was pushing on to Danzig and into Poland. Finally, in June 1807, he routed the Russians at Friedland. Peace followed within a month. Once again, sheer fighting had carried the day for Napoleon. Militarily, it was the peak of his success, though not of the formal extent of his power.

At the other end of Europe, a French army had entered Lisbon during 1807, from which the Prince Regent and the Portuguese fleet had decamped to Brazil. Napoleon had also set up a new 'Grand Duchy' of Warsaw and a new kingdom of Naples ruled over by his brother. The extremities of French power were thus demarcated. A rising in Spain in 1808 against the French soldiers whom a puppet Spanish government had allowed to pass through to Portugal helped the Austrians to decide to make yet another attempt to recover their lost ground and prestige. They did so without any help except English money. An Austrian offensive began in April 1809 and less than four weeks later Napoleon was into Hungary and had occupied Vienna. But on 21–22 May, Napoleon lost his first battle, at Aspern; it was not to be forgotten that he was not invincible, though, in the end, disappointed by the failure of a British attack aimed at Antwerp, the Austrians once more made peace at Vienna in October.

French power was now at its greatest extent. The 'Illyrian provinces' of Carniola, Carinthia, Croatia and Dalmatia were added to the French Empire. French armies occupied Spain. Napoleon had annexed the Papal States in 1808. Among great powers, only Great Britain, whose armies were confined to Portugal and Sicily, remained in the field against him. In 1810 a man could walk from Bayonne to the Elbe on imperial territory, and he could go to the Niemen, Belgrade, Calabria and the straits of Gibraltar without leaving that of French satellites or allies. The best symbol of the French hegemony thus restored by Napoleon and carried far beyond any former limits was the arrival in France in 1810 of a Habsburg princess on her way to her wedding, as Marie Antoinette had come forty years before. On 2 April Marie Louise was married to Napoleon. Their child, born the following year, was given the title of King of Rome, the traditional title of the heirs of the

Holy Roman Emperors. The Napoleonic dynasty was, it seemed, established and a new, ironic twist was given to the historic epigram on Habsburg diplomacy: 'Others may make war, but you, O happy Austria, make marriages.'

Napoleon's ascendancy, and the primacy which it gave to what he saw as the interests of France in Europe was the culmination of an assertion of French power foreshadowed under Louis xiv. But the Revolution had opened its greatest phase: it was in 1797 that Frenchmen began to speak of *la grande nation*. Yet for all the impact of French institutions and ideas, and all the weight of French arms and the disruptive and innovatory effects of French diplomacy, much went on in international life whose roots lay back well before 1789.

One example was the continuing development of the Eastern Question which, though obviously affected, was not changed fundamentally by the revolutionary and Napoleonic era. An important milestone was passed with the extinction of the kingdom of Poland, but this only indirectly concerned French power. Directly, the impact of France was greater on the Eastern Question after the Partitions, which ended its Polish chapter and opened the Ottoman one. This new French influence was not very important for a long time, except where weakness or tension already existed. The planting of a tree of liberty on Turkish soil by a French citizen (a *ci-devant* marquis) was only an insignificant ripple in the great currents of Russian expansion and the rising discontent of the subjects of the Porte. It was when French influence coincided with these that it was effective, though even then only slowly.

The first important direct effect of French policy on the Eastern Question came outside the Western World, in Egypt, formally Turkish, but ruled with great independence by the Mamelukes. An important new phase of world history was opened by a French expedition there in 1798. It provoked a British counter-expedition which was the opening move in a long Anglo-French rivalry in the Middle East, but what was more important was that the demonstrated inability of the Sultan to protect his dominions in Africa led to an assertion of independence by Mehemet Ali, the Albanian pasha of Egypt, in 1806. There followed the foundation by him of the Egyptian national state and the first eruption of Arab nationalism into Middle Eastern history. The battle of the Pyramids in which General Bonaparte destroyed Mameluke power was the first skirmish of the long wars of Turkish succession in Africa and Asia (those in Europe had begun much earlier).

The Napoleonic era also brought British policy into Middle Eastern affairs in a new way. The expedition to Egypt revealed a new sensitivity which British governments were from this time to show about routes to India. Bonaparte's descent on Egypt had repercussions across the Indian Ocean; fear of a land crossing of Suez followed by re-embarkation in the Red Sea led to the assembly of a British squadron at its mouth. The security of these routes would have to be safeguarded, in future, against both French and Russian power; by 1800 Russian fleets had twice appeared in the Mediterranean. The tendency of British policy therefore came to be to prop up the Turkish Empire against further pressure from the north-east, as had happened in 1791, when the British government vigorously opposed the Russian acquisition of Oczakov. Later, after French diplomatic activity in both Turkey and Persia, the problem took on even wider dimensions. But diplomacy was the only weapon British policy possessed, once away from the power of her fleet; it was impossible for her to resist Russian pressure on Turkey single-handed – and therefore Russian policy did well out of the Napoleonic years – but Great Britain became more and more tenacious of the sites on which her Mediterranean sea-power rested. The British retention of Malta was the centre of disputes leading to the resumption of war with France after the peace of Amiens.

Much else in the Anglo-French struggle was far from new. World conflict between the two powers is another theme which runs across the chronological boundaries of the revolutionary and Napoleonic eras. In Englishmen's eyes, the traditional enemy was only made worse by the associations of terror, rapine, looting and revolution which were the accompaniment of French occupation in Europe. The French meanwhile saw the 'new Carthage' as a commercial empire, whose self-interest made her the enemy of the whole of enlightened mankind as well as of France. The struggle between the two states was waged for the most part in three ways, in their colonies, between their economies and through Great Britain's allies in Europe.

The first was the aspect of the struggle which most obviously continued earlier eighteenth-century wars, and the entry of Spain to the war against Great Britain in 1796 confirmed this similarity. British sea-power was never threatened between 1793 and 1815 as it had been in the war of American Independence, and the colonial struggle could have only one outcome, the severing of French colonial possessions and colonial trade from France, an outcome confirmed by the destruction of the French fleet at Trafalgar in 1805. The effective end of the colonial struggle gave economic war after 1806 a new character. Napoleon's choice of economic strategy combined the assertion of French industrial and commercial interests within Europe (if necessary at the expense of his allies and satellites) with an attack on English exports by excluding English goods from continental markets. The object was not to starve the British into making peace but to ruin their industry and commerce by denying it outlets. Such a strategy was risky in three important ways: it created bitterness and opposition in other European states, it could not be completely effective against Great Britain while she was able still to look for new markets overseas (notably in South America) and it ignored the fact that the French war effort itself required some goods that only the British could supply. None the less, it hurt the United Kingdom badly.

The military conflict of the two powers in Europe was fought for the most part at second hand, although from 1793 onwards the British were always conscious of the danger of invasion by French armies and kept up large forces at home. Yet for the most part the British strategy was maritime; British power was brought to bear only upon targets capable of being reached by naval means (such as the Danish fleet, destroyed at Copenhagen), or by the maintenance of British military forces in peripheral areas. Sicily was one such; a more important theatre was the Iberian peninsula where, though it could not hope to force the French to peace, the British army nevertheless kept alive a national resistance in Spain which was a huge drain on French resources.

The only other important nation which could not be reached by French armies was the United States of America. Their importance, in any case, was debatable, and potential rather than actual; in 1789, they were still all but an irrelevance to European diplomats. Nor did Americans seek entanglements in Europe's quarrels. True, isolation could not be complete or perfect; continuing commercial ties with Great Britain and the worrying intrigues of French revolutionary diplomacy showed this as the 1790s went on. The second president of the United States, John Adams, held the Federalists in check in foreign policy (Hamilton would have happily supported war with France) but allowed them to carry out other steps hostile to France, notably through legislation to check the spread of dangerous ideas and inhibit subversive activity. Some of them identified Jeffersonian Republicanism with Jacobinism.

Many Americans then and long after shared the scepticism of Europeans about their nation and its basis in the principles of equality and popular sovereignty. No such huge experiment, after all, had ever been seen before. Some of them therefore felt fearful when the Federalist ascendancy ended and Jefferson was elected President in 1800. This year brought one very visible change when Congress moved to a new federal capital on the banks of the Potomac. It was named Washington after the first president. Its grandiose public buildings were only half-built and stood, such as they were, in a desert of mud, swamp and boarding-houses. Of more fundamental change, there was little.

In domestic affairs, Jefferson's two terms were an anticlimax. He made a major contribution to American political practice by replacing about a third of the 316 officeholders appointed by presidential authority: the men who replaced them were political allies but included also men deserving of reward. The spoils system was born. Yet his inaugural address was conciliatory. Its principles were unimpeachable and Jefferson's conduct of affairs conservative and prudent. To the proven bases of American political and social life, said the Inaugural, only one thing needed still to be secured, 'a wise and frugal Government, which shall restrain men from injuring one another, shall leave them otherwise free to regulate their own pursuits of industry and improvement, and shall not take from the mouth of labour the bread it has earned'.

Much more revolutionary was Jefferson's conduct of foreign policy, though it, too, turned out to be very different from what had been feared; at one moment even the President who was the friend of France contemplated war with her. This new departure arose in part from changes in France, when Bonaparte came to power, but its true roots lay, as might have been hoped, not in ideology or partisan politics but in American reality. Two negative facts stood out clearly. The first was that the United States, barely united and weak, could not conduct a vigorous foreign policy of intervention in the affairs of the rest of the Western World. The second was that she was not threatened by any grave danger from the outside. Geographical remoteness saved the United States from strains which could have proved fatal to an infant nation. The Union was weak, its huge territory peopled by barely six million inhabitants. Only an alliance with two great naval powers had enabled the Americans to cast off the British yoke. It was impossible, some thought, to be sure that the United States could save herself from secession and dissolution. In 1804 Jefferson speculated that the country might one day divide into two confederations, one on the Atlantic coast and one in the Mississippi valley. This was just after the most important diplomatic transaction in the whole history of the United States, the Louisiana Purchase.

The United States still had land frontiers with other great powers, ill-defined though some were. Louisiana, roughly the area from the Mississippi to the Rockies, but of unknown extent, was still Spanish in 1799. Most of it had been of little interest to Americans, whose relations with the Spanish government were shaped much more by concern that the new western states' outlet from the Mississippi, vital to them, should remain open. The right to use New Orleans as a trading port was conceded to them in 1795. Nor was Spain then greatly interested in the further west. It had always been a liability. Partly for this reason the Spanish did not much repine when Napoleon made them cede Louisiana to France in 1800.

This transformed American history. It seemed that Napoleon was thinking of reopening the closed book of French colonial expansion in North America, pushing up the Mississippi valley to establish a cordon cutting off the United States from the west. A Mississippi closed to American commerce seemed about to become a reality. Jefferson contemplated war against France with British help. Napoleon recognized that he could not hope to hold Louisiana if war broke out with Great Britain and set about agreeing to a sale. In the end, the Americans got more than expected, for the whole province passed to them by sale on 30 April 1803 for fifteen million dollars.

An area bigger than the existing United States thus changed hands. There were huge implications. In domestic politics the way was opened to the addition of state after state in the west whose influence would tell against the Atlantic seaboard. In the long run, it can now also be seen that the undisputed possession of the heartland of the continent was the decisive moment in the progress of the United States towards great power standing. The Purchase meanwhile transformed the immediate context of diplomacy by ending virtually all territorial entanglements with other great powers except Great Britain (and, for a little, with Spain, whose possession of the Floridas dragged on until 1819). Great Britain and the United States still faced almost a half-century of sporadic bickering while they cleared up leftover business. Once, too, they came to war, in 1812.

The background to this conflict was complex. To begin with, there was the difficult relationship of two countries which ceased to be enemies in 1783 but could hardly at once be friends. On the one hand, Great Britain was the former oppressor, an enemy who irritated American susceptibilities by any act – such as making difficulties over withdrawal from military posts in the north-west – which seemed to show that old pretensions were not dead. On the other, ties of culture, personal connection and, above all, economics were close. The last were being steadily strengthened, too, as England became the major supplier of manufactured goods and capital to the United States. But a new complication arose from the British use of sea-power during the Napoleonic wars. It was the supreme weapon of the United Kingdom and it was bound to cause conflict with the United States whose political non-entanglement with Europe offered important prospects of gain once colonial supplies to France were cut off. Americans might become Europe's go-betweens with the wider world. The British assertion of blockade rights and insistence on stopping and searching American merchantmen to carry off British sailors from them for enlistment in

Traditionally, French kings were crowned at Rheims and Louis XVI went there like his predecessors to be anointed from the sacred vessel which, it was said, had been used at the coronation of the Merovingian Clovis, more than a thousand years before (during the Revolution it was publicly smashed to show France's wish to break with her past). A contemporary print of part of the ceremony.

By the KING,

A PROCLAMATION,

For suppressing Rebellion and Sedition.

GEORGE R.

HEREAS many of Our Subjects in divers Parts of Our Colonies and Plantations in *North America*, misled by dangerous and ill-designing Men, and forgetting the Allegiance which they owe to the Power that has protected and sustained them, after various disorderly Acts committed in Disturbance of the Publick Peace, to the Obstruction of lawful Commerce, and to the Oppression of Our loyal Subjects carrying on the same, have at length proceeded to an open and avowed Rebellion, by arraying themselves in hostile Manner to withstand the Execution of the Law, and traitorously preparing, ordering, and levying War against Us. And whereas there is Reason to apprehend that such Rebellion hath been much promoted and encouraged by the traitorous Correspondence, Counsels, and Comfort of divers wicked and desperate Persons within this Realm: To the End therefore that none of Our Subjects may neglect or violate their Duty through Ignorance thereof, or through any Doubt of the Protection which the Law will afford to their Loyalty and Zeal; We have thought fit, by and with the Advice of Our Privy Council, to issue this Our Royal Proclamation, hereby declaring that not only all Our Officers Civil and Military are obliged to exert their utmost Endeavours to suppress such Rebellion, and to bring the Traitors to Justice; but that all Our Subjects of this Realm and the Dominions thereunto belonging are bound by Law to be aiding and assisting in the Suppression of such Rebellion, and to disclose and make known all traitorous Conspiracies and Attempts against Us, Our Crown and Dignity; And We do accordingly strictly charge and command all Our Officers as well Civil as Military, and all other Our obedient and loyal Subjects, to use their utmost Endeavours to withstand and suppress such Rebellion, and to disclose and make known all Treasons and traitorous Conspiracies which they shall know to be against Us, Our Crown and Dignity; and for that Purpose, that they transmit to One of Our Principal Secretaries of State, or other proper Officer, due and full Information of all Persons who shall be found carrying on Correspondence with, or in any Manner or Degree aiding or abetting the Persons now in open Arms and Rebellion against Our Government within any of Our Colonies and Plantations in *North America*, in order to bring to condign Punishment the Authors, Perpetrators, and Abettors of such traitorous Designs.

Given at Our Court at St. *James's*, the Twenty-third Day of *August*, One thousand seven hundred and seventy-five, in the Fifteenth Year of Our Reign.

God save the King.

The British government hardens its attitude. A proclamation issued less than a year before the Declaration of Independence, when events were already out of control.

A Declaration by the Representatives of the UNITED STATES OF AMERICA, in General Congress assembled.

When in the course of human events it becomes necessary for one people to dissolve the political bands which have connected them with another, and to ~~~~~~ assume among the powers of the earth the separate and equal ~~~~~~~~~~~~~~~~~~~~~~~ station to which the laws of nature & of nature's god entitle them, a decent respect to the opinions of mankind requires that they should declare the causes which impel them to the ~~~~~~~ the separation.

We hold these truths to be self-evident; ~~~~~~~~~~~~~~~~~~~~~~~~ that all men created equal & independent, that from that equal creation they derive in rights inherent & inalienable, among which are ~~~~~~~~~~~~~~~~~~~~~~ life, & liberty, & the pursuit of happiness; that to secure these ~~~~~, governments are instituted among men, deriving their just powers from

TOP The outline of a future: a rough draft of the Declaration of Independence, a document to have a great future as a model and inspiration for countless others.

BOTTOM The idle and industrious apprentices; a favourite theme of novelists as late as the nineteenth century, but here exploited by an eighteenth-century artist before Adam Smith attacked the apprenticeship system as a restraint on trade. Weaving in such small shops was then the rule; the factory age still lay far in the future.

THE LEICESTERSHIRE IMPROVED BREED.

To thefe various and numerous tribes of this ufeful animal, we muft add, that, by the perfevering induftry and attention of Mr Bakewell, of Difhley, in Leicefter-fhire, our breed of Sheep has been greatly improved ; and he has been followed by many eminent breeders with nearly equal fuccefs.

It feems to be generally agreed, that in Sheep, as well as in all other animals, there is a certain fymmetry or proportion of parts, which is beft adapted to the fize of each particular animal : All thofe of each kind that exceed or fall fhort of this pitch, are more or lefs difproportioned, according to the fize they attain ; and in the degree they are advanced beyond this line of perfection, we find them lefs active, weaker, and always lefs able to endure hardfhip. Thus, by felecting the handfomeft and beft proportioned of their kinds, the judicious breeder has gradually arrived at a degree of perfection in improving this animal, unknown at any former period.

Experience Aréostatique faite a Versailles le 19 Sept.ᵇʳᵉ 1783 en presence
de leurs Majestes et de la famille Royale par Mʳ. de Montgolfier avec un
Balon de 52 pieds d'hauteur sur 41 de Diamettres. Cette Superbe machine a fond
d'asur avec le Chiffre du Roi pesant 900 livres. Ce balon a ete enlevé avec
toutes l'applaudissement de tout les Spectateurs et a tombé dans le Bois de Vaucresson
Carrefour Marechal.

ABOVE Balloons became a fashionable craze
by the end of the eighteenth century. In this
print, one of the experiments of the
celebrated Montgolfier brothers is
commemorated. The aeronauts were a cock,
a sheep and a duck; Marie-Antoinette,
Louis XVI and, curiously, the young and
unknown Napoleon Buonaparte, were
present to see them ascend.

OPPOSITE A page from the *General History
of Quadrupeds* by the great engraver Thomas
Bewick, published in 1790. The
improvement of the quality of English
livestock in the eighteenth century was one
of the aspects of the agricultural advances
of the period which most struck continental
observers.

RIGHT The guillotine was named after a
deputy to the French National Assembly of
1789, Dr Ignace Guillotin, though he did
not invent it. He did, however, perish as one
of its victims, one of many who made it
notoriously the symbol of the Terror.

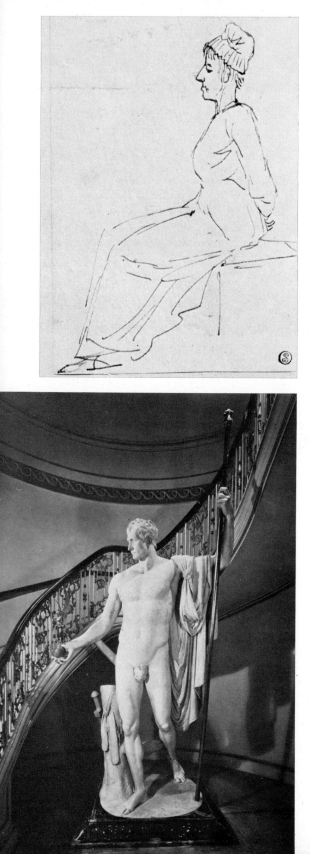

The once-beautiful Marie-Antoinette is taken to the guillotine in a cart, her hair cut short and her hands tied behind her back in preparation. This poignant sketch is by the artist Jacques-Louis David, an eye-witness.

The idealization of the hero: Canova's marble statue of the emperor Napoleon, now at Apsley House, the home of the man who defeated him at Waterloo, the Duke of Wellington.

OPPOSITE A bizarre piece of Napoleonic iconography; the former emperor is portrayed as the instrument of the Divine will: a text from the second epistle of St Peter which is cited in the margin reads, 'Moreover I will endeavour that ye may be able after my decease to have these things always in remembrance' – an invocation of the memory of a martyr.

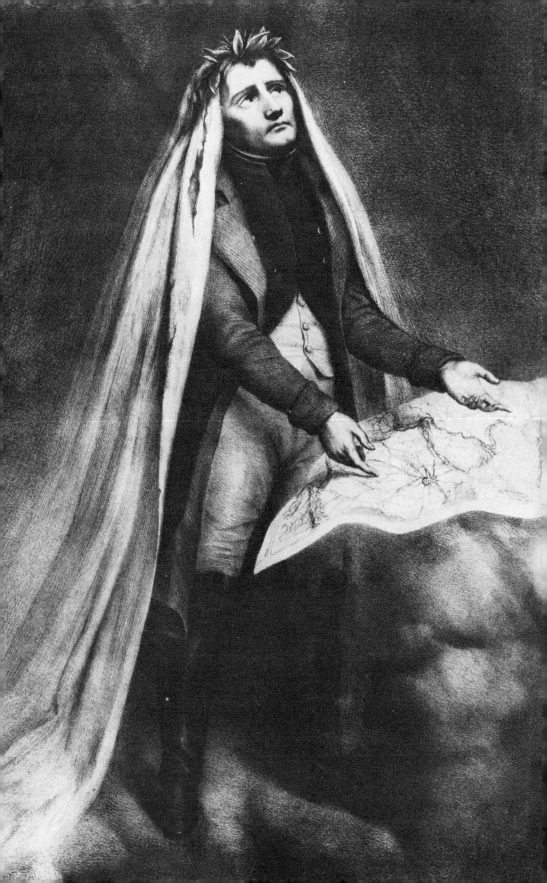

ABOVE The Russian peasant strips off the emperor's clothing and reveals the wolf within.

BELOW The railway bridge at Stockport and the London–North Western Railway going across it, in about 1830. The expansion of railway communications was essential to the success of the industries of the North. It also helped to shape the North's characteristic urban landscapes, one of which is appearing here.

The harsh face of industrialization: child-labour in a coal-mine in a print of the 1840s. Lord Shaftesbury, appalled by conditions in the collieries, took up their cause, and the Mines Act of 1842 forbade the employment of women and girls underground and that of boys under ten, and appointed inspectors to report back to a central authority.

A romanticized view of child workers in factories: an illustration from *The Life and Adventures of Michael Armstrong the Factory Boy*, published in 1840 by Frances Trollope, the mother of Anthony Trollope.

ABOVE An early design for a tug-boat – the role in which steam was at first thought to have its main contribution to make to movement at sea.

BELOW The *Comet*, a ship built on the Clyde in 1811 and used for regular passenger traffic in European waters between 1812 and 1820, when she was wrecked. She was 40 feet long, weighed about 25–30 tons and had a speed of about 5 knots.

ABOVE The hopes and disappointments of the German emigrants to the United States in the nineteenth century: a contemporary German print. They plan to build 'an earthly paradise' in their new homeland, but still have regrets about leaving the simple life they were accustomed to, and are aware of the hardships ahead of them.

RIGHT This representation of 'the causes of emigration in Ireland' which appeared in *The Lady's Newspaper* at the beginning of 1849 leaves out the famine which had devastated the province in the previous two years, but is otherwise realistic in its estimation of the pressures at work on the poor.

ABOVE 'Holeing a cane-piece': a contemporary print. Men and women alike join in the work of a sugar plantation in Antigua. Sugar, introduced to the English colonies by the Dutch, became the major industry of every colony in the West Indies, and was of course dependent on slave labour.

LEFT A cartoon dated 1848 draws attention to the hypocrisy of the United States, champions of liberty, in the matter of slavery. The caption reads: 'Oh, ain't we a deal better than other people! I guess we're a most splendid example to them thunderin' old monarchies.'

COMMERCE ANGLAIS.

ABOVE The sufferings of the Greeks were widely commiserated in Western European countries. This print depicts an incident which perhaps never occurred, but which was also used by a great artist, Delacroix, in a famous picture of the massacre at Chios.

LEFT Opium was of immense importance to the British trade with China. This anglophobe cartoon from France seizes the opportunity to satirize the self-righteousness of those who force the Chinese to poison themselves so that there will be tea enough available for the English to swill down their roast beef.

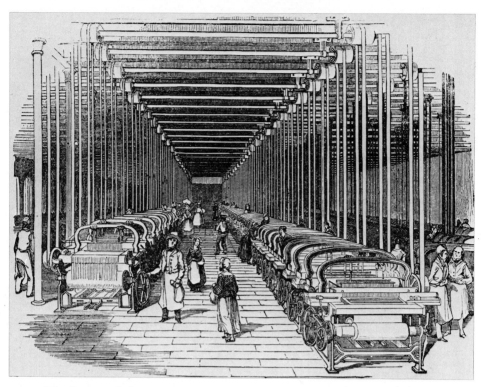

ABOVE The factory of 1845: power-looms, run from a central power-supply. The transition from the system of two or three looms in a master-craftsman's shop depicted in the print of the apprentices (see third page of illustrations) to this took little more than seventy years.

BELOW Michael Faraday, the greatest of British scientists of the nineteenth century, lectures to a popular audience of both sexes, adults and children, at the Royal Institution. Founded in 1799, the Institution became a centre not only for the diffusion of knowledge to the public, but also for original thought and investigation, under the imaginative guidance of Faraday and his mentor Humphrey Davy, inventor of the Davy lamp.

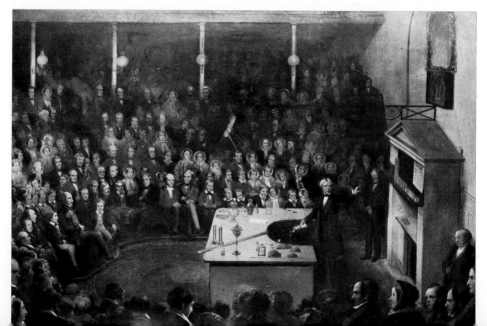

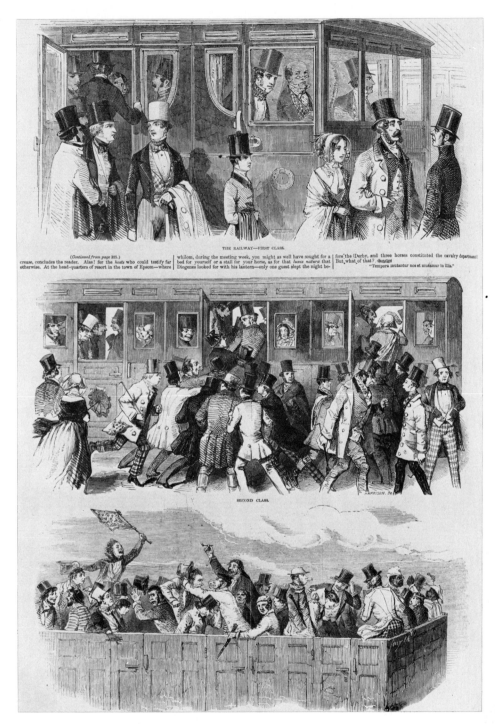

THE RAILWAY—FIRST CLASS.

(Continued from page 225.)

crease, concludes the reader. Alas! for the *hosts* who could testify far otherwise. At the head-quarters of resort in the town of Epsom—where whilom, during the meeting week, you might as well have sought for a bed for yourself or a stall for your horse, as for that *homo naturæ* that Diogenes looked for with his lantern—only one guest slept the night before the Derby, and three horses constituted the cavalry department! But what of that?

"Tempora mutantur nos et mutamur in illis."

SECOND CLASS.

The English passion for class distinction quickly got to work on the railway trains, as is depicted in this print from the 1840s of travellers to the races at Epsom.

The abbé Liszt, outstanding virtuoso of the piano and romantic composer, came for many people to typify the passionate, Romantic master of music. A well-publicized private life of Byronic excitement also did much to assure him his audiences.

the Royal Navy combined an economic threat with an outrage to the sense of independence.

Although the British attempted last-minute concessions, the fourth president, Madison, asked Congress for a declaration of war on 1 June 1812; he justified the action on maritime and commercial grounds and traditionally the war was to be represented in American schoolbooks as a war for freedom of the seas. But this was far from the whole truth. The representatives of the maritime states in Congress voted against war, while its outstanding proponents were Henry Clay, a westerner from Kentucky, one of the newest states, who had never seen the sea in his life, and John Calhoun, from the plantation state of South Carolina. There was more to the war than impressment and blockade. What was really at issue was American expansion. This was because the 'warhawks' (as those who wanted war with Great Britain were called) were sectional politicians. A tacit, informal but real agreement existed between western and southern Republicans who wanted expansion. The westerners coveted free land in Canada; they hoped also to end the threat that the British would stir the Indians up against them. In the south, war would offer the chance of picking up the Floridas from Spain (which was by 1812 an ally of Great Britain). These interests pushed a President and Secretary of State neither of whom wanted a war into conflict with Great Britain.

'The coast is to be left defenceless while men of the interior are revelling in conquest and spoil,' was the bitter comment of one Virginian opponent of war. He was only half-right; there was precious little conquest and spoil even for the men of the interior. Two years of undistinguished fighting ended in stalemate on the northern frontier. Meanwhile, British blockade took its toll of the Atlantic states' prosperity. A British raid, mounted from Bordeaux, showed what might be forthcoming once the European peace made available large numbers of Wellington's veterans; it got as far as Washington, where, on 24 August 1814, some of its officers sat down to eat a dinner cooked for President Madison. In retaliation for an American burning of the parliament house at Toronto, the British then burned the White House and some other public buildings and went away, having achieved only the creation of a new grievance. The only other notable operations culminated in a battle at New Orleans, fought after peace had actually been signed on Christmas Eve 1814. This spectacular demonstration of British folly revived memories of the failures of the War of Independence; thirteen Americans were lost in inflicting two thousand casualties on the British, including three out of four general officers dead.

The peace terms showed that there had been nothing crucial at stake in the war, however unavoidable American domestic politics had made it. Little was said about the maritime issues alleged as grounds of war, and commissions were set up to look at boundary disputes, the *status quo* being resumed until they produced solutions. The inconclusiveness of the fighting showed the difficulties of armed conflict, and the disarmament of the Lakes opened a series of agreements which produced one of the most successful political boundaries in the world simply because neither side was in the last resort willing to fight over it. In 1818 it was agreed that its line should continue west from the Lake of the Woods to the Rocky Mountains along the 49th parallel, and another great step in the delineation of American national territory was thus taken. The warhawks were discouraged by the costliness and mediocrity of their successes, and the crossing of the Mississippi was soon to offer more land for settlement than the United States could possibly absorb for decades. Thus popular excitement over Canada died down.

To the south, the interplay of Old and New Worlds was very different. From somewhere near the Red River of Texas (the exact boundary there was still disputed), Mexico, central and southern America and the Caribbean islands were all still in the hands of the traditional colonial sovereign powers in 1803, of which the most important were Spain and Portugal.

By 1789, the Spanish Empire was a much less closed and monolithic structure than it had been a half-century before. The commerce with the Indies had been diversified by the creation of chartered companies and extension to metropolitan ports other than Seville and Cadiz, and also by permission for trade among the colonies themselves. This was all legal; there was also the important growth of illegal 'interloper' trade in the eighteenth century. On a smaller scale, the Portuguese had tried to diversify and stimulate trade with Brazil. Both empires had nearly three centuries of life behind them and in each there were many *creoles* (the name applied to the native-born white colonial subjects of Spain, as opposed to the *peninsulares*, or metropolitan-born) who played an important part in government and commerce and had noted with interest the events of 1775–83 to the north. Some *creole* rebels in New Granada in the early 1780s had considerable success in winning concessions from the Spanish authorities, though they could not interest the British and French in proposals for further revolution. The French Revolution then brought Latin America into world politics.

France was at war with Spain in the 1790s when the first insurrectionary hero of Latin American liberation came to the fore, the Venezuelan *creole* Miranda. He became a French general, but sought support for revolutionary expeditions in the United States and United Kingdom as well as France. At length, the British agreed and began to make ready an expedition for which the plans were suddenly disrupted by the French invasion of Portugal in 1807. By then, a British expedition returning from the conquest of the Dutch Cape of Good Hope had already, in the interest of Miranda's plans, occupied Buenos Aires. This was the beginning of an awkward entanglement. After the over-turning of the Spanish authority embodied in the viceroy, local feeling was further excited by defeats inflicted on the British forces. These were improved by the commander of the local militia whose election as 'viceroy' by the inhabitants of the Plate area was accepted by Spain. But Spanish government at home was swept away by the French. The provisional government which tried to continue the war had no power to do more than conciliate in the colonies, but its authority was more and more questioned. Though they quarrelled furiously with one another, the *creole* politicians one by one threw off their allegiance to Spain – Chile in 1810, the Plate provinces, Paraguay, Venezuela and New Granada in 1811, Mexico in 1813. The story was substantially different only in Brazil, to which the Prince Regent of Portugal had removed the Portuguese monarchy in 1807. Royal government con-tinued, being modified importantly in 1815 by the creation of a United Kingdom of Portugal, Brazil and Algarves. Latin America thus owed a new era in its history to French action in Europe. Though the out-come was not beyond doubt in 1815, complete political independence of Europe lay ahead for a group of new nations.

Irreversible political change resulted from the French hegemony in parts of Europe, too. As in the revolutionary decade, so during the Consulate and Empire, the fundamental political catalyst was the movement of French armies. Where they went, conscription, the codes and the prefects usually followed. More obviously, they changed the map, too. A huge measure of consolidation and reconstruction in Germany followed the treaty imposed on Austria in 1801. This fore-shadowed another change five years later, when in 1806 one of the most ancient of European institutions, the Holy Roman Empire, was swept away and the Emperor Francis II formally renounced his title. With the setting-up of a 'Confederation of the Rhine' of fifteen major German states, enlarged by the booty of their smaller neighbours and predecessors, Germany began the evolution into consolidation, simplification and the elimination of Habsburg power which came to a climax in 1871.

Further east, a wraithlike Poland emerged briefly from the shadows of the Partitions when, in 1807, Napoleon formed 'The Grand Duchy of Warsaw' from parts of Prussian Poland. In 1809 he added to it some of West Galicia. It was not much, perhaps, given the hopes of Poles and the service of many of them for years in the French armies, and it was not to last, but it irritated the Tsar. In Italy, the tangle of new and old states of the revolutionary decade was sorted out by annexations to France and consolidation so that, by 1809, when the Papal States became Departments of France, there existed only two other political units in the peninsula, the kingdoms of Italy and Naples. The first included old Lombardy, Venetia, Piacenza, Emilia and the Marches; the second was the old Kingdom of the Two Sicilies minus the island, where the Bourbon court sat, protected by a British garrison.

Napoleon was sensitive to historic symbols. When in 1805 he was crowned at Milan with the crown of Lombardy he took it with the traditional speech of the Lombard kings: 'God has given it to me, woe to him who touches it.' He called his son by the traditional title of heirs of the Holy Roman Emperors. Yet Poles, Germans and Italians who admired him looked to the future. For them, the Napoleonic era was the seedtime of their nations even if the first shoots were precocious and feeble. The man whose picture was hung over their household shrines by Greek peasant women was a force far beyond the outpost lines of his armies and it was because they saw him as a liberator and inspirer of nationality that Byron and Shelley were to regret the Emperor's fall.

At the same time, Napoleon set limits to revolution abroad as at home. In effect he restored the Papacy, whose extinction seemed near when the Roman Republic had been set up in 1798 and Pius VI was carried off to die the following year, a captive in France. Napoleon might quarrel with Pius VII, and lock him up in France, too, but his own claim to stand in the heritage of Charlemagne was a tacit recognition of his fellow-monarch's power – whose reality rested on the Napoleonic reversal of a century of Church-and-State relations in Europe.

As in France, too, so abroad, making war was itself a revolutionary process. International competition (even when peaceful) is expensive and tends to generate internal change. To resist the tyrant, the European monarchies had to adapt themselves to his methods. The result was that by 1815 many changes which made modern Europe possible were irreversible.

Three ways in which this happened may be specially remarked: the attack on privilege and corporation; the adoption of revolutionary machinery and institutions; the nationalization of social life. One state where all three tendencies were at work was Prussia after Jena. The achievements of the Prussian reformers may have been exaggerated in the past (not least, by their opponents) yet they began the destruction of Prussian feudalism, created a system of municipal self-government, set up a national conscription to recruit their armies (they were much struck by the ability of the Committee of Public Safety to organize

France for victory), instituted promotion by merit in the officer corps and began to preach Prussian patriotism as something distinct from dynastic loyalty. An even more startling transformation came in Spain, though a very different one. There, nationalism joined hands with religious fervour to expel the invader and build the only great popular resistance movement to trouble Napoleon. Furthermore, the collapse of the Spanish monarchy created Spanish liberalism (a word Spain was to give to Europe). The Spanish constitution of 1812 was the fruit of a renewal of Spanish political life brought about by the need to resist. It was also to provide a shibboleth for European liberalism in the Restoration years and to give Spain herself an unhappy pre-eminence as the most turbulent of all European states of the nineteenth century.

Here, together with the aspirations of men who had enjoyed careers open to their talents and the experience of French administration and legal simplification, were realities which outlasted the French hegemony, faced by growing difficulties from 1808 onwards. The French had invaded Spain in that year, carrying off its royal family to exile and installing one of Napoleon's brothers on the throne. This aggression, however, provoked first a ferocious popular insurrection and *guerrilla* (or 'little war') against the French and then the arrival of British expeditionary forces to protect Portugal. They helped to keep alive the Spanish resistance and tied down large numbers of French soldiers in difficult country with poor communications.

These soldiers were before long needed elsewhere. A bad economic crisis in 1811 disturbed French opinion at home and played a part in bringing to a head Napoleon's dissatisfaction with Russian policy which, among other things, helped to make the blockade of English trade, the 'Continental System', ineffective. In 1812 the largest army ever gathered hitherto crossed the frontier of Russia to penetrate as far as Moscow, but then had to return to the west shattered by an appalling retreat through the Russian winter. Thereafter, Russia and the United Kingdom had Napoleon on the defensive. In 1813 they were joined by Prussia, and the weight of numbers was now decisively against France. Then the Swedes (under a king who had been one of Napoleon's marshals) and finally the Austrians came in. A series of battles in Germany culminated in October in four days' fighting round Leipzig which Germans later called the 'Battle of the Nations'. This was a misleading name; though over half a million men and four great states took part, it is doubtful if any army taking part distinguished nationality from obedience to its monarch. It was a terrible defeat for Napoleon and by the end of the year he was confined to the west bank of the Rhine.

In January 1814, proclaiming that they were fighting not the French but only their unreasonable ruler, the allies attacked France on almost every side. With his last army of young conscripts Napoleon fought for three months a brilliant winter campaign. But he could not persuade his generals and subjects to follow him any longer once the allies reached Paris, and he abdicated. Confined on the island of Elba, he escaped to trouble Europe for the last time in March 1815. Three months later he led a new army to crush the allied army in Belgium and failed in the battles which have gone down in history under the name of the Waterloo campaign. It was 'a damned close-run thing', thought Wellington, the allied commander, who in an encounter of almost tragic appropriateness fought Napoleon for the first and only time. Close-run it was, in terms of the day's fighting, but even had Napoleon won at Waterloo, it would not have followed that he had won survival as emperor, so deep was the allies' fear of him. Even France could no longer fight all Europe single-handed. He was put away safely this time, sailing away into the vast spaces of the South Atlantic to die a few years later on St Helena.

The British, Napoleon's gaolers, always referred to their prisoner as 'General Bonaparte'. This was not mere affectation. They were not pretending that the Empire had not happened but only saying that legal continuity in France was represented by the Bourbon family, whose head, Louis XVIII, brother of Louis XVI, returned to Paris finally in 1815. Many Europeans, none the less, did try to pretend that the clock had been put back to 1789, 1792 or whatever date the Revolution had first come to their countries.

As a matter of mood, and on the surface, the changes of 1814 and 1815 indeed seemed complete. Much of a past suspended or interrupted was restored. But though the King of Sardinia re-entered his capital in the powdered wig of the *ancien régime* and restored the order of precedence of his court which had existed at the moment of his departure, he ruled a new state. He was now served by civil servants trained by the French; his soldiers had learned their trade from Napoleon. Even his state's boundaries were revolutionary, for they included the ancient republic of Genoa as a compensation for his troubles; this was a symbol that the assertions of the rights of prescription and old institutions were not what really mattered in Europe in 1815. So was the failure to re-appear of the republics of Venice and Lucca. On the other hand, it was also a sign of continuity. Genoa was another leaf of the Italian artichoke at which the House of Savoy had been nibbling away for a century. More leaves would follow. Meanwhile, the acquisition of Venice was another step in the consolidation of a Habsburg preponderance in northern Italy begun with the acquisition of Milan and Mantua.

Italy was not the only place where the map reflected the irregularities of the process of restoration. In Germany, too, a simple return to 1789 was clearly barred. The old Empire which had given Germany for centuries such political unity as it possessed and kept it firmly in the Habsburg orbit could not be restored, nor could many of the states of 1801. Instead, a new Germanic Confederation of thirty-nine states was set up and was practically dominated by Vienna as eighteenth-century Germany had never been. The historic rivalry of Habsburg and Hohenzollern was in abeyance, even if it was to emerge again later. Other eighteenth-century assumptions also seemed to have gone. Scores of German cities suddenly found themselves being left alone by their rulers much as in the days before would-be enlightened despots had tried to rationalize them into centralized state structures. Germany was in practice highly localized and fragmented still, for all the consolidations. Such independent accretions of power would only crumble before railways, industrialists and Bismarck.

The Poles must have been somewhat heartened to find that restoration was not complete. Though Poznan and Galicia went back to their former rulers, the King of Prussia and the Austrian emperor, most of the former Grand Duchy became a new kingdom of Poland, with its own constitution and army, the Tsar as its monarch and Warsaw its capital. There was even a tiny independent Poland, in Cracow, which became a free city under the protection of the partitioning powers.

Restoration, therefore, had both an actual and mythological reality, though not always the one expected. But the years after Waterloo are also less distinct from their immediate predecessors than is often supposed. Not even the conscious restorers always grasped how much had happened to cut them off from the distant past they wanted to call back and to connect them, instead, indissolubly with what had just happened.

In Russia and the United Kingdom this was clearest; in these countries no restoration era can be discerned because nothing needed to be restored. Both countries emerged with their political systems intact, the one to show immense potential for change and innovation, the other an immense inertia which would make it the lynch-pin of conservative forces throughout Europe. Yet though no restoration was needed in these states, both had changed much since 1789. This was not always a matter of the most obvious and eagerly discussed innovations. The two things which had grown most spectacularly and even alarmingly under the younger Pitt, the hero of Tory patriotism and later the outstanding cult-idol of conservatism, were the National Debt and the peerage, but more fundamental changes carrying the United Kingdom to its nineteenth-century future could still be unremarked by many of his countrymen. The values and order of a still rural England seemed solid and unchanging, yet the country was by

1815 well on the way to social and economic transformation by industry, had changed its constitutional shape and political future by taking in Ireland by the Union of 1801, and had acquired an unshakeable basis for a century of world power in colonial possessions and maritime power, while watching the beginnings of a transformation and polarization of her politics at home. These things owed much to war, the greatest revolutionary force of the period. It was war, too, which had brought about the revolution in Russia's international position when her soldiers entered Paris and her Tsar became the arbiter of western as well as eastern European destinies.

We should not, therefore, lean too heavily on 1815 as a date or on 'Restoration' as a category. The most important thing about the year is that it marks a milestone in the decline of the French preponderance in western Europe. Institutionally and ideologically, 1815 is much less helpful. Sensibly, few conservatives thought that much could be done by merely political and legal change. A new world of assumptions and beliefs had come into existence and here, too, the legacy of France to Europe could not be denied.

10 Long-term change

People

The drama of the great Revolution and what followed is so powerful that it is easy to underrate forces operating less spectacularly, more slowly and at a deeper level, setting the stage on which the politicians and generals had to move. One of these forces, population change, greatly interested men throughout this period. The eighteenth century was well aware that populations could grow and decline. Broadly speaking, growth was thought a good thing and decline a bad one. Intellectuals as different as Adam Smith and Rousseau thought that a growing population was an indicator of good government and prosperity, and the article on Population in the great *Encyclopédie* insisted that liberty went with it too. It had long been obvious to monarchs that more subjects meant more taxes, more labour, more production (to say nothing of more soldiers). On different grounds, therefore, everyone could approve of a rise in population.

Nevertheless, while there was general agreement on this, there was also for a long time uncertainty about the facts; nobody could be quite sure whether population was increasing or not. Though the science of statistics had been founded in the seventeenth century, recorded data was patchy and scant. When Gibbon, pursuing an old argument about whether the ancient world had more to be proud of than the modern, put on the Roman Empire of the Antonines a figure of 120 millions and followed Voltaire in attributing 107 millions to his own Europe, both guesses were wrong. Given that two centuries' statistical work since then still can provide us with no computation of the world's population accurate to the nearest hundred million, he need not be harshly criticized. It was only in 1770 that a French minister began to publish annual figures of marriages, births and deaths, only in 1801 that the first English census was held, and only with the start of civil registration of births, marriages and deaths in the United Kingdom in 1837 that a modern demographic historian can at last find continuous solid ground in the crude data which confront him. Usually, a simple lack of technical and bureaucratic means explains the absence of data, but there were other reasons, too. An eighteenth-century English parliament turned down a proposal for a census after hearing arguments not only that such information would be useful to the king's enemies but that David's disobedience in ordering Joab to count the people of Israel brought pestilence and the death of thousands upon his people. A biblical argument was powerful cause for reflection in a religious age. Popular opposition, grounded in fear of the tax-gatherer as well as in superstition, was another grave deterrent. There were popular disorders in France as late as the 1840s over censuses.

Nevertheless, in spite of the obstacles provided by poor material, modern demographic historians have done much to construct a picture of past structures and trends whose broad outline is hard to question. It is generally agreed that about the middle of the eighteenth century Europe's population had begun to grow at an increasing rate, so that by 1850 it was nearly double what it had been a century before, and stood at about 260 millions. This represented an increased proportion of the total world population, of which Europe now contained something over one-fifth and nowhere else except in the new United States did population grow so fast. Europe could find emigrants to people other continents and still grow at about one per cent per year.

This overall picture cloaks important differences between countries. Spain had more inhabitants than Great Britain in 1800, but was left behind by her fifty years later. In Europe, British population grew fastest of all. In the century after 1750 it increased by seventy per cent, while that of Russia grew forty-two per cent and France twenty-six per cent. Clearly, there were important social and political implications in these figures. Some countries still grew very slowly long after 1800.

Nevertheless, the fact of overall growth soon provoked notice and an important change of attitude. Almost everywhere except in the United States, demographic change seemed to reveal new problems for rulers and economists, changed existing relationships and through them attitudes and ideas. The changes were neither sudden nor complete. In the 1790s it could still be proposed in the French National Assembly that celibacy should be taxed – or even deprived of political rights. Yet there were already qualifications of such views. In one of the most optimistic surveys of the human condition ever written, Condorcet conceded a theoretical possibility that population might grow so as to outrun subsistence, though he thought that growing enlightenment might bring the knowledge and disposition to overcome this. A more alarming idea had been put forward in a book of 1790 by a Venetian writer, Ortès, who noted that population grew by geometrical progression, while the possibilities of producing food were finite. This idea was given a far wider audience in an anonymous book published in England in 1798, which was to be one of the most influential works of the century. This was the *Essay on Population*, as it was soon shortly termed, of the Reverend Thomas Malthus.

Malthus's work was published at the beginning of one of the greatest creative surges of English culture and in a society already assuming the economic leadership of the world. Thus sufficiently explains its success when taken into account against the all too visible background of population growth. France was full of beggars in 1789. English villages swarmed with underfed wretches for whom there seemed to be not enough work to go round and whose plight was already leading to attacks on the system of English poor relief. Malthus attempted an overall explanation of the great paradox that a society which seemed to grow richer and richer might contain huge numbers in miserable poverty.

His argument was brutally simple and may be condensed in a few of his sentences:

The power of population is indefinitely greater than the power of the earth to produce subsistence for man. . . . Population, when unchecked, increases in a geometrical ratio. Subsistence only increases in an arithmetical ratio. . . . There are few states in which there is not a constant effort in the population to increase beyond the means of subsistence. This constant effort as constantly tends to subject the lower class of society to distress, and to prevent any great permanent melioration of their condition.

This message was instantly and continuously compelling in spite of Malthus's drab style. He revealed – or appeared to reveal – that growth was not a beneficent harbinger of plenty, as had been thought, but the spectre of coming disasters.

Malthus based his assumptions about the different rates at which population and subsistence would grow on what he believed to be the fact that human sexuality (and therefore the tendency to reproduce) was a constant pressure and that, however large it might be, there was a limit to the amount of land which might grow food. The adequacy of these assumptions is not our concern here. What matters to the historian is their impact on thought and what they reveal as symptoms. Malthus quickly became famous – or notorious – for his exposition of the laws which, he said, normally held population in check. Foremost among them were the positive checks of famine and disease. If they ceased or were not to operate, said Malthus, then only a 'preventive' check could prevent population growing to a size at which it would outrun food supply. At that point, it would initiate again the positive checks of famine and disease. By a preventive check he meant one which would not permit growth to the point at which the positive ones would operate. He summed this up as 'moral restraint', a prescription, in effect, that people should marry later; he would countenance neither abortion nor contraception (though, ironically, nineteenth-century advocates of the latter were to be called 'neo-Malthusians').

These ideas had enormous effect. His German translator called Malthus another Newton. Specifically, their impact was greatest on economics, but it was in 1838 that a naturalist, Charles Darwin, suddenly found in reading Malthus a key to the evolutionary process in the competition for survival. More generally, it gave a damaging blow to the optimistic belief in potentially limitless progress of so much advanced thought of the eighteenth century. This had been Malthus's purpose and his book's full title showed it: *An Essay on the Principle of Population as it Affects the Future Improvement of Society*. He wished to demonstrate that between Man and his perfectibility as a species lay inescapable laws of nature, whose operation, if ignored, must ensure even greater misery than if their existence were recognized. In practice, this seemed to mean that misery for some was inescapable, that the poor would always be with you, and that they ought to minimize their sufferings by cultivating prudence in the avoidance of early marriage. There can be little doubt, unfortunately, that for all Malthus's own mildness of disposition and disinterested benevolence, this was to become a powerful deterrent to political reform, for it suggested that all attempts to remove misery and poverty by institutional change were in vain.

Thus was provided a theoretical background to the mounting surge of population in the nineteenth century which has no single explanation fitting all countries. Basically, population change must be a function of variables of which the two most important are the birth-rate and the death-rate. Apart from temporary and local fluctuations the death-rate everywhere went down, though not everywhere at the same rate. It was by no means true that the birth-rate everywhere rose. It did so, it seems, only where there were reasonable opportunities of employment and therefore fewer obstacles to early marriage; this fits both industrializing England and rural Ireland where the introduction of a new crop, the potato, made it possible to support a family on a smaller plot.

A falling death-rate made itself felt in the long run most importantly through a decrease in infant mortality, as nutrition improved, the virulence of some infective organisms (such as those of scarlet fever) declined, and medicine and sanitation began to deal with some of the worst killers of the past. It is very hard to see how these factors came precisely to bear in different countries but by the 1840s, though cholera was still rife in the cities, an increased life expectancy was already general in western Europe. Mortality in Great Britain actually fell faster in the century before 1850 than in the fifty years after; it had, after all, a long way to fall in 1750. Famine, though not eliminated, became rarer after 1800. Germany and Belgium experienced it in 1846–7, but this was the end of the story for the advanced countries in peacetime; there were to be no more in France, Great Britain, Germany and the Low Countries. This decline of famine perhaps owed something to a prolonged period of international peace after 1815, something to better transport, but most to agricultural improvement (which was, of course, in some degree helped by the first two factors). The crucial economic change of modern times was the increase which was achieved in the surplus of food produced over consumption. Thus the power of some of the great positive checks discerned by Malthus was declining. Somehow, the Malthusian trap had been avoided – or, thought some, entry to it had merely been put off.

The implications and consequences of this long-term trend were profound and crop up at every turn in the history of this era. The economic consequences can be postponed but there is a striking coincidence between a surge of population and the releasing of new economic energy. Among other consequences which were important were the beginnings of a great resettlement of people of Caucasian stock the world over. Not only was Europe's own share of world population rising, but she had begun – though only just by 1847 – to export people on a scale which meant that the Caucasians who had been about twenty-two per cent of the human species in 1800, made up over a third of it in 1930. This was the bedrock of the European Age of world history. By 1847 the greatest of *Völkerwanderungen* had barely started, but even in the 1830s about a half-million European immigrants went to the United States; in the next decade there were three times as many.

An important consequence of uneven growth between nations was a new distribution of population inside Europe. Already by 1847 the heavily populated belt which stretches across north-west Europe from Manchester to the Ruhr was beginning to appear. There was nothing new about cities as such, what was new was that existing cities were often getting bigger, as population grew, and that a new kind of urban area, closely related to the growth of manufactures, was also appearing. Huge percentage increases in the populations of both old and new cities were recorded in the 1830s and 1840s. It seems probable that Paris reached a million just before 1848, and that made it about half the size of London; London grew by 130,000 in the 1830s alone, Manchester by nearly seventy thousand. In 1851 England had nine cities of more than a hundred thousand people and at this time Russia, with a much greater population, had only two, the same number as the United States and Germany. But it was the middling towns whose distribution on the map showed where the backbone of the future industrial Europe lay. England had fifty-four cities of more than twenty thousand and less than a hundred thousand people in 1851, where Russia had twenty-one in a much greater area. France had led in this category in the eighteenth century.

The nature and bearing of all of these changes was in 1847 still far from clear; England was the only country where the process of industrialization and urbanization had yet gone very far. But as this process advanced, it would further emphasize the existing division of Europe into a progressive west and a more reactionary east. To the layers of ethnic, cultural, religious and political differentiation laid down by a thousand years of history would be added a differentiation of wealth between two zones divided by a line running, roughly, from Stettin to Trieste.

Meanwhile, in countries where population growth was already a great fact, a change of structure was implied. Eventually, a slowing of reproduction rates and a continued fall in death rates would produce a population in which there were large numbers of elderly people. In 1847, the Western World was still full of youngsters; the drop in infant mortality had begun but the diseases and mischances of adulthood were still far from retreating. This had been even more true at the beginning of the century. Given the new political, economic and intellectual possibilities and frustrations of the age, the presence of large numbers of young people was a dynamic element of great importance to the era. It was the age of the first angry young men. One of them was Napoleon Bonaparte, dead at fifty-two, but ruler of France at thirty. France was not the only young society; Wellington was only three months older than Napoleon and would not die until 1851. Thus his life outspans this book at both ends: it is worth remembering that many of the men who made the age of Revolution and Improvement were themselves made by the *ancien régime*.

The Economy

From somewhere about 2,000 BC until the last decades of the nineteenth century, the lives of most Europeans and Americans were dominated very visibly and obviously by the land. In 1847 as in 1775 most people in the Western World still got their living directly or indirectly from it even if they were craftsmen, shopkeepers and servants of the rich who lived in cities. The rich employed great numbers of attendants and suppliers, and overwhelmingly the rich got their incomes from land. Everywhere, therefore, weather regulated the economy; it was not until after 1850 that a bad harvest in France ceased to be followed automatically by commercial and industrial depression, and even English statesmen long continued to note a good harvest with relief. The Physiocrats and Adam Smith alike had preached the primacy of agriculture in the creation of wealth; manufacturing was intimately mixed up with agriculture not only because much of its raw material came from farms – hemp, hides, wool, madder and the sources of alcohol – but because the actual processes of manufacture were often scattered among the cottages of the agricultural labour force. In the cotton districts of Normandy, for example, or those of Bohemia where flax was turned into linen, spinning and weaving provided an indispensable part of the peasant's income.

Since time immemorial agriculture had enjoyed this primacy. Yet within the decades surveyed in this book, there was a great and fundamental change. Agriculture was displaced as the major source of wealth in only a very few places – even in England, the leading industrial country, it was still in 1850 the largest single employer of labour – but from being a brake on the advance of civilization, agriculture turned into its propellant in the first half of the nineteenth century. It is perfectly reasonable to call this change an 'agricultural revolution'. It was a change of scale and quality comparable to the invention of agriculture in the first place, back in the early Neolithic Age.

Essentially, what happened was an enormous increase in productivity. This began well before 1775, but it is in the second half of the eighteenth century and the first half of the next that its decisive effect was registered, even though it was to roll on to even greater successes in the twentieth century. Though it brought larger crops which might have industrial use, the heart of the change was a huge growth in the production of food. A summary but revealing calculation shows that from about 1800, the average increase of agricultural productivity in Europe was about one per cent per year. This dwarfed all previous growth, which had not only been much slower but had been interrupted by recurrent setbacks and recessions.

Another way of looking at this is in terms of man's power to produce a surplus above his needs. In traditional agriculture, it seems likely that in terms of calories a worker produced foodstuffs roughly equivalent to about twenty or thirty per cent more than the needs of himself and his family. This narrow surplus provided the beam on which stood civilization. During the eighteenth and early nineteenth centuries, the surplus was increased to something like fifty per cent, and it continued to grow. This was a turning-point in world history. For the first time, food supply over a large area was carried beyond the point at which hunger was a real check on population, and it happened first in the Western World. It removed not only a check on population but one which had held back the economy and the growth of civilization as a whole. The way was open to seemingly uninterruptable and certainly accelerating progress.

The most striking change was in what Europeans ate. Though there was still a long way to go in 1850, European nutrition had improved startlingly in the previous seventy-five years. In the west (and in North America) famine disappeared, even if it endured in eastern Europe into the twentieth century. Bread became plentiful and cheaper. In 1775 it had usually been dear, sometimes was not available at all and was normally made not from wheat but from rye, buckwheat or barley, the staple grain crops. There was little else to eat which could supply sufficient energy – meat was rare because animal feeding was expensive. By 1847, though men in all countries might still go to bed hungry, there had been a huge change. Wheat acreage exceeded that of rye in France after 1815. Dr Johnson had reminded the Scotch that even in his day they ate food that Englishmen gave to horses; by 1800 already, almost all English bread was made of wheat flour.

New foods appeared, too. The most important was the potato, known for centuries but before 1800 little eaten except in Ireland and parts of England and Germany. From being scoffed at as fit only for animals and the destitute, it spread to become a staple of European diet by 1850. This meant that many more could be fed from a given area of land. There were other innovations in root crops, too; one of them, beet, was to transform the supply of sugar. Even greater strides would be made in the later nineteenth century, when almost the whole world would be able to supply food to Europe, thanks to railways and steamships.

The great changes which underlay this deserve more than a moment's consideration because they had enormous repercussions on the relations of states to one another, on social structures, on institutions and even on ideas, let alone on other sectors of the economy. The story had deep roots; its suddenness must not be exaggerated because they can be traced at least as far back as the sixteenth century. They can be conveniently grouped under two heads: changes in knowledge and technique which gave higher productivity, and changes in society and law which gave this increase and knowledge full play.

By the middle of the eighteenth century there was really only one country in which the pattern of events which was to shape the future had really begun to unfold, England, the country where the word 'Improvment' was first applied to agriculture. By then she had already an important surplus of agricultural produce; the dismal vision of the poverty-stricken landscape of early seventeenth-century England, when emigration was advocated as a way of relieving population pressure, had given way to a different image. For all her poverty, England seemed to herself and to foreigners a fat country, where men ate beef, white bread and cheese, and drank strong beer. The reality behind the myth was shown by the figures for grain exports; with a rising population, England could nevertheless export a quantity of grain equal to about thirteen per cent of her domestic consumption and she kept this up until the nineteenth century. Only after 1850 was England to become wholly dependent on foreign food.

This success produced admiration and imitation. By 1789 foreigners could already see in the contrasts between the English landscape and the beasts which grazed in it and their own the dramatic results of new techniques, scientific study and the intensive application of capital. The book from which the main wave of agricultural reform in Germany is dated was published in 1798 under the revealing title *Introduction to the Knowledge of English Agriculture*. Foreigners came to English fairs and farms to buy stock; they joined agricultural societies and subscribed to English periodicals to learn lessons to apply at home.

The result was a sure but slow advance of better agricultural practice. It was uneven, too; while Improvement had still to make its first appearance in many countries in 1800, in others change was irreversibly advanced, as it had been in England, Flanders and the Netherlands even before 1775. Different stages of development could also exist in the same country. Arthur Young, touring France in the late 1780s, found model farms in some places which were experimenting with the newest techniques of cultivation and husbandry while in other provinces he found poverty and backwardness. Even greater contrasts existed in Italy or eastern Europe where there were landlords or amateurs of agronomy reading and contributing papers to the English *Annals of Agriculture* from estates near others where the agriculture of the Middle Ages was still in full swing.

Generalization can only be suggestive and approximate, but improvement had made a significant impact in England already in 1775, in France, North America, Switzerland, Denmark and Germany by 1800 and in Austria, Italy and Sweden in the next few decades. The Low Countries are a special case: they had in some ways begun the whole thing in the fifteenth century and were as highly evolved in somewhat special circumstances as was England. Technically, the most common innovations were new methods, new crops, new land.

Continuous rotations of crops and the ending of fallow was increasingly widespread; it went with the introduction of new vegetable and cereal crops, with new tools and implements (the first all-iron plough appeared only in 1771). Machinery began to be used, at first usually for threshing, then for cultivating and drilling. Artificial meadows were sown with clover and lucerne. Selective improvement of both seed and livestock was another growing practice. Average weight rose and the killing age of stock came down. Animals were differently employed, too, the more efficient and more easily manageable horse gradually replacing oxen. Finally, an increase of agricultural production followed from bringing new land into cultivation. Marsh, waste and woodland were drained, irrigated and cleared. But this process, old as it was (it had probably accounted for most of the increase in food supply in Europe before 1600), was now pursued with better technical means and improved knowledge. Agriculture was entering, slowly, its scientific era.

Of course it is important not to exaggerate what had happened by 1850. Everywhere, a primitive technology survived. Small peasant exploiters resisted innovations but the crucial advances had been made in principle in most of non-Mediterranean Europe by 1850, even if more spectacular ones still were to follow. An agricultural worker in the United Kingdom was already producing twice the vegetable-based calories of his French equivalent in 1810: by 1840 he had bettered his output by another twenty-five per cent though the Frenchman's production had in the same time increased by almost sixty per cent, so that the gap between them had narrowed. Output on the best Prussian farms increased a hundred per cent in the first half of the century. Another way of measuring the change which was in train would be to assess the labour needed for a given return. In 1800, it seems, an American had to work for 373 hours to produce a hundred bushels of wheat; in 1840 he could do it in 233 hours.

Another expression of the technical agricultural revolution was observable in the beginnings of specialized roles in international trade in agricultural produce. This, too, still had far to go after 1850 (by then even England took less than fifteen per cent of her food from abroad) but Europe was already emerging from the highly local markets imposed by eighteenth-century communications. Sometimes this set in motion forces which would reverberate far into the future; Romania's future poverty-stricken peasantry clinging to holdings too small to support its families emerged from the new wheatfields of the Danubian provinces which had already by 1850 produced a great surge of population. In the context of international economics, the abandonment by the United Kingdom of protection against cheap foreign grain for her own farmers was a significant indicator.

Some social consequences of agricultural change soon excited alarm. Conservatives felt uneasy when the proportion of the population engaged in agriculture began to fall, tiny as the drop seems in the light of what was to come later. Only in England was less than a quarter of the working population engaged in agriculture in 1850; in the Netherlands about half the people worked on the land, in the United States about two-thirds and in Spain over three-quarters. Men were right, none the less, to sense that much more was involved in 'Improvement' than a simple increase of production. It would, in the end, transform society, too.

Improvement had first appeared in areas of relatively dense population and it penetrated the emptier spaces of eastern Europe only gradually. As it spread, it encountered everywhere an agriculture more deeply embedded in traditional practice and social bonds than was the English. Governmental, legal and customary barriers stood in the way of, for example, breaking into the age-old rotation of crops and eliminating fallow. In all European countries except in the Netherlands and, perhaps, Lombardy, agricultural improvement quickly ran into tough opposition. Seigneurial tenures, an unfree labour force, common lands, rights of turbary and grazing – in different parts of Europe these institutions and many others were tenaciously defended by men who felt their livelihood threatened by the innovators who demanded their removal. Improvement – even in its most acceptable sense of increasing the supply of food – was inevitably linked with social change and therefore with political and social struggle. New methods challenged an agriculture which had been set for centuries in a topographical mould by soil and climate and had thrown up social and legal institutions of immense tenacity and strength. From the difficulties presented by history and environment had evolved European rural societies which often differed greatly from one another but also shared important common features. In greater or less degree they were marked by personal dependence on lord and community and sometimes by servitude to the first. Legally this found expression in a mass of rights and usages standing in the way of exploitation of the land in the most profitable and rational way once new knowledge and techniques became available. Ignorance reinforced conservatism and collective regulation; there was little idealization of the peasant in the eighteenth-century literature of continental Europe.

The obstacles which the past thus presented to the new agriculture could be removed only by institutional as well as technical revolution. But an even more dramatic force making for institutional change was at work at the same time and it, too, was inextricably tied to agriculture. This was what was labelled while it was still unrolling as 'industrial revolution' and, arguably, it did more to shape the Western World than anything since the coming of Christianity.

We have already touched on the way in which manufacturing and agriculture were mixed up under the *ancien régime*. An eighteenth-century industrial area was not one of large towns, as it was later, but one where domestic manufacture was a large part of the livelihood of agricultural workers. Its presence was not marked by a forest of smoking chimneys but by looms and spinning-wheels in almost every country hovel and cottage. The 'putting-out' of materials to workers in their own homes was the basic form of industrial capitalism in the cotton areas of Normandy and Lancashire, the wool areas of Alsace and Yorkshire, the flax-spinning areas of Bohemia and Ulster.

Yet agriculture was from the start linked to industrialization in another way which was probably even more important. This was as a contributor to investment and demand. There is a rough chronology relating early improvement in agriculture to early industrialization in the modern sense. Great Britain and Belgium both show this. In part it is a matter of the generation of profits, the provision of capital for investment in industrial expansion and even of the provision of entre-preneurial manpower; the agricultural origins of many early industrial-ists have often been remarked. But increased productivity in agriculture was also expressed in demand. There was in the first place specialized technical requirement. More iron goods were wanted as tools became more common and more necessary; there is already detectable a surge of iron-using in eighteenth-century Great Britain which much ante-dates the railway builders' boom of the next century. There were still no public railways in England in 1824, but the country then already produced half a million tons of pig iron a year. Iron ploughs, the shoeing of the greatly increased numbers of horses used on farms and the development of specialized tools all helped to sustain demand. In the second place, agricultural development created demand for consumer goods, too. It seems likely that the English agricultural labourer's productivity doubled in the eighteenth century; that of the French increased by about a quarter in the last half of the eighteenth century and by over a third in the first half of the next. The new margin of profit could not be retained solely by the employer and, after all, many millions of European (and still more North American) peasants at this time were their own masters. It was bound to work through the econ-omy as an increase of demand and, as this eventually expressed itself in ways other than the consumption of more and better food, notably in a demand for cheap textiles. This process is easier to sense in the early nineteenth, rather than the late eighteenth, century. It has been calculated that in every important country in Europe, including England, agricultural wages fell in real terms to a low point somewhere about 1790; rising cereal prices had just shot ahead and reduced peasant purchasing-power below earlier levels. But this again emphasizes the importance of agricultural improvement in the first half of the nineteenth century.

Though we may properly speak of an 'Agricultural Revolution' because of the magnitude of change which it brought about and the important implications concealed in it, 'Improvement' is a term whose connotations of a slower rhythm better conveys the sense of what was actually happening in the countryside. 'Industrial Revolution', on the other hand, is appropriate to both the importance and the drama of what it denoted. It expressed a sudden and dazzling acceleration in the production of wealth, whether measured in terms of energy or of manufactured goods. The phrase was coined, it seems, in the 1830s, but the acceleration had begun in England long before this and was to go on even faster to a point at which by 1900 Europe and North America contained almost all the industrial power of the world. At first, it did not seem to require large-scale social change. The first response to an increased demand for industrial products was usually to develop still further the putting-out system: industry, largely confined to the towns in the Middle Ages, spread out in the form of looms and sewing-shops from town to countryside. In the 1770s there were getting on for a quarter of a million flax-spinners in Bohemia, most at work in their own homes. Such industrial areas were often areas of poor soil: they therefore offered cheap labour.

The mature industrialization process changed all this (and often did terrible damage to the home-workers in the process). It rested on other factors and finished by consummating a social revolution. It was not compatible with domestic working or serfdom, and it once more urbanized industry – but did so not by drawing it back to towns but by throwing out new towns and housing about its manufacturing centres. The total result was the creation of a new world.

This huge change runs through the history of these years, shaping and diverting them at many points, a great historical agent, only in part apprehended by contemporaries, let alone understood by them, certainly neither controlled nor the result of volition. It is one of the constants at work behind all the political upheavals of the age. Amid the welter of varied consequences flowing from it and expressions of it, the essential matters seem to be four. The industrialization process was a matter of changing sources of power, of new techniques, of new forms of social and economic organization and, above all, of a growth in new wealth so important as to mean a qualitative as well as a quantitative change in world history.

The skill with which new sources of power were sought and exploited has some spectacular embodiments and says much for the ingenuity of the innovators of the period. In only one decade, the 1780s, the Mont-golfier brothers made the first ascent by balloon, the English Channel was crossed by air for the first time and Coulomb carried out the experiments which were to show that forces between magnetic poles, like those between charges of electricity, were inversely proportional to the square of the distance between them. Yet though both the beginnings of human flight and the sudden interest in electricity (also shown by the fashionable world who flocked to receive shocks from Leyden jars and by Benjamin Franklin's kite-flying) were the precursors of forces transforming the world in our own day, it was not in them, ingenious manifestations of the inquiring mind though they were, that the pattern of the immediate future lay. Western society picked up in the science and technology of its day the things which could be exploited in the existing economic and technological environment. The most important of these was steam.

Water was a long familiar source of power. Besides its agricultural employment, it had been used in fulling, paper-making, metallurgy and timber-working (to name only a few applications). Usually it was tapped by using a mill-wheel. It had also, more recently and especially in England, become one of the most important supports of the inland transport system. A great age of canal-building testified to its economic importance as a means of supplying cheap transport.

Both of these uses of water were fundamental to industrialization. As a source of power for machinery, more important and reliable than wind, it continued to predominate even in the most advanced industrial economy in the world until well into the nineteenth century. Canals were to carry huge volumes of traffic long after the appearance of the railway. But it was the turning of water into steam-power which, in the end, did most to advance and shape the pattern of industrialization.

The dates of inventions do not by themselves say very much; everything depends on how quickly a new device is taken up and diffused. Given the point at which this book opens, though, there is a certain interest in noting that it was in 1774 that techniques were developed by an Englishman, Wilkinson (affectionately called 'iron-mad' by his admiring countrymen), which permitted the boring of much better cylinders. This removed one of the most important hindrances to the development of the steam-engine, whose principle had long been known. It was in the following year that James Watt brought together flywheel, throttle and centrifugal governor – a new device and the first industrial application of the principle of feedback – in the first steam-engine capable of operating steadily and efficiently with variable loads. It took time for these devices to spread, but the time-scale was a short one and the next century was to be the age of steam.

There had already been applications of steam to transport – in 1776 a steam paddle-boat sailed on the Doubs, and stationary engines were soon used to haul trucks on rails – but the real herald of the future was the appearance in 1804 of the first locomotive. This was to be the revolutionary agent of transport, making bulk land carriage easier and faster than it had ever been. In 1825, the Stockton and Darlington railway was opened, the first to provide carriage to the public. Meanwhile the industrial application of the engine also went ahead. The first locomotive had itself been created to meet the needs of mining, and long before this stationary engines had been employed for pumping and hauling. The great new application of the nineteenth century was to manufacturing; steam-engines were gradually harnessed to drive more and more machinery.

Though this second revolutionary impact of steam was a reality by the middle of the century, its ascendancy was then far from absolute. Until the second quarter of the century, power from running water still predominated industrially over power from steam in Great Britain, and was still the main source for American manufacturing until the 1860s. In the United States, as in England, the earliest industrial use of steam had been in mining; the first application of steam to other machinery seems to have been in a New York saw-mill in 1803. But textile manufacturers took up steam rapidly. By 1850, two-thirds of the power used in woollen-mills in the United Kingdom and seven-eighths of that in cotton-mills came from steam. The thousand or so engines which seem to have existed in 1800 in British mining and metallurgy probably produced between them about ten thousand horsepower (a figure which shows the low capacity of early engines). By 1850, Great Britain could raise some 500,000 hp from stationary and 790,000 hp from mobile engines. The huge advance which this represents is put in perspective by considering Prussia, one-third of the area of Germany; in 1846 the total horsepower of Prussian steam-engines was twenty-two thousand, of which fourteen thousand were employed in mining or metallurgy.

Steam had other important implications for mining. Coal-firing was usual in Great Britain, and the results can be seen in a part of the rise in the output of coal. The 11·2 million tons raised in 1800 became an annual averge of 50·2 millions in the early 1850s. More iron was needed, too; though the new machines were far from being the only important consumer, the building of railways had an enormous impact. One estimate is that the forty-three miles of public track which existed in 1825 turned into 9,747 miles in 1850. At that moment, Germany contained about 5,800 miles, and was the next best-equipped European country, while the United States had 8,600.

Finally, steam changed men's minds. The movement of information, goods and men made its first great advance since the coming of the sailing-ship, deep in ancient times. An important contribution was also made in the transfer of information by the new technology of telegraphy. This was first of all a matter of visual signals between chains of stations; the semaphore code was invented in 1793. Interestingly, its first important application was strategic. The French government linked itself to the battlefields of the northern frontier by this means and the British admiralty built a chain of stations to the south-coast naval ports. It was not until 1833 that German scientists built an electric telegraph. Eleven years later, Samuel Morse sent the opening message along the first telegraph line in the United States. This was an enormous advance; it took the communication of information a giant stride away from dependence on physical carriage or good visibility.

The telegraph, none the less, was the only significant contribution to communication not dependent on steam, whose harnessing produced a true revolution in transport. On land, for all the magnificence of the great highways built by the French monarchy in the eighteenth century, most of Europe in 1775 had main roads far worse than those of the Age of the Antonines to which Gibbon looked back as a golden era. The armies of France in the 1790s would enter Rome, but when there, communicated with Paris by couriers who took as long as those of Julius Caesar. Across the Atlantic, things were even worse; news of the Declaration of Independence took twenty-nine days to reach Charleston from Philadelphia. For bulky goods, water transport was always preferable (as the canal-building of the eighteenth century showed) and when Jane Austen described in *Sense and Sensibility* the Dashwoods' removal from Sussex to Devon, she assumed that the family's belongings would be sent round by sea. The railway brought an end to this state of affairs. Though many misgivings were at first expressed about the dangers of travelling at so high a speed as thirty miles an hour, commerce and human experience were soon transformed by the growing availability of land transport. Water journeys were changed almost as rapidly. A paddle-steamer was made for Robert Fulton by Boulton and Watt in England and put to work in 1807 on the Hudson. For a long time such steamers were small and were limited in use to river and coastal traffic, or to acting as tugs. The *Comet* working on the Clyde in 1812 was of twenty-five tons. There was difficulty in building large engines not only for technical reasons but because a steamer had to carry its own fuel. Nevertheless, the first steamship to cross the Atlantic (under sail most of the way) did so in 1819 and just over twenty years later the invention of the screw propellor was successful enough for the first Atlantic crossing to be made by a screw-driven ship. Lafayette went up the Ohio in 1825 in a steamboat; alas, he was ship-wrecked.

Steam at sea made bad weather and unfriendly winds more manageable, and greatly cut costs; faster voyages turned money over more quickly and reduced the expense and hazards of emigration. Steam was to change naval warfare, too. Above all, together with the telegraph and railway, it tied together a world economy much more closely knit and greater in scale than any that had hitherto existed. It is not surprising that steam had important mental and even ideological expressions. Like gas-lighting, it became something of a shibboleth of the progressive and advanced thinker, still confident of the blessings of material progress discerned by the eighteenth-century thinkers of the Enlightenment and, perhaps, sometimes aware of the possibilities of social and political change which must follow from throwing different areas and peoples together as never before. It was consistent with his own sense of where the future lay, though not, perhaps, with a later age's notion of the poetical nature, that Shelley should decide to put money into a scheme for a steamboat to run between Leghorn and Marseilles. Equally consistently, the Lombard liberal Confalonieri pushed ahead his schemes for his country's improvement not only politically and educationally but by experimenting with steamers on the Po.

The changing sources of power blur the boundaries of the technical innovation in this period. For the most part this was a matter of machinery and its use (though it was in 1774 that a German chemist discovered the bleaching action of chlorine, whose industrial application quickly followed). More machines of every kind were to be seen and increasingly gripped the imagination of the age. For the whole of this period England led the way in making them. By the 1840s she was already the 'workshop of the world'. Until 1815, the war combined with laws against the export of machinery, which was not completely legal until 1843, to give England her lead. After 1815, there was an increasing penetration of the Continent by English mechanics, *entrepreneurs* and their knowledge, in particular in Belgium.

The first sign of what was coming had been in textiles, even before 1789, when some French *cahiers* denounced 'English machines' as unfair competition. Many of the most important inventions in textile machinery came in the 1760s, but (another convenient date) 1774 brought the invention of a new spinning machine, the 'mule', by Samuel Crompton, which incorporated earlier advances and made possible the production of yarn finer than anything yet available outside Asia. Cotton fibres lent themselves to mechanical handling. This fact, together with the stimulus of a ready market for fine goods at prices lower than the luxurious imports from India sustained a rapid, indeed revolutionary expansion. Cotton was king in Lancashire long before it ruled the southern states of the United States of America. By 1840 three-quarters of British industrial workers were employed in textiles and two-thirds of these were in cotton. The pace of expansion which followed the introduction of more machinery, though much of it was still water-driven, can be seen by Great Britain's consumption of raw cotton. The 2·5 million pounds imported in 1760 became twenty-two million in 1787, and 366 million fifty years later.

One function of technical change was the grouping of machinery in factories and the closing down of the old domestic system of industrial working, though its retreat was a slow and painful one. Again, the first industry to display the new pattern was textiles. Soon there were some conspicuous examples in England of very large manufacturing units. They tended to be grouped near power, labour or good communications resources; the result was concentration at another level, too, and the first new industrial areas began to appear. By 1800 people in England were already familiar with the term 'manufacturing districts'. Even forty years later and in England, though, they were not like the huge conurbations of today, but rather were areas of relatively small industrial towns sprawling into closer proximity with one another; a Manchester was unusual.

The overall effect of such changes was to bring to an end the *ancien régime* in its social and economic aspects. Society changed from a cellular structure of families, estates and corporations to one in which a mass of individuals were linked to one another predominantly by economic ties and shared only the common status of equal submission to the legal powers of the State. The basis of this change was the complete mobility of labour and national prices beginning to be discernible in Great Britain already by 1800. Little more than thirty years later, Thomas Carlyle coined the phrase 'cash nexus' to characterize a society in which the payment of money for labour or goods remained the only tie between men. The substitution of economic for social and legal traditional ties between men seemed to be accompanied, too, by the division of society into opposed camps: those who had nothing to sell but their labour, and those who hired that labour. A future Prime Minister of Great Britain dramatically and romantically pictured this divided society as 'Two Nations', a striking phrase in an era when the better-off among Englishmen were perhaps more intensely aware of their patriotic unity than ever before. Disraeli's answer to the problem in his novel *Sybil* was perhaps hardly persuasive, but he had touched a sensitive nerve and was not the only artist to exploit the theme. The social and moral consequences of industrialization soon presented urgent problems. The traditional Christian morality seemed unable to grapple with social change on the scale it faced in new manufacturing districts. The novels of social protest, or others which had social distress in new and pressing forms as their background, were a cultural registration of specific historical facts; that England was the first society to experience industrialization in full without the checks which the *ancien régime* provided elsewhere.

So disruptive a process was bound to provoke resistance. This did not only come from those who believed themselves to be the exploited; it also came from among the possessing classes who were shielded from at least the worst effects of what was going on. But there is a difficulty here in disentangling the roots of what was to become the most important component of the coalition resisting social change, the movement called, broadly, Socialism.

If Socialism is, as some of its exponents have said, fundamentally an assertion of the primacy of economic equality above other social values, then there was plenty of it about before industrialization occurred on a significant scale anywhere. Moreover, it was not in the countries where industrialization went fastest that there was most heard about Socialism in the nineteenth century. The word itself has eighteenth-century origins, but first began to be applied widely to criticism of society from an egalitarian standpoint in France in the 1830s. What those who then called themselves Socialists were attacking was by no means an industrialized society, even by contemporary British standards, but a commercialized one.

They could sometimes get political support from spontaneous movements of resistance and protest by those who suffered from industrialization. These could take many forms, however. These were, for example, workers in particular trades which looked backwards to the days when they had successfully regulated their conditions of employment and the supply of protected markets, and enjoyed prestige and respect. In France the guilds went down before the legal changes of the Revolution; Germany's survived until the 1860s, doggedly fighting a rearguard action against the coming of the market economy. It is beside the point to criticize such institutions for not adapting themselves to the new order and not taking advantage of new processes and new markets: they were not there for that purpose, but for the regulation of the interests of self-conscious groups within the social framework of the *ancien régime*.

More specifically in conflict with industrialization in one of its most obvious and characteristic forms was the phenomenon of popular protest usually given a name it acquired in England, Luddism. This usually took the form of attacks on machines or plant. It was not merely blind rage at innovation, though when such innovation threatened livelihood, the rage is comprehensible. It was also often the expression of objection to the replacement of one form of industrial society by another, of, for example, the rural domestic industry which was in some parts of Europe absolutely necessary as a support to meagre earnings from agriculture if people were to survive at all. Particularly in an area of poor soil such as Bohemia, for example, the landless peasant found domestic industrial earnings absolutely necessary. Often the target of his hatred was the machine: there are plenty of examples in the French *cahiers* of 1789 of objections in the textile areas of Normandy to innovations in the form of 'English machines'. But though the tendency of machinery to make labour redundant was taken as a fundmental explanation of Luddism by many of those responsible for law and order, particularly in England, it was by no means all that Luddism was about. Sometimes, Luddites seem to have ignored machines they might have attacked. Significantly, Luddism appeared and was mingled with many other disturbances, in the worst economic crisis faced by the British economy in this period, when the war with France had helped to produce a fall of about a third in English exports. The consequent dislocation and unemployment came at the end of a decade of almost continually rising bread prices. In the circumstances, machine-breaking took its place alongside protests against many things other than machines, notably the riots to sell food at a fair price which were the English version of the *taxation populaire* of the 'Flour War'.

Luddism should therefore probably not be thought of as a 'movement' at all, for its manifestations were varied and reflect archaic social attitudes far more than future class-warfare. Much in it looked back to attitudes rooted in the old corporate organization of society rather than forward to the new Trades Unions which would emerge in the nineteenth century. Both, in industrializing countries, were often under legal attack during the years covered in this book. This is another much misunderstood phenomenon, thanks largely to later Socialist mythologists who wished to see in the struggles of the oppressed of all ages struggles organically connected with those of their own day. The early trades unions or 'combinations' of the first era of industrialization were discriminated against at law for many reasons, but not only because they were seen as the enemies of a new industrial capitalism. In most of continental Europe, for example, the traditions of Roman Law treated all voluntary association suspiciously. It was central to the jurisprudence of many European states to assume that association for any purpose required specific authorization, whether this was to be given by the sovereign power or by long custom and prescriptive right. Any spontaneously formed association for any purpose which did not seek authorization was, if not illegal, *ipso facto* suspect. This tipped the balance against combinations for economic purposes from the outset. The situation in England was very different. It was and remains a principle of English law that an act which is not illegal when committed by one man does not become so when committed by men acting in concert, unless specific statutory authority to the contrary exists. This meant that England had to set about legislation in the 1790s, when people became alarmed about conspiracy because of revolution in France and the sufferings of the manufacturing classes. France was passing her own combination laws at about the same time. The most important was the *Loi le Chapelier*, named after the radical deputy who introduced it to the French Assembly, some of the provisions of which (notably that requiring the French workman to carry a work-record card which made possible reports on his conduct) remained on the statute-book until the 1890s.

As in the case of England, the legislators were being influenced by much more than a simple wish to hold down wages by weakening the bargaining power of labour, however attractive that prospect may have been. In England the threat of revolution was the spur to legislation and in France those who passed the law were voting against the past as well as against the future; they were putting the seal on the abolition of the old trades guilds. Turgot's policies were at length achieved. Another consideration also influenced some of those who voted for the *Loi le Chapelier*; they believed that subordinate associations within the state could only weaken the unity of its general will and therefore the national community and the national sovereign, by providing other foci of loyalty.

Many other institutional changes accompanied economic expansion. Banks multiplied and their regulation became more complex; the law changed to take account of limited liability and new forms of association. There was also an important growth in new media of exchange as more and more commercial and governmental paper was used. All currencies were gold-based, but in this era several experiments with paper currency were made, often under pressure and usually with unfavourable results. Above all, there was the terrifying memory of the French *assignats*. These were bonds, at first interest-bearing, but later not, issued by the French government to enable it to liquidate rapidly the capital it confiscated from the Church in the Revolution. The *assignats* were bought by people who wished to buy the former Church lands at auction, where they could be used to pay for the purchase. Soon the government agreed to accept them in payment of taxes and then they became a general currency, being issued in lower and lower denominations as inflation drove coin more and more off the market. The result was a depreciation which led to two bankruptcies before a gold-based currency was successfully re-established by Napoleon.

The spectacle of French inflation was a grave warning. Yet English commerce depended importantly upon paper by the end of the eighteenth century, though it was not legal tender. The Bank of England had in 1789 some ten or eleven millions of its notes in circulation and in addition there were more than three hundred other private banks in the country which issued their own. Furthermore, there was a great mass of instruments of credit of other kinds also in circulation. The cheque had been invented in 1781. With the war not only did banknotes become legal tender but the increase in the National Debt created a great new mass of government obligations which augmented the supply of negotiable paper.

Yet these important and striking changes were only incidental to the greatest change of all in those years which is the simple increase in wealth. By 1847 it had already become remarkable enough for it to be clear that there had been a decisive change in world history. It has been estimated, for example, that the world's output of one of industry's basic needs, pig-iron, increased by eighty per cent in the 1820s, by fifty per cent in the 1830s, and by nearly seventy-five per cent in the 1840s. Its output in the most advanced industrial society, Great Britain, went up forty-fold in terms of annual averages between 1780 and 1850. British coal output was quintupled in the first half of the nineteenth century alone. At somewhere near the other end of the scale was Russia, but even there increase was notable; her pig-iron producing plants more than doubled in number in the second half of the eighteenth century, though their size remained small and an output of 9·7 million *poods* in 1800 rose to 13·8 million in 1850. Though Russia was well behind in the race towards industrialization, she could show spectacular growth in textiles, almost universally the leading sector. The number of workers in her woollen producing plants doubled between 1815 and 1852 and in the same time her imports of cotton fibre, for working in her new factories, rose from thirty-two thousand to 1·8 million *poods* a year.

After 1815, world trade expanded with only temporary setbacks for over a century. In the era before industrialization it had rested on the exchange of surplus products for luxuries. Most nations were for most of the time self-sufficient in their basic needs, which remained at a low level. Industrialization brought a qualitative as well as a quantitative change to this situation. The industrializing countries now began to look for their livelihood to external trade. Manufactures were more and more made from imported materials (of which cotton was the first outstanding example) and those who made them began to depend more and more on imported food. This was to end with a change in the shape of world trade which has produced the global interdependence of today. All nations appeared to share in this expansion. The value of Russia's imports and exports between 1802 and 1840 increased from 31·1 million to 163·5 million roubles; that of the United States from annual averages of $100 million dollars in the 1790s to $244 millions in the 1840s and the annual average international trade of the United Kingdom rose from £61 millions in 1801–5 to £132 millions in 1846–50.

Yet this new wealth was shared unequally. The Western World enjoyed it exclusively, while traditional societies elsewhere remained in near stable economies modified only by periodic disaster. But even within the Western World, there were important differences in the extent to which different countries shared in it. Russia, given her size, fell behind dramatically in her share of the new wealth; her industrial sector certainly grew, but it remained tiny, given the needs of Russian society and the overwhelming preponderance of agriculture. France fell behind relatively, though in the eighteenth century her economic growth had roughly kept pace with that of Great Britain. Though her woollen industry did not do badly, her metallurgy lagged; she was turning out nearly 150,000 tons of pig-iron annually in the 1780s and only 560,000 in the early 1850s. The five thousand steam-engines of France in 1847 produced between them only about sixty thousand horse power. The United States, on the other hand, was a spectacular example of growth which in some respects matched that of Great Britain, but presented great diversities between regions; in 1850, the Middle Atlantic and New England states, with less than a third of the population of over twenty-three millions provided seventy-five per cent of the country's manufacturing employment. There were by then more than 8,500 miles of railway in the Union, a figure which can perhaps be most meaningfully compared with that for countries with comparable problems of size: Russia in 1850 had 501 miles of track and Canada sixty-six.

The country which was in every sense the leader in the race for growth which was beginning was the United Kingdom. In the small area of the islands were more than 9,700 miles of railway. British ports handled over a fifth of the world's total international trade and the country was first among trading communities. In 1843 there were more than twenty-three thousand ships under the British flag; this was more than three million tons of shipping, nearly twice as much as was floated by France, Germany, the Scandinavian countries and the Netherlands together. British iron-working which, in the eighteenth century, had produced little more than Sweden (from which the country drew four-fifths of its imports of pig-iron) was in the later 1840s making 2·7 million tons of pig-iron a year, a figure which was again the largest in the world. Blessed in her position on the belt of easily accessible coal which runs round the northern hemisphere, the United Kingdom raised more than fifty million tons a year in the early 1850s; Germany was far behind with 9·2 million tons and Belgium further still with 6·8 million.

All these figures were to be surpassed by far in the later nineteenth century, but visible in them is the groundplan of the future. By 1850, the era of national specialization within a world economy had begun. Great Britain first made the transition from being a self-sufficing economy in essentials and by 1850 had to import food for which she paid in manufactured goods and services. She was the first country to complete the characteristic demographic transition of industrialization, in which the majority of the population ceases to be dependent upon agriculture for a living and becomes dependent on wages earned in industry. No other country had gone so far. The specialist producers of raw materials and food were already emerging, too. Russian grain was to be her main source of foreign earnings while she built up her own industrial equipment. The best early example, perhaps, was the United States. By 1850, seventy-six per cent of the value of her exports was provided by one commodity, cotton, and most of it went to the mills of England. A crop of just over five million pounds annually in the 1790s had become one of more than eleven hundred million pounds sixty years later.

This huge transformation (which was to prove to be irreversible) struck contemporaries into attitudes of pride and awe. Some of the more farsighted glimpsed the even greater possibilities ahead, but few were unimpressed by the revolutionary exchanges which the years since the American Revolution had brought. So many of the relics of this great change are still with us in patterns of manufacture and trade, and in the geography and architecture of the great industrial areas, that there is probably no danger of underestimating its importance. What may therefore be worth recall at the close of a brief survey is that much had still not changed in many parts of even the most developed world. Thousands of German towns, of no great size, still enjoyed something near to economic self-sufficiency and would have to wait for the coming of the railways to awake them, so many Sleeping Beauties left behind by the *ancien régime*. Steam trains would integrate them with the new world in the making but had not done so by 1847. To take another indicator, even in the British merchant marine, most sailors worked in sailing ships, not steamers. In 1850 only 168,000 tons of the three and a half millions of British overseas shipping was steam-propelled. Finally, though it was perhaps the sector which, in most countries, saw the most sweeping changes, agriculture still dominated in the economics of most countries and was still in some places heavily encumbered by backwardness both technical and social. The scythe had still not replaced the sickle on French farms in 1847 and even in the Western World, most men were then still peasants and long would be.

Wars and Warfare

The years from 1775 to 1815 were in one way much like most earlier modern history in that they saw almost continuous conflict between major states of the Western World. In 1775 the war of American Independence began and before its close Holland, Spain and France were drawn in. In 1778 Prussia and Austria went to war, albeit almost bloodlessly and briefly. From May 1784 Europe and America were once more formally at peace, but only until 1787 when the Prussians invaded Holland and war again began between Russia and Turkey, who were soon joined by Austria and Sweden. This war did not end until January 1792, when Europe returned to a formal peace which lasted a little more than three months. There then began twenty-three years of warfare, sometimes worldwide, and interrupted only for a little more than a year in 1802–3.

The contrast after 1815 is very striking. The reasons for a long era of almost continuous peace can be discussed later. What matters here is that war ceased to be an important factor making for change though the capacity to make war, on the other hand, was as important as ever, because it was part of the basic data of international politics. From close quarters, the relations of states appear to change like patterns in a kaleidoscope. In a longer perspective, they evolve much more slowly. This is because they rest upon constants, such as geography, or near-constants which change very slowly, such as historical tradition and national character, or such fundamental facts as those just considered, population, wealth and technology. Nations compete to safeguard their interests and achieve their goals in two main ways. One is by negotiating with one another and the other is by fighting – by diplomacy and by war. As, until the twentieth century, both the goals they sought and the resources they employed only changed very slowly, it is easy to forget that developments in the nature of warfare itself are as much a source of historic change as those in politics or economics.

At first sight, war did not alter much between 1775 and 1847 although its incidence was strikingly different in the first and second halves of this period. There was an obvious great new ideological force at work from the 1790s onwards, but this did not much affect comparative strength once governments had taken it into account. For this reason the relative war-making capacity of great powers did not seem very different in the middle of the nineteenth century from what it had been in the eighteenth. France was still the greatest land-power in western Europe and Russia in the east. Land-power depended upon numbers and it was only in the second half of the nineteenth century that population trends meant that France had lost the military supremacy she enjoyed for so long because of large numbers. Sea-power was more obviously linked to wealth and technology and here Great Britain was well-placed, even if she did not always appear to exploit her assets fully. Great Britain's naval superiority to all other powers had been increased and confirmed by 1847.

Overall, technological innovation did not produce significant changes in warfare and therefore in the relative war-making power of nations in this period. After 1815 there was no important campaign fought by one of the great powers against another (though there was colonial fighting on a considerable scale in Algeria and India in the 1830s) and when European armies next met one another, in 1848, battlefields looked much as they had done a half-century before. Muzzle-loading cannon and muskets were still normal. The rifle had been used as early as the American War of Independence, but its management and slow rate of fire while it depended on muzzle-loading made it a weapon only for highly trained elite units with a limited tactical role until 1841 when the Prussian army adopted the 'needle-gun', a breach-loading rifle, capable of being fired and loaded easily by a man lying down, who could, if competent, get off seven shots a minute with it. This weapon opened a new era of infantry armament which transformed fighting in the second half of the century. Apart from this, improvements in weaponry produced only marginal change (only in 1840 was the percussion musket adopted by the British army) and the basic tactics of the battlefield still rested upon the co-ordination of the three traditional arms – horse, guns and foot – to produce superiority of shock or firepower at decisive points. Technological change in communication was probably more important than changes in weapons on land, though the electric telegraph and railway had not been tested as adjuncts to field operations before 1847. Moltke, however, saw what lay ahead in the coming decades which were, indeed, to provide decades of railway wars.

At sea, technology was a little more important. This was less because of changes in weapons than in the ships which carried them. One flash revealing a distant future was soon overtaken by oblivion. In September 1776 an American serjeant navigated single-handed an extraordinary vessel into New York harbour where it made the first submarine attack. The target was HMS *Asia*, to which the attacker failed to attach an explosive charge. In the following year, a similar attack again failed to reach the frigate which was its target but blew up a small schooner, which thus became the first victim of submarine warfare. The experiment was not thought successful enough to justify further efforts and was not followed by others. Interest in submarine warfare languished. Perhaps the most interesting thing about this beginning was its illustration of an important strategical truth: that the submarine, when made effective, would be the obvious weapon for the weaker of two contending naval powers.

Much more important was the change brought to sea-power by technology's effect on the design of surface ships. Here the crucial innovations were the coming of steam and iron. Steam-engines spread more rapidly to merchant than to fighting navies. Although Fulton built a steam warship for the United States in 1814, no steamship saw service in the Napoleonic wars. The Royal Navy's first was a paddle-driven tug, commissioned in 1821; it was used to overcome problems of wind and water by getting the sailing battleships out of harbour in adverse weather. The invention which really changed things was the screw propellor, which had none of the vulnerability to gunfire of the fragile paddle-boxes. The United States had the screwship *Princeton* in 1842, but it was not until 1850 that the first ship of the line with a screw was launched (by the French). Though steam had therefore already changed naval warfare more than war on land, it had by mid-century therefore still not produced a revolution. Nor had iron, though the East India Company had its first two iron gunboats in 1839 and the Royal Navy its first iron ship in the following year. The great days of the armoured and iron-built warship lay ahead; it needed better guns and projectiles to demonstrate its value, as the Royal Navy's reversion to wood construction after gunnery trials at the end of the 1840s showed.

Given the general stability of weapons (virtually untroubled by innovation before 1815), it is scarcely surprising that tactical innovation, too, was slight. Later idolization of Napoleon obscured this fact; he was supposed to have been an innovator of unparalleled stature in tactical matters. This is exaggerated to the point of distortion. He was a strategical genius whose *forte* was the swift concentration of superior numbers at a decisive point. On the battlefield he tried to do the same and displayed also a mastery of artillery management. He was by training a gunner and here displayed his technical skill and professional flair at its best, but he stood on the shoulders of those who had written the manuals and reformed the artillery of the *ancien régime*.

When Napoleon – or General Bonaparte, as he was then – fought his first great campaign in 1796, the army he commanded had already been transformed by the Revolution in a way which affected its tactical handling, being diluted by mass conscription which produced great numbers of recruits but of a quality quite unsuited to the standard military practice of pre-revolutionary days. This practice was seen at its fullest development and peak in the armies of Frederick the Great. Its essence was the drilling of long-service professional soldiers to the point at which they could fire volleys from the cumbersome musket of the day more rapidly and regularly than any opposing force and carry out complicated manœuvres under fire with great precision. The drill-serjeants' role was not to prepare men for the parade-ground, but to use the parade-ground to provide regiments which could do what their commanders wanted under fire. Armies of such men won Frederick's victories but suffered from two limitations. One was imposed by the wastage of prolonged fighting; professional soldiers were made by years of drill and could not quickly be replaced. The other was that, as the British learned in the American forests and at Bunker Hill, they could not fight advantageously in broken country or against entrenchments containing even small numbers of men armed with precision weapons such as the slow-firing but very accurate muzzle-loading rifle.

The first of these limitations goes far to explain the victories of Napoleon. For many years, he had greater numbers of men to call upon than his opponents. French tactics capitalized on this by abandoning the attack in line of professional armies – which the conscripts of the revolution could not have been relied upon to carry out – adopting instead a formation of dense columns. Their leading ranks presented a relatively small target and their weight and cohesion enabled them to buffalo their way through opposition. Even before the Revolution, column had been powerfully advocated by some writers, but the recipe was not infallible and came to disaster when careful selection of ground and a reasonable balance of numbers were combined with the old professional standards of discipline and fire control by Wellington in Spain.

The last great battle of a whole era of warfare was Waterloo. There, two armies armed with eighteenth-century weapons (if a few spectacular but ineffective British rockets are discounted) and commanded by eighteenth-century soldiers, fought with one side employing tactics well-known before 1789, and the other those of the Revolution. It was important in differentiating the overall generalship of Napoleon and his conqueror, Wellington, that they had served their apprenticeship in different theatres, one in Europe and one in India, but neither had fundamental innovations to make on the battlefield. Napoleon proved the less flexible of the two. After the first battle he commanded against the French, in 1808, at Vimeiro in Portugal, Wellington (then Sir Arthur Wellesley) remarked 'I received them in line, which they were not accustomed to.' The story was not much different at Waterloo, where the allied army lay mainly behind a low ridge which protected them from French gunnery, and spent a long day throwing itself into line and square alternately as the French cavalry raged about them and the French infantry stormed up the slope in dense masses against them. The end of the story was the shredding of the last attack like the first by the shatteringly regular volleys of troops still well in hand and then attack in line. As Wellington remarked of the Emperor, 'He just moved forward in the old style, in columns, and was driven off in the old style.'

Waterloo was the last great battle between Western states until the middle of the century. It may stand, therefore, as a climax of an age when technology and tactical innovation changed warfare very little. This meant, therefore, that calculations about the relative power of states, which in the last resort meant their capacity to fight in defence of their interests, still rested fundamentally on numbers. But this index needed qualification. Men had to be mobilized, equipped, trained and delivered to the right place at the right time. Superiority might turn therefore on organizational, political, moral and even cultural facts, in so far as those last affected the competence of those directing operations. It was in these areas that war changed its nature most during these years.

Change spread from France. The royal army was terribly dislocated by revolution. The pre-1789 reforms had produced a renovation of tactical doctrine but the destruction of the cohesion of the officer corps and a deterioration of discipline greatly impaired its fighting value. When war broke out, it was soon being badly defeated. This led to its transformation by drafting into it large numbers of volunteers from the National Guard, a part-time security force which had been formed in 1789, and then by the imposition of conscription in 1793. This was decisive. Although conscription never worked perfectly – later, under Napoleon, many of those who should have served never turned up, or deserted on the way to their units – it gave France the numbers of men which again made her the leading military power. Other countries, of which the most notable was Prussia, adopted the device. Significantly, the United Kingdom did not (though the press-gang was used in the ports) but since the Napoleonic era Europe has never been without at least one great power which employs the principle of a universal obligation of males to man its armed forces.

It was a step which went far beyond the mere matter of numbers.

Conscription marked a great widening of the powers of governments over their subjects and helped to change the character of war. From being a conflict of professional armies, sharing many assumptions about the conduct of fighting, war moved towards becoming a conflict of societies, in which national and ideological passions destroyed restraints formerly holding brutality in check. Before 1792, when the wars of the French Revolution began, civilized powers fought wars with armies led by leaders usually drawn from the same social class. Indisputably, though he might have no hereditary title, even the rebel General Washington was a gentleman, and had, indeed, once held the King's Commission. Frederick the Great would only reluctantly expand his officer corps to incorporate men not of noble birth under the dire pressure of wartime needs, and tried quickly to restore its exclusiveness once peace was made. In the early 1780s regulations were made in France restricting the possibilities of promotion earlier open to those who were not noblemen.

Whatever the technical results of this social homogeneity, its moral importance was considerable. All officers operated against a background of assumptions which supposed war to be a limited business, with important restraints on what might be done. Honour was at stake as well as defeat or victory, and war was conducted at times rather like a great public duel, due order and decency being observed according to known rules. The coming of conscription (and other innovations) blew this away. In the first place it involved directly many more people, since armies now had a more homogeneous and national composition (eighteenth-century armies frequently relied heavily upon foreign soldiers, whether recruited singly or in batches hired from mercenary kings). It also changed things because new forces had to be brought to bear to persuade people to fight. Ideological factors again began to loom large as they had not done since the seventeenth century. This combined with nationalism to intensify a change in the character of war marked by greater popular participation. Remarkable examples were given by popular resistance to the French in Spain and Russia and in the enthusiasm with which the peoples of other German states applauded Prussian operations against Napoleon in 1813. The spirit in which the wars of peoples were conducted was to be very different from, say, that which prompted the American and French governments' orders to their naval commanders that if they came across Captain Cook, then busy exploring the Pacific, they were not to fight him but to treat him as a benefactor of mankind, whose researches would be of value to all.

Changes in warfare were one of the reasons for a new attention to its theoretical aspects. This expressed itself in reforms which improved the training and quality of commanders and founded the idea of the professional staff. The regeneration of Prussia's army after defeat by Napoleon was the outstanding example. But it was a Prussian officer who also provided the first philosophical treatment of war to be made in the West. Clausewitz was the first student of war to treat it as more than a technical matter of ideal manœuvres and barrack-square training. He grasped that from being a matter of the struggles of sovereign with sovereign, war was becoming one of peoples with peoples and was approaching what he termed 'absolute' war in its nature.

Book IV

The New Worlds of the Nineteenth Century

11 A new Balance of Power

For all the personal drama of Napoleon's fall, the collapse of the French imperial structure and the psychological shock to thousands of Europeans, the continuities running across 1815 were soon clear in international relations. The great powers of 1815 were still those of 1789; Spain's marginal status was somewhat more obvious, that was all. Their interests, too, were hardly changed, except that France was now much less concerned with overseas trade and empire. This was the outcome of the final round of a century and a half of oceanic rivalry with Great Britain. Both powers, on the other hand, were as interested as ever in the Netherlands, the Rhine and the Mediterranean. Such matters, like the Eastern powers' interest in a subjugated Poland and the future of the Balkans were founded in inescapable geographical and historical facts.

Yet there were also important changes in international life. Gradually, they transformed the political and psychological situation within which statesmen had to work. Some of them were material, the demographic changes, for example, which eroded the military preponderance of France, or the economic which brought more and more wealth to England. These would produce their greatest impact only in a longer run than can be dealt with in this book. Other forces were non-material and some of them produced change much more rapidly. Nationality was something statesmen had to take more account of in 1815 than in 1775, whether or not they were sympathetic to nationalism, whose claims were based upon it. The word 'international', reflecting a change of emphasis from relations between rulers to those between nations, had made its appearance in 1802. New political forces such as conservatism and liberalism, or the new romanticism, some of whose expressions infected and coloured political behaviour, injected ideological considerations into diplomacy which had not been there in 1789.

Finally, there was the simple legacy of the Great Interruption itself, a dislocation of the normal course of things and of the institutions of

173

the *ancien régime*. The wars of the revolutionary and Napoleonic era had produced deep shock, placing in jeopardy all thrones and properties. Some ancient institutions were gone for ever (such as the Holy Roman Empire and the Republic of Venice) and revolutionary adjustments had been made within states which survived. This helps to explain much of the long success of the great powers after 1815 in avoiding war with one another. There was too much at stake to contemplate lightly the prospect of another war between great powers for war might again release revolution.

No one was more aware of this than the Austrian chancellor, Metternich. Whatever Austria and the Habsburgs had suffered, and whatever the concessions they had been required to make – including the marriage of Marie Louise to an upstart – Austria had finished on the right side, the winning one. She had recovered her Italian provinces and seemed to have shaken off the uncertainties and weaknesses of the eighteenth century. Prussian competition was in abeyance since 1790. Austria was top dog in central Europe and now began to exercise a remarkable and long-lasting grasp of the diplomatic initiative. From the peace congress held there in 1815, Vienna under Metternich was a major focus of European diplomacy for more than thirty years.

Though Austria was still a great German power in 1847, her international position was already by then much changed from that of 1775. The Austrian Netherlands had been given up, but they had always been an embarrassment. Apart from them and a few scattered bits and pieces in Germany and Galicia, the Habsburgs regained in 1815 all that they had lost during the wars and more. Venetia, Dalmatia and Salzburg were new acquisitions. In the east some of the Ukraine and modern Romania had by then come under Austrian rule. The empire had by 1815 the second largest population among European states. Fear of revolution had bound local notabilities more closely to the government, and the state was much stronger than it had been in the days of Joseph II. Many of his officials, too, were still there to push forwards the bureaucratic centralization he had stood for.

Metternich could therefore look out on Europe from a base much stronger than that of Joseph II. Its weaknesses were less obvious. A shift in the centre of gravity of the empire had occurred; Germany was less important after the disappearance of the Holy Roman Empire and the impalpable influence which it carried. Italy was now more important. It was accepted by the allies of 1815 that Austria should have a free hand in the peninsula, but this understanding might one day change. It was in any case improbable that France would forever acquiesce in this. As Italy also contained a number of governments which were to attract sharp criticism from among their subjects and breed revolutionaries expecially successful in publicizing their cause, there was good reason for the disquiet Metternich was always to show about demands with liberal or national implications from Italians. They threatened stability in a region now of new importance to Austria.

Another potential weakness (for all the populousness of the empire) was over-extension. The imperial armies stood guard on the Ticino and Po in Italy and in a few garrisons beyond them. In the south they faced the Ottomans on the Save and Danube, the Russians on the Dniester. Galicia had to be garrisoned, too. This huge area contained a great diversity of peoples and that was dangerous in an era when new ideas and forces had been set loose in Europe by the revolutionary and Napoleonic wars. Finally, for all the devotion of some of the imperial servants, there was an uncompromising rigidity about the structure of government which boded ill for its future when new challenges might arise rapidly. Only in 1817 was there any attempt to reform the structure, and in the end it boiled down to very little. This was a part of what lay behind a famous and bitter remark by Metternich that he had governed Europe sometimes, but Austria never. Another part was the personality of his imperial master, the Emperor Francis.

The most dramatic change in the Habsburg position had come in Germany. In 1786 the great humiliator of the dynasty, Frederick the Great, had died and his successors had played second fiddle to Austria from 1790 onwards. The result was a Germany in which Austria's influence was paramount. Yet though Metternich was determined to avoid a united Germany, or further progress towards it, the 1815 settlement had to recognize the practical consequences of the previous quarter-century. The result was a new German Confederation, in which were associated the thirty-nine states into which Germany was now divided (and of which Austria was one in respect of her German lands). No fundamental change in it or in the constitutions of its components was permitted except by the unanimous decision of its representative bodies, in which the Austrian representative was always to preside. The Confederation was a union much less strong than even that of the United States before 1789, but it had a practical conservative value in that it was dominated by Austria. It turned out to be little more than a diplomatic device for the co-ordination of the affairs of German states in the interests of Austria.

Within the Confederation, the only possible counterweight to Austria remained Prussia. Practically subservient to Habsburg policy after 1815, she was potentially very strong and the future was to show that she would dominate Germany. Her administrative structure had been given a great shock in the dark days of the war; it stimulated a burst of centralization and rationalization which equipped the State with a bureaucracy the model of Europe. The army had undergone similar improvement and from Stein's era onwards, legislation began the transformation of Prussian society away from the feudal and patriarchal model.

Prussia had done well at the peace; her population was doubled, to nearly eleven millions. Although her king did not obtain (as he had hoped) the electorate of Saxony, a part of its territory came to Prussia, her Polish lands were restored to her and, most importantly, a huge block of territory straddling the old Prussian territories of Cleves and running from the Hanoverian frontier with Westphalia to the Saar and Luxembourg frontier in the south. There were weaknesses in the grouping under one crown of such disparate territories and old loyalties. Western Prussia, ruled by French law and institutions in the Napoleonic era, was more distinct than ever from the agrarian, still feudal east and in Prussia's new lands lay the keys to future power. To the Silesian gains of the previous century was now added the Ruhr, an area rich in coal, with excellent water communications; it was to be the German Black Country. For the realization of Prussia's economic potential, two things were necessary. One of them, the completion of a railway network to tie together the German states in an economy centred on Prussia, existed only in outline in 1847. The other, the integration of German tariff policies in a common marketing area was by then virtually complete.

The process began with internal legislation of 1818 which made the fragmented Prussian lands one Free Trade area. A year later the first of several smaller German states to do so entered this structure of shared tariffs. The little state of Schwarzburg-Sondershausen was followed in the next ten years by others in northern Germany. In 1828 the *Zollverein*, as the customs union was called, was paid the tribute of the sincerest form of flattery; Bavaria and Württemberg led a movement which formed a customs union for the south, and Saxony one of the middle states. These were anti-Prussian measures, and by the middle of the next decade they were in ruins, and Bavaria and Saxony were inside the *Zollverein*. Though a few remained outside, the major German states were now and remained united in a Free Trade area from which Austria was excluded. Here was a sign of the new source of Prussian power, the growing material interest shared with other German states. It was also a new source of Germanic self-consciousness in which Austria had no part. From the *Zollverein* Austria looked less and less a German, and more and more an Italian, Danubian and Balkan power.

For three-quarters of a century after 1815, good relations with Russia remained the cornerstone of Prussian foreign policy. The two countries were linked by the need to hold down the Poles, but Prussia was also impressed by the sheer preponderance of Russian landpower. She had something like four hundred miles of frontier in common with this colossus, the only great power with a population larger than Austria's. Russian armies in Germany in 1813 had been the preconditions of survival and recovery for Prussia. Their movements then stirred memories of their earlier visitation of Germany, in a less acceptable role during the Seven Years' War.

Man-power was one foundation of Russia's ability to shoulder the burden of being policeman to Europe after 1815. Where her armies could reach, she could in the end get her way. In 1815 her military strength was at its peak. It remained there so long as huge numbers moving on foot or horse-dominated land warfare. The slowness of changes in military technique in the early nineteenth century prolonged a Russian military supremacy which rested on sheer weight of numbers, but a lasting peace between great powers concealed the weaknesses which were to emerge later. Until then, Russian armies were the ultimate argument of the Holy Alliance.

The real decline in Russia's relative strength in these years was thus hidden; in 1847 she was still the citadel of conservative principle in Europe. Secure at home, her rulers watched revolutionary waves rising and breaking abroad, confident that they could be mastered as were the Poles in 1830. A special ideological bent had been given to the Russian regime by the historical traditions grouped round the peculiar nature of the Russian autocracy and by the alarm caused by troubles following some feeble dabblings by Alexander I with ideas of liberal reform. Russia's history in consequence reflects little of either Revolution or Improvement in these years; her civil progress under Nicholas I has been summed up in Herzen's bitter phrase – 'the plague-zone of Russian history'. In a great Asiatic and agrarian society like Russia, the virus of liberal, individual ideas might, within a framework of enlightened despotism (as in British India), have produced a healthy stimulus to peaceful change, but if left uncontrolled would probably lead to social disruption; under Nicholas I, conscious of his role, confident of the military simplicities of his thought and alarmed by the revelations of a conspiracy in 1825, the year of his accession, the experiment of directed liberalism was not to be tried.

The regime instead coupled an attempt to maintain stability at all costs at home with an ideological foreign policy. The second was, of course, an impossibility in pure terms, if Russia were to survive and uphold her historic interests. Reactionary alliances with other interested parties made sense in Poland, where a revolutionary threat to Russia was a threat to the other partitioning powers, or in western Europe, where a threat to general peace (such as was long feared might follow another revolution in France) was a threat that revolution might spread once more through the lands of allies. But they had nothing to do and might even conflict, with, say, Russia's historic drive to the south-east. Catherine the Great had set the precedent of employing the revolutionary weapon of subversion against the Turks, and a tempting constituency for political warfare existed in the Christian subjects of the Ottoman Empire. Further complications were introduced when the likely or indicated reactions of other powers to these developments were taken into consideration. Beyond the Turkish frontier lay the mouths of the Danube, the waterway to the heart of Habsburg Europe, and beyond them the Straits, the Aegean and the Mediterranean, where the appearance of a Russian fleet had already alarmed Englishmen in the 1770s. Further east, relations with Persia again concerned the British and, further still, in her contacts with China, Russia was herself a revolutionary force, one of those beginning in the 1840s to awake a country which Napoleon had suggested might be better left to sleep undisturbed.

In the immediate aftermath of victory, ideological principle none the less seemed to dominate Russian diplomacy. No doubt this owed much to the character of Alexander I, a ruler given to emotional and expansive gestures both personal and public. The Tsar's exalted temperament and Metternich's anxiety to permit intervention in the internal affairs of states whose troubles might threaten revolution added the Holy Alliance to the Quadruple Alliance of the victorious allies on which rested the defence of the peace settlement. It was a symbol of fundamental agreement on conservative principles by what British diplomatic terminology referred to as 'the Northern Courts' of Vienna, St Petersburg and Berlin for more than thirty years. The instrument on which it rested united their monarchs in 'the bonds of a true and indissoluble brotherhood ... to protect religion, peace and justice'. The Pope did not endorse this attempt to write religion into the diplomacy of Europe, and the British government sceptically but politely refrained from signing.

The importance of the Holy Alliance was mainly psychological and mythical. It satisfied the Tsar's conscience by sanctifying the fact of great power predominance (though even Metternich had jibbed at its originally abject spirituality and had an unbecoming reference to the 'penitence' of the victorious powers struck out). It eased the transition of Alexander's personal preferences from a vague liberalism in the immediate aftermath of victory to the conservatism which he showed increasingly in a series of conferences of great powers beginning in 1818. These brought the Holy Alliance as near as it ever came to action as a European fire brigade of revolution in 1820–1. But the cost of this, demonstrated in a congress held at Verona in 1822, was the withdrawal of Great Britain from regular co-operation in concert with other states. It became apparent that the suppression of revolution by the three eastern states would be possible only in cases where Great Britain and France acquiesced – whether because they wanted to or had to. Nevertheless, the term 'Holy Alliance', which in fact represented little of the real basis of co-operation between the eastern states, was a rallying slogan for liberals who sought political change in Europe for the next forty years. All that they opposed they attributed to its malign influence. It was supposed to have a substantive reality it never possessed, and was personified as 'international capitalism' and 'international communism' have been in more recent times.

In the 1830s, there was talk of a grouping of supposedly liberal states opposed to the Holy Alliance. The reality behind this was the co-operation (sometimes very uneasy) of Great Britain and France to protect constitutional regimes in Spain and Portugal; there was another Quadruple Alliance between these four states in 1834. Well before this, the two great powers of this quartet were regarded with deep distrust by Metternich. In the case of France, his suspicions are understandable. In 1789, France had shown an explosive capacity which he never forgot. His misgivings were not allayed by the over-throw of Napoleon and the restoration of the Bourbons to the French throne.

Some of the terms of the restoration were set by the subjects of Louis XVIII, some by the allies. Restoration France was, therefore, constitutional France. It had guarantees of personal liberty, representative government and equality before the law. This did not satisfy all Frenchmen. But it gave France fifteen years of peace, troubled though they were by plots, assassination and scuffles with rioting peasants or Luddite weavers. Then, in 1830, Paris again suddenly gave France a government. The result was only just a revolution in France and its effervescence was quickly contained; Paris was not allowed to re-establish its dictatorship of 1793. The dynasty was changed; the junior branch of the house of Bourbon, the Orleans line, was called to the throne in the person of Louis Philippe, former member of the Jacobin Club and officer in the revolutionary army, son of the man on whose dynastic ambitions some blamed the Great Revolution itself, a walking monument of the history of the last forty years.

Apart from constitutional monarchy, the demand for institutional change was focussed in 1830 on the suffrage and the change was small;

the French electorate after the Revolution was still a smaller proportion of the population than was the unreformed electorate of England of the English. Louis Philippe himself was a more reassuring figure and he soon began to behave in a reassuring way. The rule of the men of the *juste milieu* followed; those who wanted more were again driven to secret societies, plots and clandestine newspapers, or were shot down in the streets like the Lyonnais in 1834. Under the July Monarchy France changed meanwhile but only very slowly. She was still the greatest of western European powers, but grew rich less rapidly than Great Britain or Belgium. It seems that the period in which the rural population of France was the largest in relation to the whole was in the last decade of the July Monarchy.

Great Britain changed more and changed faster. She underwent two great psychological experiences, an intensification of national self-consciousness and patriotism, and that of industrialization. The wars that ended in 1814 had been an experience of huge importance. First of all, the outcome was a great victory: Englishmen were proud to have stood alone and weathered the storm. Second, victory was a great deliverance. This left a legacy of distrust in their attitude to the Continent. Even when military monarchy was replaced first by chartered legitimacy and then by constitutional monarchy, English statesmen distrusted France. They remembered the terrible power demonstrated in twenty years of warfare and were afraid that French governments, whatever their colour, could again easily be pushed on to the road to conquest. Behind this, too, lay the history of rivalry for world power on which Trafalgar had set the seal in 1805 and opened almost a century of unchallenged world power for Great Britain.

Except in India, where the frontier of empire moved steadily forward, this did not involve large acquisitions of territory. After the wars, Great Britain handed back many of her colonial conquests. Those she kept were usually, like the Cape of Good Hope or Mauritius, of strategic importance. Ceylon was taken mainly because the harbour at Trincomalee was the only safe port on the western shores of the Bay of Bengal during the monsoon. The Dutch got back Indonesia, on the other hand, and the French their sugar colonies. After the peace, naval bases and trading-ports still made up most of the story of British expansion.

By 1847 Great Britain was literally the only world power in the sense that she had great interests in every ocean and continent. Her standing in Europe rested on this, in the sense that they contributed to her wealth, rather than to her military and naval strength, which, though great, had important limitations. British sea-power could sweep enemy commerce from the seas and deliver land forces to virtually any spot on the globe without interference. This was the enviable legacy of Trafalgar. But on the mainland of Europe, this power ranged only so far as the cannon of the British battleships; blockade, bombardment or the destruction of shipping could only be effective against a limited number of European states. It was Russian numbers which finally defeated Napoleon. The heavy drain imposed on him by the presence of a British army in Spain was strategically very important, but British victory there could not have overthrown the Emperor had he not been defeated in Germany and eastern France. British power in Europe was diplomatic, economic and naval: if military action were needed, she required an ally.

Another aspect to British power was moral and exemplary, and here it is perhaps better to speak of England, which was what Europeans saw when they looked across the Channel, rather than the backward wastes of Wales and Scotland, far less the rural slums of Ireland. England had by 1847 created a new sort of society, and for many Europeans it was one which represented modernity and the future – whether they welcomed or strove to avoid it; in England Europeans could see the future and how it worked. This was the culmination of a period of a century and a half in which England often profoundly influenced Europe. Envy of her wealth, enduring institutions and a high level of general culture; the provocation of her commercial competition; the pontifications of her statesmen about illiberal regimes abroad; her export of capital and industrial skill; the ramifications of a worldwide commercial system resting on the Royal Navy – these were some of the ways in which England, for good or ill, influenced Europe before 1847.

These influences arose in part from England's own changing nature. She was, in 1847, a fast-growing nation; her population was then nearly two-thirds that of France and in 1789 it had been only about one-third. Her landscape registered the fact that more than any other nation she was an industrializing and urbanizing power. Her relative economic lead grew even greater. Bigger towns and more factories accompanied an enormous expansion of overseas trade. The country grew wealthier and wealthier. By mid-century there would be no doubt about the *per capita* measurement of this, and the worst social suffering of industrialization was past; England was, in the phrase of the 1840s, 'the workshop of the world'. Yet though the British were becoming a town-dwelling people, their machinery of government and the values which dominated their lives (even if only formally) were still very much those of a rural society. Agriculture, measured against individual manufacturing industries, was still the biggest single employer.

The balance of social power was none the less shifting away from land. The old eighteenth-century antithesis of land versus trade had given way to the new one of land versus industry, even though the embodiment of this distinction in class differences was blurred and qualified by the growth of the professions and by the traditional readiness of the English landed classes to inter-marry with business and allow their younger sons to go into it. Such a change in social power could be symbolized in a single dramatic event – such as the so-called 'Repeal' of the Corn Laws of 1846, when the government proposed and carried a bill to reduce to a nominal sum duties on imported grains and to introduce this change gradually – but it was reflected only slowly in the composition of the House of Commons. Landed wealth would long be strong enough to provoke radical outcry, and in 1847 a real property qualification was still a formal requirement for election to the House of Commons.

One other political fact is pre-eminent in these years: whatever the fear of revolution, England never had one. There were waves of alarm. In the early 1790s, in the years after Waterloo and in the early 1840s excitement combined with hard times to produce uneasiness among the ruling classes and hope among the would-be English Jacobins. The postwar years, too, were particularly bad. Corn Laws to keep up grain prices, deflationary currency policies which produced unemployment, a reversion from income tax to the indirect taxation brought in by higher duties, the suspension of the Habeas Corpus Act for the first time in its history and finally the derisively named 'Peterloo massacre' brought radical feeling to a pitch never again reached. It is hardly surprising that there was a new gunpowder plot, though this time the target was not the King and Parliament, but a Cabinet dinner-party. In the 1820s, government policy became less flint-faced. Important reforms were made but the reformers in the country concentrated more and more upon a change in the representative system as the key to all other desirable things. In 1832 they had their greatest triumph when the Reform Act was passed as a result of something near to a naked threat of revolution if it did not.

Many radicals found this victory empty; giving the vote to middle-class townsmen and transferring seats to under-represented but populous new urban areas did not produce a very different House of Commons. But even after hard times in the early 1840s, the Chartists, the greatest radical movement yet seen in England, had not by 1847 secured any of their demands. In that year Englishmen found themselves still with a structure of politics organically and naturally much like that many of them had lived under in 1789. The monarchy, though sometimes threatened, was still there, and much the same oligarchy retained power and made up governments as in 1789, though under Pitt there had been an infusion of new peers and, it was complained, men of obscure birth. Property still ruled England, even if it did not do so quite so mechanically as in the eighteenth century. The electorate was still not a very large one, and it voted by open ballot. The importance of 1832 was not what it changed but the road it opened to change. It was a great precedent (Cromwell, the last great remodeller of the House of Commons, had been a dubious forerunner) and, sooner or later, more parliamentary reform would follow.

So much real and implied change could not leave untouched the confused, rich tapestry of assumption and prejudice, idealism and fatuity which makes up a national outlook. Englishmen in this period acquired or confirmed a sense of themselves as top dogs which they were long to hold and slow to lose. It was the revolutionary and Napoleonic wars – significantly, called by them the 'Great War' – which first made most Englishmen aware that England was a great power, though this was an immense reinforcement of a patriotism which already existed. After 1815 there was widespread assumption, which greatly benefited continental liberalism, that the voice of England should be heard in European affairs. It grew stronger and stronger as the century proceeded, and the interest in foreign affairs of the man on the top of the Clapham omnibus was fanned by the newspaper Press and the flamboyance of Palmerston. Yet (and this may seem surprising in the twentieth century) there was in this small place for overt domination over other races and what was later to be called imperialism. Englishmen were conservative about colonies; they might be interesting or even necessary, but their worth had to be demonstrated as strategic, demographic or commercial goods, for they were likely to prove a burden, a drain and perhaps a disaster. There is a good indicator in India: it exercised nothing like the grip on the English imagination which it was later to have. Commercial, not political, supremacy was the idol of the early Victorian Englishman. What has been called the 'Imperialism of Free Trade' opened to him the markets in which he and his colleagues, unconsciously arrogant in their assumption that their possession of twenty years' advantage over their European rivals was permanent, sold their wares.

Even so slight a sketch suggests the complexity of currents shaping international life. It is impossible to reduce it meaningfully to such simplicities as the struggle of Holy Alliance and Revolution. Of course, many men, some conservatively and some progressively inclined, could and did see the operation of the European system in such terms. But much more complicated forces were in operation to sustain the balance of power, even when it was troubled by the appearance of new nations.

They presented statesmen with a Third World both *de facto* in that some now came into independent existence and further complicated old relationships and *in posse* in that others clamoured – or were alleged to clamour, which could be quite as troublesome – for an independent existence. Any equilibrium of a liberal western Europe and a conservative and autocratic eastern Europe was always liable to be disturbed by this.

The oldest new nation and first member of the ex-colonial club was, of course, the United States. Three powers, Spain, Great Britain and Russia, continued to be much more affected than any others by the growth of the new republic. The United States first annexed Spanish west Florida, in 1810, and then bullied the Spanish into ceding the rest bit by bit, the last in 1819. This extinguished Spanish claims to lands forming part of the future territories of the United States on the mainland east of Texas. But this by no means ended the entanglement of Spain with the United States. As far back as 1787, when Jefferson was American minister in Paris, he had carefully reported attempts by a Brazilian and a Mexican to interest the United States in aiding revolution in their countries. At the time, he wished his government to hold its hand; thirty years later, the time came to do more. The future of Latin America had been transformed by the French invasions of Spain and Portugal. In the colonies, independence *de facto* aroused demands for independence *de jure*. In 1815, the only independent state south of the United States was Haiti; by 1822 the whole of central and southern America, except for the Caribbean islands, part of Honduras, the Guianas and Bolivia, was under independent governments. Most of this area had been Spanish, and the attitude of the United States towards its former and rebellious colonists was therefore of great importance to Spain, whose Crown hoped to recover at least some of its former possessions.

American policy was important to Russia and Great Britain for different reasons. Russia had long been an Asiatic power, and under Alexander I took steps towards being a Pacific one as well, thus antedating an American political presence on that ocean's shores. A Russian settlement at Kodiak in 1784 was followed in 1799 by a company with monopoly rights to manage Russia's American trade. Except for its valuable furs and fishing, the area was uninviting, but from it Russian settlement pushed further south, eventually as far as a fort in San Francisco Bay. In 1821 the Tsar decreed that Alaskan territory ran as far as fifty-one degrees North; this was not far north of Vancouver, in what was called the Oregon territory, where the extent of British and American claims was as yet uncertain. Perhaps the Tsar thought that the Americans would not mind after his benevolent reception of the news of the American acquisition of Florida two years before with the words: 'We are all getting a little bigger nowadays.'

Such a claim was in fact alarming to Americans already disturbed by the Tsar's interest in the restoration of Spanish rule in South America by the arms of the Holy Alliance. Such a scheme was very unwelcome to the British, too, though for different reasons. The separation of South America from Europe had brought the final collapse of the once closed system of colonial commerce which reserved its trade in principle to Spaniards and Portuguese. The volume of British exports to South America had grown rapidly, so rapidly, indeed, that it helped to offset the damage done to British trade by the Napoleonic blockade which attempted to exclude it from Europe. A possible loss of South American markets could not be contemplated without dismay in the depressed conditions of the 1820s.

The matter came to a head when the French invaded Spain to help the king against his constitutionalist subjects in 1823. The British proposed to the Americans a joint warning against a Franco-Spanish attempt to recover the Latin American colonies, but jibbed at recognition for the new republics. Yet the Americans knew that the British were not prepared to tolerate intervention and had the sea-power to prevent it. Seizing the opportunity at the same time to appear independent of Great Britain, denounce the Holy Alliance, warn off the Tsar from Alaska and encourage the new neighbour of the United States in the belief that they had a protector, President Monroe informed the world by a message to Congress of 2 December 1823 that the 'hemisphere' (an undefined zone) was not in the future to be regarded as an area for the extension of their political systems, nor the American continents as a place for colonization by European powers, and that Europe's affairs were not the business of the United States. Many years later, this would become known as the 'Monroe Doctrine' and was presumed to justify an American hegemony in hemisphere affairs, thus taking on the characteristics of positive law. It was one side of the expansionist coin which bore on its reverse the words 'Manifest Destiny'; it set out a claim, not yet enforceable, to an American sphere of influence beyond the homeland.

American territorial expansion was immediately more significant than the Monroe doctrine. Much of this was a matter of consolidating and organizing territory already legally American; some of it involved aggression against others. Between 1803, when Ohio became a state, and Missouri's admission in 1821, seven new states west of the Alleghenies were added to the Union and only one east of them, Maine. In 1800 there were less than four hundred thousand Americans west of the mountains – about one-fifteenth of the total population. By 1820 there were more than two millions out of a total population of nine and a half. Both the figures and the proportion continued to rise.[1] They implied a transformation of the politics and sociology of the Union, and marked the change in America's international position which was the logical outcome of the Louisiana Purchase. She became unquestionably the dominant power of the western hemisphere and was by 1847 firmly and legally established on the Pacific coast and had begun her history as a two-ocean power. Finally, although its implications long went unrecognized by most European statesmen, the base was being laid for the later vast economy of industrial America.

This expansion was made easier by improvements in communication. The steamboat was the most obvious – by 1819 there were sixty stern-wheelers working between New Orleans and Louisville, Kentucky. Freight charges from the upper Ohio to the mouth of the Mississippi were less than half those of the trip to Baltimore or Philadelphia. Canals, too, were being built. But the main impetus of territorial expansion was provided by spreading waves of settlement, informal and disorganized though following well-defined geographical routes, as people sought free land. The idea of a national destiny was reinforced by such changes. The war of 1812 had done much for the patriotic pride of Americans – the *Star-spangled banner* and the caricaturists' figure of Uncle Sam both emerged from it to take a permanent place in American symbolism – and there were more and more to be heard suggestions that a great destiny lay ahead. 'We are the pioneers of the world,' wrote the novelist Melville. Many could identify their people's future with such a myth. The phrase 'Manifest Destiny', with its implications of overriding right, came into use in the 1840s as the crystallization and cant expression of such feelings. It summed up a strenuous era in which de Tocqueville saw the essence of the nation in the psychology of the pioneer: 'Before him lies a boundless continent, and he urges forward as if time pressed and he was afraid of finding no room for his exertions.'

Of seven states admitted to the Union between 1836 and 1850, three were formerly Spanish territory. Florida was the first. The next, Texas, was part of the new republic of Mexico and under its rule had attracted settlers from the United States. By the middle of the 1830s

[1] *Rounded figures in thousands.*

	Total US pop.	Western pop.
1800	5,300	380
1810	7,200	1,070
1820	9,600	2,230
1830	12,800	3,670
1840	17,000	6,370

there were about twenty thousand there and they had grievances in the unsatisfactory state of law and order under Mexican government. Perhaps more important, they lived under Spanish law which was, from some points of view, unsatisfactory in so far as the ownership of slaves was concerned. Finally, when an attempt was made to introduce some greater degree of centralization into Mexican government, the Americans in Texas reacted as had the colonists of the 1760s to British centralization, and a revolt took place. There emerged an independent Texas, the 'Lone Star Republic'. When it asked for annexation to the United States, this was refused, because of the dispute which it provoked about the admission to the Union of another state in which slave-owning would be legal. While matters hung fire, politicians battled for support in the United States. In 1845 an election was fought almost solely on the issue of territorial expansion, and the expansionists won. Congress voted to admit Texas, the Mexicans protested and a war took place from which the United States emerged not only with Texas but with California and the territory of the future state of New Mexico as well, in 1848.

This discreditable episode demonstrated the importance of American imperialism as a vote-catcher and also its connection with sectional balance, which lay behind the slavery question. It confirmed the United States' future as a Pacific power; even before California was acquired, the United States had made its first treaty with China. In fact, the Mexican War, overtly over a dispute about the boundaries of Texas, was about California, whose seizure could be made possible only by war with Mexico. It stood in relation to Texans' wishes in 1845 much as the dream of expansion in Canada stood in relation to maritime grievances in 1812.

Like the south of the Columbia and Vancouver Sound, California had long been of interest to sailors and New England merchants who had long pressed for more secure ports and harbours there, and therefore for expansive annexations. Their efforts, together with those of explorers, quickly awoke awareness of a Pacific destiny. 'We border on Russia, on Japan, on China,' urged one naval officer in 1814. A decade later, two hundred American ships were engaged in whaling and sealing in the Pacific. The status of much of California was doubtful, or at least obscure, after Mexico succeeded to the Spanish possessions. The key point was the fine harbour of San Francisco, where Americans traded with cattle-breeders for hides. In the 1840s, American immigrants began to arrive overland in California, too, swelling the largely Spanish-speaking indigenous population. Yet they were few and though Mexican government was not a reality, there was small chance that an American majority could establish itself and play the Texans' game. But there was a huge American interest and investment in the Pacific trade; in 1845 the building of a transcontinental railway to San Francisco was already being considered. A war with Mexico might anticipate a danger of the British moving into a territory Mexico did not appear able to control. So, in the end, California became American, its acquisition the clearest announcement yet given of the future Pacific destiny of the United States.

Though there were dangerous moments, expansion on the northern flank of the United States was more peaceable; notwithstanding the violent language of some politicians. Great prizes were at stake in the north-west, too, and it was here that most difficulty arose (though the frontier of Maine was not agreed until 1842). In the 'Oregon territory', both British and American claims were at first very big (those of Spain had been renounced in 1819), but both nations recalled the unpromising experience of 1812–14, which made war an unlikely outcome. The British also had the advantage of an early start. The first explorers to cross the continent had been Canadians, not Americans, and the British North-West Company threw out a thin but sufficiently continuous line of trading posts from Lake Superior to the Columbia River at a time when only a few individual Americans penetrated the North-West to look for pelts. The Americans who knew most about the area were the Boston sailors who scoured the coast looking for whales and the valuable sea otter. It was only late in the day that John Jacob Astor and the Missouri fur traders got into the act by the long land route to the Columbia valley, at whose mouth, hoped one senator, 'a modern Tyre' would rise to dominate the trade of China and America.

The Oregon question was finally entangled by politics with that of the south-west, for it raised the possibility of compromise on sectional balance. The huffing and puffing of the 1845 election provided the last obfuscation of the logic of eventual compromise in that area, but in the end the war with Mexico forced realism on the United States. It was agreed that the northern boundary should run west of the Rockies as it did to the east, along the forty-ninth parallel, Vancouver island remaining to the British. By this time serious immigration of farming families overland into Oregon had begun, following an agricultural depression and collapse of farm prices in the late 1830s. Yet even in 1845 Oregon had less than ten thousand settlers, against a hundred thousand in Texas.

American foreign policy shows the dynamic effect of nationalism on international relations in an especially pure form; yet in Europe the idea seemed more profoundly disturbing. The most obvious danger was provided by what many people regarded as the most blatant and atrocious example of its frustration, in Poland. A nation with a long history of independence – much of it resting on Polish domination over other peoples – Poland had in the end failed to re-emerge from the false dawn of Napoleon's Grand Duchy. Because of their disappointment then, some Poles were at first disposed to welcome the decisions of the Congress of Vienna, especially the creation of a new kingdom of Poland. But its king was the Russian Tsar, who appointed his brother viceroy. It soon became clear that the constitution was not likely to be respected by the Russians (the promised Diet, for example, was not called). Under Nicholas I, there was even less to hope for. Polish patriotism was finally detonated by his hope of using the Polish army to suppress the 1830 revolution in Belgium and France; at this, there was a Polish revolution which succeeded briefly in expelling the Russian forces before succumbing in September 1831. This was the end of the Polish constitution.

In the eighteenth century, Poland's fate had been part of the Eastern Question. In the next, the fundamental themes of Turkish weakness and Austro-Russian greed were joined by the complicating third of nationalism inside the Ottoman Empire, a new worry for statesmen. The beginnings of significant and ordered resistance to Ottoman rule first became apparent in Serbia during the Napoleonic era. This primitive country was antagonized by its especially ruthless treatment by the Ottoman janissaries, whose interests were by no means identical with those of the Sultan. To him, therefore, the Serbs appealed for protection. But Serb Christians also disliked the fact that the only road to high office was by apostasy; often those who tormented them were Christian renegades. Against this background it was especially galling that Serbs who lived across the border under Habsburg rule were at that moment courted and favoured. A particularly ferocious attempt by Turkish forces to intimidate the leaders of the Serb clans by executions led at last to revolt in 1804. Like everything else, it turned out that the Eastern Question, too, was affected by the French Revolution; when the Serbs looked to Austria and Russia for help, they found them at that moment mainly concerned to win Turkish help against France. The diplomatic story of the rebellion is therefore tangled, following the shifts of the policy of Russia (soon at war with Turkey again) and all the while Serbian leaders were aware that the final endorsement of their independence had to be Napoleon's.

Eventually, in 1813, a new leader emerged in Serbia. Two years later he made a successful peace with the Porte, giving Serbia an autonomous status within the Ottoman Empire, the Turks retaining possession of only a few places. This ruler, Milosz Obrenovich, was soon sending the heads of predecessors and rivals to Constantinople as an earnest of his goodwill. None the less, for all Milosz's respectful loyalty (rewarded in due course by recognition by the Sultan of his hereditary status), Serbia's autonomy was the first loss of sovereignty suffered by the Ottoman Empire as a result primarily of an internal revolt by its Christian subjects. Moreover, Serbia was at the end of the day neither Russian nor Austrian.

Against this background and that of Mehemet Ali's successful usurpation in Egypt, the Ottoman government confronted a more serious rebellion among its Greek subjects. Unlike the Serbian rising, this burst straight into the main current of international relations with huge effect. As a start, it provided the occasion or excuse for the end of the co-operation of the victorious allies of 1815 and France (soon admitted to their number) which had produced the series of conferences and congresses between 1818 and 1824. They expressed, according to your point of view, either the successful working of the 'Concert of Europe' or the machinations of the Holy Alliance.

Viewed abstractly, the Greek war of independence was a simple case of rebellion against established authority; Metternich would have liked to have had this straightforward conservative proposition accepted by his colleagues. Unfortunately, behind rebellion stretched the great chain of complicating circumstances of the Eastern Question: who was to rule at the Straits if the Turkish Empire crumbled away? Austro-Russian rivalry loomed up, but so did a new British concern: since Bonaparte's expedition to Egypt in 1798, the attention of British policy to the Straits (which, in unfriendly hands, might provide a sally-port for a threat to the land routes to India) was much more intense. The British had not forgotten the reluctance of their Russian allies of 1799 to give up the Ionian islands which they had then occupied. There were implications too for other subject peoples in the Balkans, especially those nearer to Austrian borders.

Then there was the practical difficulty presented by the curious phenomenon of Philhellenism. To educated men in many countries (but especially in England, France and the United States), the revival of interest in Greek antiquity which had begun with Winckelmann coupled with the classical content of their education to excite admiration and a vision of the Greeks who fought their Turkish overlords as sons of Hellas. Better still, they were Christian, too. It was well-known that Turkish rule was barbaric and wicked and the result was the glamorizing of brigands and pirates to make them fill the role of modern successors of Leonidas, subscriptions by professors to buy guns and the rehabilitation of Lord Byron's reputation. Romanian landlords, Albanian cut-throats and Aegean pirates were the improbable beneficiaries of the first of those high-minded liberal orgies of international goodwill which were to be so potent a source of confusion and trouble in the future.

In the end a new independent state emerged, the first in Europe to be founded on nationality, and this was a blatant affront to legitimist principle. Many Greeks can hardly have expected this outcome. In 1800 they were distinguished not by being a nation but by their faith; a Greek in the Ottoman Empire (and there were about thirteen million of them, making up about a quarter of its total population) was a Christian whose community had as its head the Patriarch in Istanbul. Greeks looked to him for their social coherence above the level of village community and class. Regional distinctions were strong between the Phanariots of Constantinople and the Danubian principalities, the poverty-stricken peasants of the Peloponnese and the prosperous merchants and trading captains of the islands. Distinctions between Greeks were often as important as divisions between Greek and Turk in determining what happened when fighting began. Broadly speaking, the educated Greeks of the principalities thought in terms of autonomy within the Empire and Russian patronage, the peasants of the Peloponnese were hungry for an independence which would end Turkish landowning and the islanders wanted to be free to combine piracy and trade.

On the other hand, religion was the seedbed of Greek nationality and there were Greeks who identified the two. Anachronistically but sincerely, they saw themselves as the heirs of those who, it was believed, had not surrendered with the officials of the Byzantine empire in 1453 but had continued a popular struggle against the new pagan masters. This was given plausibility by the undying tradition of banditry and resistance to the tax-gatherer. Widely scattered through the Ottoman Empire but linked in religion, Greeks were important both to its administration and to its internal trade. Many of the lesser merchants and traders belonged also to the 'Friendly Society', a secret and conspiratorial organization founded on Russian soil in 1816. Circumstances were to turn the strong, if incoherent, sense of brotherhood which such facts fostered in some men into nationality.

The Greek future, none the less, had to be worked out in the context of great power politics. In the background lay the Russian claim, going back to Kainardji, of a right of intervention in the interests of the Christian subjects of the Porte. In the early nineteenth century, Greek priests were being trained in Russia and sent back into the Ottoman Empire to propound the case for looking to the Tsar for protection. In 1812 the possibility of such intervention became much easier for Russia, for by the treaty of Bucharest Bessarabia passed into Russian possession. From the new frontier on the Pruth Russian armies looked across to the provinces of Moldavia and Wallachia where, in fact, they had been on occupation duties since 1806. This was a position of enormous leverage as was shown by Alexander's successful insistence that the Turks should not participate in the Congress of Vienna. His relations with the Ottoman Empire were in his eyes domestic matters in which no European power should intervene; the claim to a special sphere of interest was a sort of Russian Monroe doctrine. Unfortunately for Russia, while Great Britain was prepared to underwrite the American claim, she was emphatically not prepared to endorse the claims of Russia about her southern and south-eastern neighbour.

The Greeks set the pace for the powers. For all that was later said about diplomatic provocation and revolutionary plotting, it is impossible to believe that Turkish government was by 1815 capable of maintaining its grip on the Balkan peninsula without provoking rebellion. Turkish government depended upon local governors, *pashas*, who raised taxes and delivered recruits to the central government while providing a system of justice and police for the local inhabitants. The *pashas* were not unlike medieval marcher barons in western Europe; their indispensability and remoteness from a central government which in the end could check them only by armed force made some of them virtually independent princelings. Some behaved like it. Mehemet Ali was the first to go further and claim independence, while the Serbian rebellion had been begun by a local notable who, though not a *pasha*, sought, as did his more successful successor, this sort of status. In 1820 Ali Pasha (1750–1828), the virtually independent governor of the Epirus and central Greece, rebelled against his master. This detonated the Greek revolt, for it suddenly put a heavy demand on the Turkish army.

A history of bad government and the persistence of traditional banditry explain much of the atrocious and bloody nature of the war when it came. The *klepht* had been for centuries a respected figure, a bandit who could be seen as a sort of Robin Hood, with whom the local population (whose language he spoke and whose religion he shared) could identify against an alien authority. The mixture of social banditry, local patriotism and simple criminality among the *klephts* cannot be disentangled. Not that the Ottoman government did not set thieves to catch thieves; it often recruited *klepht* leaders and their bands and renamed them as units of the *gendarmerie*. Between their barbarities and those of their opponents there was nothing to choose. This was another concession by the Ottomans to the realities of Balkan life and did not really strengthen it, for *klephts*-turned-policemen in fact continued to behave as bandits, since this was often the only way of assuring their pay. In other places, notably the Morea, where the Greek population was more agricultural and somewhat thicker on the ground, the Turks worked through the Greek headmen and ecclesiastical authorities. But even here, there were areas where, if the test of government is tax-collection, the Ottomans had not ruled for years. Finally, there were the islands, whose Greek population ran and manned an important merchant marine of hundreds of vessels. They were prosperous and had important communities abroad, in Odessa, Trieste, Marseilles and London. From them, too, the Sultan's authority was able to exact only a small tribute each year.

Against such a background, it is not really surprising that Ali Pasha's revolt prompted some Greeks to think that the moment had come to stage a general rising. Such men were few and had been influenced by ideas of nationality and hopes of Russian support since the 1790s. They were to be disappointed in the Danubian principalities, where revolt had begun prematurely in 1820 only to be crushed the following year, but in the Morea the community sustained a rebellion launched by the Metropolitan of Patros in April 1821 and it was speedily reinforced by the help of the Greek islanders.

The sea-power brought to the help of the rebellion by the islands may well have ensured its survival. At sea, the Greeks were masters. This threw the Turks back upon land communications and made it easier for the Greeks to hold on to the Peloponnese. They needed to survive, for defeat would be followed by appalling retribution. No doubt the background of *klepht* warfare made it inevitable, but the Greeks had begun their rising with a massacre of thousands of Moslems. This set the tone for what was to follow and, indeed, for a tradition of Turco-Greek struggle which has had a long life. A massacre of Greeks in Constantinople and the hanging of the Patriarch was only a first reprisal. For seven years massacre, roastings alive, impalements and torture were the lot of Greece, until the Turkish forces withdrew from the Morea in 1828. Only in 1831 was the story of the revolt ended, when the new and independent kingdom of Greece which appeared in that year was demarcated to include Livadia and Euboeia and the Cyclades, as well as Morea and the Peloponnese. By that time, Greeks had been bitterly divided from one another, too. Not all the horrors were the work of the Turks, and civil war brought Greek atrocities against fellow-Greeks to match those with which they earlier harried the Turk.

Turkish counter-measures had soon stirred up Russian diplomacy, but whatever was going on in Greece, it was certainly revolution. Not only did Metternich deplore this in principle; there was a tradition of Austrian wariness about the spread of revolutionary ideas in the Balkans, as the treatment of Rigas Pheraeos had shown. It was also feared in Vienna that a general war would follow Russian attacks on

Turkey. For a time, Austrian diplomacy successfully contained the danger; at Laibach in 1821 the revolt was condemned by the Great Powers. But the British soon fell out of step. In March 1823 the Greeks were recognized as belligerents by the British government, which was especially impressed by their success at sea and the complications which would ensue if their disruption of Turkish sea-communications had to be treated as piracy. There was growing public sympathy for the Greeks in the west, too. Such a recognition implied another change in the diplomatic situation. Besides preventing Russia from gaining territory whose loss would fatally weaken Turkey, there now existed an infant Christian nation whose first steps to statehood had been approved by a great power. If due care were not exercised, however, it was likely that this new nation would become a Russian satellite – one with a Mediterranean coastline, too. Austria, reluctantly, was soon proposing the recognition of Greece as an independent state.

While the powers haggled, the Sultan turned to an older rebel for help. In return for a promise of Syria and Crete, Mehemet Ali in 1825 sent his son Ibrahim with a powerful fleet and army to conquer the Morea for the Sultan. He succeeded so well and behaved so ruthlessly that men believed he proposed to exterminate the population of the Morea and replant it with Africans. But his brutal success fanned sympathy abroad and meant an end to non-intervention. The British, unwilling to leave Russia to act alone, as Nicholas showed every sign of doing, agreed to a joint demand that Greece should be constituted an autonomous state tributary to the Sultan. The Austrians and Prussians objected, but all the time that the Greek ulcer continued to run, the Turks, as Canning well knew, were under pressure to make dangerous concessions to Russia in the Black Sea and the Caucasus. When the Sultan refused the Anglo-Russian proposal, therefore, he was willing to act with Russia to enforce it. The two powers' agreement was now joined by France, where enthusiasm for an oppressed Christian people united liberals and conservatives to improve their situation, if necessary by force.

A naval blockade of the Morea began which, helpful to the Greeks, was acknowledged by them and therefore directed against the Turkish – that is, Egyptian – fleet alone. On 20 October 1827 that fleet was destroyed at Navarino, the only naval battle between Trafalgar and Tsushima which may be said to have been decisive, though it seems to have begun by accident or Turkish error. Codrington, the British admiral, was congratulated enthusiastically by his chief, the Lord High Admiral and future King William IV (though it has not been confirmed that he had previously been encouraged by a private message attached to his instructions which said 'Go it, my boy!') but the British government thought otherwise: he was recalled and dismissed. Still, enough damage had been done to ensure that the last chapter of the crisis opened.

It did so with the Sultan's declaration of Holy War against the infidel. Soon Russian armies crossed the Danube into Bulgaria and then Rumelia. They made a slower progress than hoped, but in 1829 were threatening Constantinople. A French army had by then arrived in the Morea but as Ibrahim had by then agreed to withdraw his army, it had no fighting to do. The result was another victorious Russian treaty with Turkey, signed in September 1829 at Adrianople. Greece got its tributary autonomy, though the Greek president, Capodistrias, thought the territory too small and rejected the terms. Russia took nothing more in Europe, but pushed forward her frontier in the Caucasus by taking Armenia and the Black Sea coast as far south as Poti. Beyond the Pruth, Moldavia and Wallachia became virtually independent principalities, in which no Moslems were to be allowed to reside. Finally, Russia's merchant ships were to have the right of unimpeded passage through the Bosphorus and the Straits.

This was not quite the end of the most important changes in the European balance between 1815 and 1847. There was the problem of Greece itself, which the British were unwilling to strengthen for fear of Russian influence and which was in uproar (in the middle of which Capodistrias, suspected to be a Russian agent, was murdered in 1831). Events in the west, where the French revolution of 1830 seemed likely to raise new problems, disposed the powers to settle quickly, and in 1833 there emerged at last a kingdom of Greece, whose first king, a nineteen-year-old Bavarian prince, arrived at Nauplion with a train of his countrymen to provide the officials and soldiers on whom would rest the future of the first experiment in constitutional monarchy to be made in the Balkans. It was not to prove a happy enterprise and a revolution ten years later forced King Otto to surrender much of his power, but this began a period in which constitutional monarchy was regularly prescribed for new nations – much as parliamentary democracy was after 1945.

This closed the most important Turkish crisis before 1847. Alarmed by revolutions in the West in 1830, the Eastern Powers agreed in 1833 to uphold the integrity of the Turkish Empire (against Mehemet Ali, who had seized Syria). Austria had her special fears of the spread of revolution northwards. Though suspicious of what was believed to be a continuing Russian policy of undermining Turkey, and ignorant of the Eastern Powers' agreement, this in fact coincided with British aims. When, therefore, Turkish attempts to control Mehemet Ali led eventually to military disaster in 1839, only France was available to resist the other great powers' determination not to let the Turkish Empire go under. They made the Sultan give Mehemet Ali the hereditary pashalik of Egypt, but that was all. After this experience of co-operation all the powers were able to agree in 1841 that the Dardanelles should be closed to the warships of any state: Russia, therefore, acquiesced in her exclusion from Mediterranean naval power, and Great Britain in hers from direct access to Constantinople for her battleships. Though the mid-1840s brought Russian soundings in London of what British intentions would be if (as seemed likely) Ottoman power continued to decline, the Eastern Question was, for a while, stabilized.

The importance of this question was immense and justifies giving it much space. Yet just after 1830, events elsewhere preoccupied statesmen more. A new revolutionary wave had exploded in that year and the July revolution in France revived fears of a new revolutionary republic. An *émeute* in Amiens or Lyons would not trouble Europe, but one in Paris could. A French change of a government might mean a change of French foreign policy; in any case, it encouraged revolutionaries all over Europe. The July revolution acted as a detonator to revolt in Poland and even, in small measure, in Italy; it distracted attention from a revolt by the Belgians against the incorporation in the kingdom of the Netherlands imposed on them in 1815 and so was to ensure the survival of the second European state to come into existence since the peace of 1815; finally, it set up a constitutional regime in France which was, for the next eighteen years, in spite of troubles and friction, to provide a partner for Great Britain in something like an International of liberal states. In eastern Europe, liberalism could do nothing and the Poles were crushed, but in Spain and Portugal two wicked uncles did not prevail; by 1840 both Don Carlos and Dom Miguel were in exile and the young queens Isabella and Maria were seemingly secure on their thrones. The later history of those two countries may well give rise to incredulity that an optimistic view could be taken of the future of liberalism in the Iberian peninsula, but that was how it looked at the time. Elsewhere, reaction redoubled its efforts and soon seemed unshaken in the saddle once more.

An informed observer of European affairs who looked about him in 1847 would therefore have felt that he lived in a world transformed since 1775, but not, perhaps, one changed unrecognizably since 1815. The international balance was remarkably unchanged in thirty-two years in appearance, nor was it much changed in substance. A system of great powers to which the United States was only peripheral was still often divided into three eastern and two western states. France was still usually isolated and unable to exercise the weight which had once been hers, while, of course, her real demographic and economic growth was all the time so slow as to prefigure a role even more diminished in the no-longer distant future. Of the three eastern states, Russia was still the greatest, and the most obvious changes of these years had come in her relationship with Turkey. The Treaty of Adrianople and the later Straits Agreement had made the Black Sea the Russian lake whose eventual emergence had been made possible at Kainardji. Imponderably, too, her advantages *vis-à-vis* Austria had grown. Bessarabia was hers, Moldavia and Wallachia were really out of Turkish control, and Greece was independent. These real and potential gains were unmatched by corresponding Austrian advantage.

Austria, indeed, seemed to have prospered, but by allowing her traditional Danubian interests to go by default while she upheld her power elsewhere. Most successfully, this had been done in Italy and Germany. Though surprised by the election of a 'liberal Pope' in 1846, the Austrian ascendancy in Italy was unshaken. The same was apparently true in Germany, though there were danger-signs. Though the formal and diplomatic subordination of Prussia to Austria continued, the growth of the *Zollverein* and the association of Austria with the thwarting of German nationality was slowly building a basis upon which a Prussian leadership of Germany would emerge far more dangerous than that of the days of Frederick the Great.

Nationalism and nationality had been throughout these years the forces which most obviously threatened the European balance. They had, in the Greek revolt, begun at last to complicate the historic interests of the great powers in the most backward part of Europe. The next country there whose national independence was likely to raise an international problem was Romania, whose self-determination and consolidation had taken another and important step forwards as a result of the Greek war. Soon after, it was undergoing economic transformation as a more or less tribal society crumbled with the new possibilities of exporting grain through the Straits which were created by the treaty of Adrianople. The increased cultivation which followed as the steppes were cut into by farmers doubled the population of the principalities between 1800 and 1850. Here was a problem in the making for a nation itself yet to be made. It was in western and central Europe, though, that, in 1847, men were most conscious of what nationalism might do. In part because of their high cultural level and literacy, it was beginning to be widely felt in Germany and Italy that national demands required to be taken account of. In Slav lands, too, such demands were crystallizing.

12 From Status to Contract

One of the most bitter critics of the reforms of Stein was the Prussian conservative von Marwitz. From the other side of a great ideological divide he denounced the reformer in language and a range of examples which goes to the heart of the social revolution in the Western World which was consummated in this era. Stein had inaugurated, said his critic,

the revolutionizing of our fatherland; the war of the propertyless against property, of industry against agriculture, of fluidity against stability, of crass materialism against divinely ordained institutions, of (so-called) utility against law, of the present against the past and future, of the individual against the family, of the speculators and money-changers against the land and the trades, of desk-bred theories against conditions rooted in the country's history, of book-learning and self-styled talents against virtue, honour and character.

In such passion, there speaks the anxiety of a whole society. He identified with great accuracy several key expressions of the fundamental revolution of his day, one more dangerous to traditional society than any mere rebellion of discontent. Von Marwitz identified the issue of the age, the choice between the two views of society differentiated at almost every point.

The end of the story was the victory of the new conception, which we may call market society. The essence of what was involved can be summed up in a famous phrase as one 'from status to contract', the coming of the idea that relations between men are more properly regulated by contractual obligations voluntarily undertaken than in any other way. The most obvious expression of this was economic, the new assumption that men should work or provide services in consideration of anticipated economic gain, and not because they occupied a certain position in society. Yet much more was involved than economic life alone and this is why the term 'market society' may be misleading if unqualified. More was involved, too, than can be contained in another historical portmanteau, that indicated by words like 'capitalism' or 'capitalist society'. Useful though such phrases can sometimes be, they are too restrictive (as well as often being misleading) to be used as general terms. The vision of individual men as exploiters of themselves, their capital, their skills and their opportunities – the ideal of the *carrière ouverte aux talents* – is fundamental to the change in society's economic organization, but affects much more than this. At its broadest, it gives the individual a new dignity and significance. Legal and institutional expressions of this are perhaps the most obvious and provide a good starting-point. Many examples could be given, from the individual rights enshrined in the Declaration of 1789, to the gratification of younger sons by the extension to them of rights of inheritance hitherto confined by primogeniture, or the liberation of the individual craft worker from the rules of the guild. Women hardly gained from this, an important limitation; still, at least the advocacy of their rights as individuals began in these years.

Legal rights only partly defined new spheres of action to the individual; new assumptions about what he could do with them are also important, though less easy to delineate. As men were released from the restrictions (and protection) of family, Estates, *Stände* or corporations which had defined their social relations under the *ancien régime*, ambition became more respectable, though, at the same time, conservative denunciation of it mounted. One cultural expression is worth a moment's attention: the young man in a hurry made his appearance in European literature. He had no eighteenth-century equivalent; the 'adventurer' of the *ancien régime* was nothing like him. Merit and desert could now be thought to justify untrammelled advancement. They combined with Romanticism's denunciation of the artifice and corruption which repressed the natural virtue of the good heart to produce the archetypal literary hero and bore of the next century and a half, the young man at loggerheads with his environment. One example and precedent above all pointed to what he might hope for if he were successful; Stendhal's Julien Sorel kept Bonaparte's picture under his mattress.

The idealization of revolt and liberation and the cult of the young which began at about this time were to produce extraordinary paradoxes. The nineteenth and twentieth centuries were to prove time and time again that the most telling criticisms of the world which replaced the *ancien régime* were to come from those who had enjoyed its privileges. The new order seemed to institutionalize the notion of criticism which Kant had seen as the central idea of his age, and even the idea of revolt. A young Jewish Rhinelander, the middle-class Karl Marx, was the living refutation of his own teaching that being preceded consciousness and that ideology was determined by social class. By 1847 he was a revolutionist seeking to accelerate the collapse of an industrial society not yet in existence anywhere outside the British Isles. The young Gladstone reared in Toryism and a man who was to go on to be the most romantic, even nostalgic, of all British prime ministers, was already in 1847 a zealous reformer, though his greatest hours as the liberator of the individual from the shackles of faith, tradition and history were still to come. In fiction, Stendhal again provides a touchstone of his age: Lucien Leuwen, his young hero, circulates exasperatedly in the world of French politics and finance, resenting the compromises it imposes upon him and seeking opportunities of rebellion when, after all (and to his rage), it is only his father's fortune that makes his career possible.

The idealization of revolt was an extreme example of a new mobility and fluidity within society. This was masked by the survival of the symbols and trappings of the past. The titled hierarchies of 1775 seemed still intact seventy-five years later. So, in form, they were, but contemporaries knew that the survival of the forms still did not mean there had not been important change.

William Cobbett was an English radical. In 1803 he was complaining that 'the ancient nobility and gentry of the kingdom have, with very few exceptions, been thrust out of all public employments.' This now seems an odd thing for a radical to deplore and it is not made much more comprehensible by his further remark that 'a race of merchants and manufacturers and bankers and loan jobbers and contractors have usurped their place.' This is not how many of us now see English society of his day, or that for many decades afterwards, dominated as its commanding heights seem to be by landed aristocracy and landed aristocratic values. Yet it is an important indicator. Cobbett was not making something up. However he exaggerated it, he rightly sensed a transformation at the roots of English society, even if the great families still dominated it.

England was the country where social change went furthest and fastest in this period (and, in justification of Cobbett, it may be noticed that Pitt's inflation of the peerage went unsurpassed until the buoyant days of Lloyd George). At first sight, continental nobilities were less changed. In 1847, even if a Protestant commoner was prime minister of France, titled aristocrats still dominated the higher reaches of government everywhere. In France the abolition of legal nobility had proved only temporary. Noblemen were still the great landowners of Restoration society, in which land was still the main source of wealth and social power. The forms of nobility were in fact more obvious and sometimes more insistent in a world newly conscious of the danger of disrespect for historic institutions. In France the old nobility was actually consolidated by the Revolution; distinctions and divisions within it had less significance after the Revolution than before. In Germany and Italy, too, the Napoleonic era brought great changes to nobility, but did not decrease its apparent importance. Even before the Revolution, Frederick the Great's dislike of ennobling commoner officers in the army and civil service had been abandoned and this meant more people with noble status, not fewer. The practice went so far that when, in 1840, Frederick William IV proposed to ennoble only those who owned land and to guarantee inheritance of their titles only if the property connected with it was maintained intact, he had to abandon the idea because of the outcry from civil servants. By then, hard times had driven many of the old landed and *Junker* families to seek places in the civil service, so that the old distinction so much felt by the reformers of the Stein era between the landed and service nobilities was much blurred. An increase in the number of noblemen and the pervasiveness of noble influence was the result.

Forms persisted in constitutional detail, though the duke of Wellington does not seem to have been as impressed as his Spanish companions by the revelation that as a Grandee of Spain he could keep his hat on in the royal presence. The glamour, the continuing aristocratic flavour of European society and the pageantry of hereditary rank none the less masked an important change in social power. In part, this is hinted at by the fact of dilution already remarked. There was no more talk, as in earlier times, of closing nobilities to further entrants. Moreover, though Europe's noblemen continued to fill the highest posts of administration and the armed services, they had lost their near-monopoly of important office by 1850 in many countries.

In part this was because of the bureaucratic evolution of the State; more and more jobs were created. In part it was because the barriers of privilege had been lowered or destroyed. Already in 1775, the grip of the Swedish nobility on the civil service had loosened to the point where more than half of those in its highest ranks were commoners, though the leading officials were still noblemen. By the middle of the nineteenth century almost half of the leading posts, too, were lost to them. On every front, the social changes of the era bring us back to the diminution of the importance of legal status, for all its prominence. The decreasing role of Orders and Estates as political realities was another sign.

In many countries, status had defined economic opportunity under the *ancien régime*. Formally, though the prohibition had largely fallen into desuetude before 1789, a French nobleman might not lawfully practice certain gainful occupations. In Prussia (and some other countries) there were lands which might belong only to noblemen and could not legally be sold to commoners by them (though economic pressure was making nonsense of this already in the early years of the nineteenth century). This again raises the question of the economic dimension of the great, if slow, revolution which was going forward. It was as economic liberation that the idea of individual self-assertion achieved some of its most striking expressions. It was the core of market society, embodied in the idea of the 'cash nexus' and the belief that the individual was the best judge of his own interests.

The new economic order offered men a rapid expansion of the community's wealth in return for the abandonment of old ideas and institutions. Social man, tied by a multitude of inherited and historically determined usages to the obligations of that station to which God had been pleased to call him, turned into economic man, rationally self-directed towards the maximization of his welfare. Scientific capitalist farming replaced the collective working of divided fields and the ties of service and justice between landlord and peasant. In the name of economic rationality governments were urged to abandon the regulation of economic life in pursuit of non-economic ends and tended to give up, together with the control of marketing and supply, many traditional social duties. Above all, property took on a new aspect. Its old collective, moral, quasi-tribal aspects dropped away as laws against entail, primogeniture, mortmain or collective exploitation gradually spread across Europe. It is not always easy to see through the tangle of legal qualifications which surrounds what is going on (English land law, above all, remained a jungle in which there lurked the survivals of an older view of property until the great Victorian reforms) but the essence of the process was that land was being turned into a commodity like any other. Not only would the industrialization of agriculture follow but a whole social order in the countryside would die. It was the sense that this lay ahead that so deeply wounded conservatives.

This whole complex change so far sketched in outline was deplored by many critics whom, like Marwitz, we have tended to forget because they stood on the Right of the spectrum of politics created by the French Revolution. Yet there were many of them. Lord Shaftesbury, the English factory-reformer who yet opposed the extension of the franchise, was an example. So was Carlyle, who recognized the justice of much popular agitation and affirmed in 1837 that *laissez-faire*, the economic doctrine which vulgarly symbolized the new world, was already out of date. (The phrase had, when he wrote, less than a half a century of life behind it, so fast had change been in England, the most advanced industrial society.) The later denunciations by Marx of social arrangements whose essentials he believed to reside in their capitalist foundation – the private possession and therefore control of the means of production – got its moral force, ironically, from something he shared with conservatives, anger at the rise of individualism and the decline of community.

Besides Great Britain and France, where new social forms were most obvious, the United States provided the most completely developed example of a society based on the individual. This accounted for much of the hostility felt towards the republic in Europe. The *ancien régime* had been in 1775 already even more completely extinct in North America than in the United Kingdom. Such marks of it as remained had been finally extirpated in a revolution which swept away quit-rents, tithes, entails and primogeniture. The United States knew no hereditary and titled status, nor an established Church except in parts of New England. In America men could already see before 1800 a nation which was socially quite different from any other in the world and owed little but its independence to revolution. Except in minor matters American society was not made by revolution; rather, the Revolution had been made because the society was already unlike any elsewhere.

The United States' historical heritage, though complex and rich, thus did not impede change, and the social consequences of geographical expansion and economic growth were not long in asserting themselves. They made American society even more unlike European. The practice soon began of paying a visit to the United States and then returning to Europe to deplore in print what had been seen. For the most part, such foreign commentators were content with the superficial and easy judgment that American life lacked refinement and the higher manifestations of culture and connected this with the absence of a formal social hierarchy such as that of Europe. One observer went much further and wrote a sociological masterpiece: this was Alexis de Tocqueville, whose *Democracy in America* appeared in 1835. The title was significant; de Tocqueville directed his attention to the working-out in the American environment of what he regarded as the key principle of the society which had taken root there, democracy. In the United States he believed he discerned the most important expression of a trend towards democracy which he believed to be worldwide, and it rested on the passion for equality.

In Europe, England and France were generally agreed to be the major states which most strongly expressed a break with the past, though England seemed to have got there by evolution, France by revolution. In each country, unfriendly critics noticed the assertiveness of the middle class, or, as the French called it, the *bourgeoisie*. In England this was easy to see; there was a vigorous assertion of its self-respect by those who believed themselves to be part of it. A Lord Chancellor spoke of the middle classes as the best part of the nation. The idealization of the middle class reached its apogee in these years; though, later, middle-class Englishmen were anxious to blur the distinctions between themselves and the representatives of landed wealth, in the 1830s and 1840s they gloried in it; if politics ever was about class in the United Kingdom, it was then, and by and large the division ran between the middle class and the landed gentry. In both of the major political debates of the early nineteenth century, over parliamentary reform and free trade, there was a conscious struggle of two societies, that of urban, commercial, industrialized England, against rural, agricultural, aristocratic England.

Less of such a conflict was to be seen in France. There, the *bourgeoisie* was an idea narrower in scope than the English 'middle class', which could be stretched far down the scale of wealth; indeed, it was almost a moral, rather than a sociological category. The French *bourgeoisie* of the July Monarchy, the era when it enjoyed most power and prestige, consisted of those who were not members of the nobility but who had considerable wealth derived predominantly from financial or commercial, but sometimes from industrial, enterprise. Members of this class, though often mocked for doing so, seem to have sought assimilation to the traditional hierarchies of French society much more eagerly than their English counterparts. Many historical circumstances would have to be taken into account in explaining the difference between the two countries. One would be the predominance in France of the habit of investing as soon as possible in land, rather than ploughing back profits into business. Another was the absence there of a respectable form of religious dissent with anything like the numerical importance of the British nonconformist connections which did so much to give moral identity to the British middle class; French Protestantism might be unrepresentatively prominent in the ranks of French business, but it was no such widely spread social force as nonconformity across the Channel.

Many recognized the importance of the middle classes in the evolving civilization of the nineteenth century. Like the Americans, they were mocked for their lack of taste and elegance, for their materialism and vulgarity, for their philistinism and obtuseness, especially in France. The cost of the society they were creating was often to be pointed out more or less explicitly – by Carlyle, Dickens, Proudhon and Marx, to name only a handful – but even such criticism could be combined with recognition of the positive achievement which went with it. Along with his denunciation of the power that had created the slums of Manchester, Marx also set out a grudging and bitter, but admiring, recognition of what the *bourgeoisie* had achieved, in *The Communist Manifesto* (which did not appear until 1848 but was commissioned in 1847).

Whatever the *bourgeoisie* was and whether it was responsible for them or not, most people could agree that it was in its growing cities that the new society of the nineteenth century showed its most striking novelty, and also its most repellent face. Something must be allowed for judgments made in a tradition formed by rural values. Traditionalists were likely to be biassed against city life in any form. After the Revolution it was additionally linked in their eyes with 'Enlightenment', sedition and the destruction of old social ties. Within a few years, in England they could see that a world of horrors was arising which justified an even greater sense of outrage and dismay. The eighteenth-century town was by no means always a pleasant place. It was usually filthy, smelly and ill-lit (though there were exceptions: London's whale-oil lamps were celebrated and admired). Behind noble façades and attractive piazzas lurked dreadful squalour. But this squalour became more squalid and the nastiness nastier as population growth laid new burdens on administration and police. Drains barely adequate for their eighteenth-century populations could not deal with the problems presented by the vastly greater London and Paris of the nineteenth century. The result was, among other things, a worsening of conditions already nearly intolerable. Most cities under the *ancien régime* shared two characteristics with fashionable watering-places and spas in this century: their death-rates were always higher than their birth-rates, and the population grew by immigration from elsewhere. Until very recently most European town-dwellers were probably immigrants or the children of immigrants from the countryside. There was not a very large chance that children born in the eighteenth-century city would survive, and the chance diminished in the early nineteenth century. Half the children born then in England failed to reach the age of five, and when the general expectancy of life at birth was about thirty-eight in England, that in Manchester was twenty-four. Existing diseases (cholera, for example) became more lethal as the population rose and as the population they attacked lived in yet dirtier and more crowded conditions. Building nowhere kept pace with population growth. Lodging-houses in Paris commonly let rooms to eight or nine men or women each, and Engels reported a group of twelve houses inhabited by Irish workers in London lived in by 461 persons, each with 175 cubic feet of space. In the yards and streets there swarmed livestock (milking-cattle were still normally kept in London). Overcrowding, in turn, brought the rudimentary cleansing and sanitary services of the day yet nearer to complete collapse. Things were made worse by medical ignorance (it was not known how infectious disease was transmitted) and by administrative machinery which rested on a structure designed for a different world. With a tradition of governmental initiative lacking in England, the French at first did best in tackling this, as readers of the almost lyrical description of the Paris sewers in Hugo's *Les Misérables* will recall. In 1847, London had 250,000 cesspools under its houses; they were emptied twice a year. For the surface drainage which was the main purpose of the sewers, Londoners still relied upon the Thames being able to perform as effectively as a drain as it already did as a water-supply. Napoleon had constructed a purification plant on the Seine above Paris, so here, too, the Parisians were better served.

In the end, the problems of a new urbanism required a revolution in the whole structure of English local government. This was a process which rolled on to completion only long after 1847. But by then a new confidence was already observable in English provincial towns transformed by industrialization which were the foci of the manufacturing areas which so struck foreign observers. This, rather than the slums of London and Paris, was where the new urbanism of market society was to be seen. They were amazed by the landscape of the new industrial areas, where the factory with smoking chimneys had replaced the spire of church or cathedral which was the dominant and equally characteristic visual feature of towns in an older era. It is easy to forget, so dramatic was this change, that big manufacturing units were not the typical expression of the early stages of industrialization, but an unusual one.

In the new manufacturing areas, where social and political hierarchies were unbuttressed by the old certainties of land, rank and religion, there gathered a new sort of working population, and this was one of the clearest signs that more than a change in the material fabric of society was going forward. This was the spectacle which for many observers most strongly epitomized the new society whose arrival they deplored. It struck them as heartless and cruel that men should live in conditions such as those Engels found in Manchester, and it seemed also to threaten civilization with violence and lawlessness from 'dangerous classes' huddled in the depths of a society conscious of the fragility of its police. The obliteration of the old patterns of community had gone furthest in Great Britain where a new sort of working population was most obvious. One test was the old parochial system of the Church; it was incapable of working as an effective framework of social organizations in the new manufacturing districts. In France it had been the peasants whose violence destroyed the old order in 1789, but in England frightened conservatives turned their gaze towards the new towns. The people who lived in them, feared as insubordinate and fractious, were taken as a model of what the future proletariat must become. This was somewhat misleading, for any such view paid scant regard to the evidence this population itself provided, in the suddenness with which it emerged, of the dynamism of the economy which had called it up and therefore to its possibilities of creating well-being. To be pessimistic about its unchanging nature was to underestimate the likelihood of change in the future. It was also to underestimate the variety within this population and to assume too easily that it could be summed up in easy generalizations, and second that it could be expected to show a self-conscious solidarity.

Modern historians have sometimes followed nineteenth-century reactionaries and revolutionaries in their simplifications, often because of ideological concern: they have been drawn to study the social impact of early industrialization by interest in the origins of popular movements and ideas. One recent expression of this has been a great effort which proceeded from an initial assumption that it was permissible to speak of 'a working class' in industrializing Great Britain to provide an index of its exploitation and abuse by its rulers in terms of the worsening of its conditions of life. There is now a large literature on what happened to the standard of living in England during the process of industrialization which a non-specialist is tempted to sum up as follows: the fact of an overall long-term increase in the country's consumption is unquestioned; in the long run people ate more and had more consumer goods; local, occupational and temporary aberrations and the difficulty of agreeing on what is the significant period make this an unhelpful statement if (as many historians feel) it is necessary to follow it with conclusions about the exploitation (or otherwise) of people involved in the process; in any case, consumption cannot take us very far as an index of well-being and we must also consider conditions of work, some of which were appalling, especially for women and children; these conditions, too, require to be seen in a very complex way, taking account of, for example, differences between emerging and declining trades; finally, the cultural and emotional conditions of town life in the early nineteenth century have to be compared to the primitive and restricted life of most countrymen if we are to assess changes in well-being – an almost impossible task. The whole controversy has had very valuable results in promoting investigation of many topics; there are signs, however, that it is now running out of steam. Perhaps this is just as well, since there are plenty of other questions about early industrialization which need scrutiny. Curiously, the basic controversy seems to be of little interest to the historians of industrialization in other countries; perhaps it tells us in the last resort as much about twentieth-century as about nineteenth-century Great Britain.

Whose lot grew worse and whose better may remain obscure, but it is unquestionable that, in the United Kingdom first and later elsewhere, labour in these years was more and more coming to be bought and sold solely with reference to the mechanism of the market. Thus labour followed land; specially protected and regulated by the law of the *ancien régime*, it was in the new world of the market a commodity like any other. This had been implicit in Turgot's abolition of the *jurandes* in 1776, to release enterprise and labour from the protective barriers erected by the skilled and thus bring into operation the beneficial and cheapening force of competition. He failed, but the generation of Le Chapelier succeeded. Their success came, in turn, to operate against new forms of self-defence with which working-men were experimenting to protect them against the effects of industrialism.

England began to shake off hostility to working-class organizations earlier than continental countries. Its Combination Acts were repealed in 1824 and thereafter trade unions were legal, though still restricted in the methods they might employ to gain their ends. This liberalization came about more because of different national rates of economic change and because of different legal traditions. The persistent distrust of voluntary association in France was to throw the town-dwelling workingman more and more into a position in which he was conscious of the law as an opponent to which he felt hostility, the law of the propertied and the employer, not his. He had a constant irritant in the legal requirement to produce a work record, endorsed by previous employers with their comments, when seeking new employment. Germany by 1847, on the other hand, had barely begun to shake its inheritance of corporate institutions. Long apprenticeship to a craft, restrictive practices and close municipal supervision of industrial life were still, broadly, the prevalent norms.

Apart from the new city, the factory was a striking symbol of a new world, though in the middle of the century it was still only in textiles that great agglomerations of labour were to be found under one roof. Even in 1847, the majority of English industrial workers were employed in groups of less than fifty. The huge Lancashire cotton-mills which first gave that industrial area a visual and urban character distinct from that of earlier manufacturing towns were unusual. The rhythms and patterns of work of the new society, on the other hand, were by then much more widely diffused. A different pattern of free time and holidays was required for the economical use of machinery. Artificial light – made easier by gas – liberated the manufacturer from the limits imposed by sunrise and sunset, and shift-working became possible. Traditional holidays became less important; factories ceased to close to take account of them. In continental Europe this was slowed down by the influence of the Roman Church, but the secularization of society sapped this resistance, too. In the second half of the nineteenth century, an examination of work-patterns in Hamburg showed that free time had by then become confined to Sundays only.

Another change was in the employment of women and children in manufacturing. There was nothing new about this in principle: domestic industry depended heavily on them (and so, for that matter, did the booming English agriculture of the Napoleonic War). What was new was the employment of large numbers of women and children in a new role as machine-tenders in factories for wages. They were an indispensable part of a rapidly expanding labour force as their greatly increased use in unskilled work in coal-mines showed. The resultant evils were soon remarked and rather less soon attacked by legislation. Not until the twentieth century were they eliminated in the Western World. By then they had done great damage. They were one of the most flagrant and tragic instances of the brutal indifference of market principles when applied to labour.

All these phenomena were symptoms of the basic change to market society. It was visibly and hugely different from the past and it felt different, too. Those who lived through the changes which produced it were conscious of a new dynamism; life was unstable and unpredictable in ways quite different from the past. It was increasingly affected by an economy which fluctuated much more readily and violently than formerly; profits, turn-over, employment, share-prices all swung about wildly and produced sudden and dramatic changes in men's fortunes, some of them disastrous. The cycle of short-term commercial boom and slump made its appearance. Yet perhaps the deepest and most disruptive impact was produced in a social and economic sector where change went most slowly of all, the countryside.

In 1775 the *ancien régime* was most firmly entrenched in the country-side, where most Europeans then lived, as they did still in 1847. The greatest social revolution of all between these years was the slow, incomplete, untidy one which broke up irreparably the traditional structures of rural Europe. It is very hard to describe in general terms, though its technical and economic aspects have been touched on; its social forms now call for attention because it was the most vivid demonstration that the *ancien régime* was dying and that a new society based on individualism and economic ties was coming into existence.

Its most striking manifestation was the retreat of seigneurial institutions – feudalism, as they were usually summed up – and the economics and technology that went with them. Criticism of them by humanitarians, free-trade theorists and royal lawyers had been going on for a long time and they were much eroded already in some countries by 1789, but the revolutionary wars were decisive in generalizing this change;

slowly, it began to roll eastward. Much more was involved than formal lordship; the whole traditional rural community was in question. The picture of what was going forward in the countryside is clearest and can be indicated by two words: emancipation and individualism. The first was much used in Germany to characterize agrarian change in this period. Land and peasant alike were being freed, not only from legal servitude and personal dependence but from the disciplines of communal practice and tradition. Property was increasingly held by individuals who had independent control of its exploitation, whether or not they enjoyed outright freehold possession. This was most obvious in the spread of enclosed or demarcated ground where there had been common fields.

A great impulse was given to this development by technical change. Even to follow a new rotation at once involved an innovator in a tangle of obstacles. Law and custom, popular prejudice and ignorance, could be cut through only at great cost and often could not be cut through at all without action by the state. This is why half the story of the agriculture revolution is social change, no less drastic and innovatory than industrialization because it was longer drawn-out, but the great variety of environments involved makes description in general terms difficult. Violent and startling contrasts could be found in the status of the peasant, in his degree of freedom or bondage, in the demands which might legally be made upon him in cash, kind or labour, in his practical independence to exploit his holding.

Within the great open field area which ran from the English Midlands and the Seine up across northern Germany to southern Sweden and Denmark, the usual holding in 1775 had been everywhere a scattered collection of strips. In this area there were plenty of landless peasants, but they were not so common as in Italy or southern Spain. In northern Spain and southern France, more consolidated peasant holdings could be found, many of them farmed by share-cropping. In much of western and southern Germany more consolidated units were the rule. Status varied just as much. There were, formally, serfs in Holland, but they looked just like prosperous small-holders in other countries and did not labour under any but the most formal of legal disabilities. In Poland, on the other hand, serfdom had a very bitter and depressing character; the Polish peasants were probably the worst-off in both real and legal terms of any in Europe. In eastern Germany, too, across the Elbe, servile status was normal and some peasants lived precarious lives, bound to the soil if they wanted to move, but evictable at will. Some could even be sold, like the Russian serf, and the service obligations to render service with their own beast as well as their labour extended to the provision of household and general services by their families. Broadly speaking, the obligation to do labour in the landlords' fields – *Robot* – was general to the east of the Elbe and in the Habsburg dominions other than Italy and Austria. These complicated relationships stood in the way of effective exploitation of existing knowledge and resources. No single change was sufficient to deal with the problems they presented, and any particular solution would produce very different results in the different environments in which it was deployed. 'Emancipation' was increasingly seen as the answer, but it meant many different things in practice.

The rolling back of both bonded labour and feudal dues before 1847 is far from complete but is a clear general trend. The degree of the peasant's liberation from his community is less easy to generalize about. The restraints which it laid upon him in his exploitation of his land, for example, were unbreakable so long as the open-field system of strips persisted, whoever formally owned them. The separation of the peasant's property rights from the community as well as from lordship was, therefore, essential. This might mean the consolidation of strips, the break-up of the old field pattern and the alienation of common rights to individuals. To some, therefore, emancipation came as a burden. Common rights made it possible for a poor man to keep a few geese or pigs, and meant perhaps the difference between subsistence and starvation. Emancipation bore heavily upon him. It meant the emancipation of the landlord, too. As he was more and more concerned with the simple renting of land, the fewer obstacles to improvement the better, and that could mean clearances.

England, the Netherlands and to a lesser extent France in the eighteenth century were ahead of other countries in this movement as they were in their relative technical advance. English agriculture had been shedding its medieval incumbrances since the fifteenth century. The most obvious legal and social evidence by 1775 was the enclosure of commons and waste. Enclosure Acts made up much of the work of parliament (there were more than five thousand in the eighteenth century) and the rate of enclosure came to a peak around 1800. For all practical purposes, the internal English grain trade was by then completely free, though magistrates had sometimes set prices in the recent past. Bounties were paid to exporters in the eighteenth century as a way of getting rid of a surplus at the expense of the taxpayer; this was a distortion of the free market, but, of course, like the 'Corn Laws' introduced in the years after 1815, it was in the interest of the most powerful of English pressure groups, the landlords whose rents were thought to be in jeopardy without it. To this extent, English regulation of the grain trade was different from that practised in other European countries before the era of modern tariff policy; it registers a modern political world of interest groups.

In France enclosure had been legal and even encouraged by official policy from the 1760s onwards. Yet, like the freeing of the grain trade, it had run into deep popular opposition. After Turgot, other attempts had been made to liberate the grain trade, notably and unhappily on the eve of the Revolution. They too ran aground and were abandoned once food shortages became grave enough to cause alarm. The French revolution itself brought only a temporary change in this respect. Though in 1791 the law freed the cultivator from any restraint upon the growing and marketing of grain, popular outcry within two years resulted in the introduction of the first *Maximum*, an attempt to control prices. This was to look backwards to the *ancien régime* rather than forward to post-revolutionary France, though it was an understandable response by a government to exigencies created by war, natural dearth and civil disorder. A similar pattern of advance followed by partial retreat can be seen in the matter of common lands. In 1792 it was decreed that except for woodlands they should all be divided between the inhabitants of the commune. Soon this division was made optional, and then in 1803 further alienation of communal property was forbidden. Much, of course, had been sold by then. France therefore moved more slowly towards the domination of the market in her rural life than did Great Britain.

The Revolution had, on the other hand, brought to France a great rearrangement of property. A huge amount of land changed hands, for the state confiscated not only the possessions of the church but also those of many enemies of the state and emigrants who had gone abroad to avoid living under the Revolution. Not all of this came up for sale in the end, though much did. It is still not accurately measured, but the rough effect of the Revolution on the distribution of landed property was that it added substantially to the holdings of men already rich before the Revolution, gave many more peasants than before 1789 enough land to make viable small farms, added very little to the amount of land held by those who already held very little and brought virtually nothing to those who had nothing at all. Coupled with the effect of French laws of inheritance, this seems to have had a restrictive effect on agricultural practice. The pattern of exploitation in France continued to be that of the small-holding, often but not always consolidated, and the entrenchment of the peasant was to prove everywhere a barrier to technical innovation, emancipated though he might be from seigneurial or communal restraint. The pace of agricultural change in France might have been quicker had not the better-off peasant done well in the Revolution. He had an insurance against disaster (and therefore a disposition not to innovate) in his secure possession of a viable unit of exploitation. Almost all the important advance of French agriculture was the work, at least to begin with, of landowners of substantial estates, such as Lafayette, the hero of two worlds, who is virtually unknown for his least qualified success, the introduction of the Merino sheep to the Orléanais.

German agrarian development started from a different background. Germany was already by 1800 visibly divided into two zones of husbandry, the west and the east, the boundary between them very roughly on the Elbe. Within each of these zones there were manifold varieties of governmental policy at work before the French Revolution, which itself had a double effect. In the first place French occupation led in many places to the direct application of the laws abolishing feudalism, serfdom and so on. Second, the wars stimulated a reform movement, notably in Prussia, where there was launched in 1807 the most firmly pressed and far-reaching of all governmental programmes of emancipation. As, after 1815, Prussia's superficial area was something like a third of that of the German Confederation, and also included a huge tract of territory in the east which lay outside it, it had important consequences.

On the actual property of the Prussian Crown, much could be done without legislative change at all, but elsewhere reform had to wait until the shock of a great disaster had destroyed the confidence of conservatism. This came with the overthrow of the famed Prussian military power at Jena in 1806, which followed a persistent agricultural crisis leading to sales of noble estates in the early years of the century. An important conditioning fact was Prussia's membership of two Europes. West of the Elbe, her social and agrarian structure was much the same as that of France; this was the open-field zone of peasants living in various practical degrees of independence of lords who might formally be feudal seigneurs, but were not usefully described as such. In some parts of these territories the physical presence of French law and administration had already made some liberalization possible. East of the Elbe, in the March of Brandenburg, but much more beyond the Oder, in Prussia proper, Pomerania and East Prussia, society was very different. This was a land of medieval frontier colonization and here the manorial estate was still a social, administrative and judicial reality as the nineteenth century began. The *Junkers* were feudal lords, the descendants of conquerors who had held knights' fees; their peasants were bound to their estates, and economic reality was reinforced by the landlord's jurisdiction and police power. Though formally antiquated, this structure was agriculturally efficient; unlike many French landlords, the *Junker* squires were usually direct exploiters of their own land, farmers in their own right, interested in the development of their estates as a productive unit unencumbered by restraints upon profit. Paradoxically, they were therefore ready for the introduction of new methods and

213

were to prove by 1847 the pioneers of German agricultural improvement. It was in the German east that the great strides of German
agriculture were to be made, not among the smallholders of the west,
whose low productivity and poverty still troubled German governments
in the twentieth century.

From 1807 to 1821 a series of Prussian edicts brought about the legal
emancipation from the manor; the next thirty years saw the working
out of what this meant in the reassembly of holdings and estates from the
strips and enclosed common lands. They made possible the ending of
servile status, the separation of the individual from the communal
holding, the separation of the land of lord from that of peasant, the
ending of manorial justice, but they also deprived the peasant of the
protection which the connection with the land by a legal tie had hitherto given him in many places.

The effects of this legislation accentuated even more the contrast of
east and west. In western Prussia, the peasant's new independence in a
zone where traditional cultivation was dominant put fresh obstacles in
the way of consolidation. In east Prussian lands the peasant population
was divided sharply by the reforms. The effect on the more prosperous
peasants – those with the biggest holdings – was not very different from
that in France: their share of land in separations of communal property
increased their relative advantage. The disappearance of the feudal
order cleared the way for the beginning of a substantial class of yeomen.
The poorer peasants, on the other hand, were liable to sink towards the
class of landless labourer, for they were deprived of the supplementation
of their livelihood which communal rights had provided.

In the other German states, in most of which there was a preponderance of peasant holdings, eighteenth-century reform by enlightened
despots had not gone far, though there were areas (Alsace and Austrian
Swabia, for example) where serfdom had long been abolished. In the
Rhineland, French occupation did more to break up the grip of traditional cropping routines. In the 1830s, servitude was abolished in
Saxony and Hanover. Yet the general effect of liberalizing legislation
which followed the Prussian lead was small before 1847. The crucial
tests of the extent of enclosure and the rearrangement of holdings show
that little progress had been made by mid-century in Bavaria or
Württemberg; strip holdings were still usual in Wiesbaden in the 1840s.
By 1847 rural Germany – and this meant most of Germany – was much
less removed from the Middle Ages than was rural France, for all the
survivals of open grazing that could be found there. This was a great
contrast with England, where the smallholder's disappearance proceeded almost *pari passu* with improvement.

This picture of variety could be amplified by citing examples drawn from other countries. Feudalism existed in 1775 in Savoy and Piedmont, but the process of liberation began there with the governments of the *ancien régime* which introduced legislation in the 1770s and 1780s. Enlightened despotism played a big part in change in Denmark. Enclosure legislation in the eighteenth century was followed by substantial rearrangements, often by agreement, and consolidation of individual holdings. Although there were still some formal feudal survivals to be found in 1847, the Danish rural economy then rested basically upon a population of free peasants paying rent. Poland presented a very different picture. The legislation which applied to other Prussian lands was deliberately not applied in Prussian Poland so that Polish peasants might have some protection against their own landlords.

The result is a confusing picture. But it draws attention at least to important negative facts. One is that the actual ownership of land is often a misleading formality; what mattered was freedom of exploitation. Above all, though the achievement of European agriculture is great in this period, it is really the achievement of only a part of Europe. There were increasingly less impressive economic results the further one went down the scale of ownership and exploitation. Progress was something to be looked for on big farms, not on peasant holdings. Arthur Young's optimistic dictum that 'the magic of property turns sand to gold' was by no means borne out universally. Extremes of practice varied between the high farming of an English tenant or a Prussian *Junker*, and those parts of Russia and Poland where, even in the nineteenth century, a money economy had barely begun to establish itself. In much of Europe, therefore, for all the reality of the long-term upward curve in productivity, the material basis of agriculture must have appeared little changed by 1847.

What would have been much more noticeable would have been the institutional changes in rural society. These were widespread and were expressed both in striking changes in legal relationships and in changes in the ownership of land. It was these changes, summed up in the word 'emancipation', which constituted a rural revolution, for they signalled the coming of an economic order which would tie the countryside into capitalist society, breaking down traditional obstacles and ending a rural order once the norm almost everywhere. The effects on the peasants were fundamental. It has been said that from about 1500 to about 1850 the great social question in Europe was about what should be the peasants' place in society. The second date marks an epoch not because that place had by then everywhere radically changed from what it had been in the Middle Ages but because by then it was clear that emancipation into the status of the free individual exploiter or the free competitor in a free labour-market was what lay ahead.

Meanwhile, few peasants were better-off. The multiplication of smallholders tended to impose a deadweight of conservative practice; land in Europe for decades after 1800 and well into the twentieth century was still tilled as it had been immemorially. Sir John Clapham was unequivocal about the overall picture in France and West Germany: 'Broadly speaking, no general and thorough-going improvement can be registered in peasant agriculture before the railway age.' In other places, where emancipation brought more landlessness, technical improvement could be seen side by side with poverty. In the Baltic lands, wealthy Germany landlords and prosperous Latvian and Esthonian kulaks lived side by side while below them was a growing population of poor, landless peasants whose turn would not come until after 1918. In East Prussia, the effects of legal reform in breaking up traditional social practice led to greater freedom of choice in marriage and trade: by mid-century this helped to produce a boom which doubled population, and then men began to worry about employment. The multiplication of smallholdings made possible by the introduction of the potato was fundamental in producing the contemporaneous and disastrous rise in the Irish population which met its Malthusian nemesis in a great famine in 1846.

In the long run, a social and political revolution was implied almost everywhere in eastern Europe and the Danube valley by population growth. There would follow clashes of nationalities and demands for a political voice. In these parts increasing population was not offset by industrialization; the result were the so-called 'dwarf' peasants whose holdings were too small to support them and the landless who provided cheap migrant labour. The story of south Italy, Sicily or Andalusia was similar; though in these areas there were no national differences to channel discontent, the great rural slums of the future were in the making by 1850, as the peasantry multiplied and was more and more driven down to the status of wage-earners. These were to be the areas of continuing unrest and violence, tempered by the outlet, more and more accessible, of emigration, either across the seas or to the growing cities. The old notion that the rural community was responsible for its own collapsed before the strains which rising populations and growing poverty placed upon it, but the old idea of settlement could nowhere be altogether abandoned until better transport and industrialization made the movement of labour easy and therefore a free labour-market a reality. One sort of community was being hammered to pieces before another could be put together. Even in England, where social change went fastest, the problem of rural poverty was insoluble within the old framework by 1800, but it was only in the 1830s that the principles of a new sort of society were put into practice in a new form of poor relief.

The political consequences of distress were by no means always likely to find expression in demands for further extension of the benefits of emancipation. Rural Europe had never been a quiet and orderly place and it had long been little policed by the State. Peasants were often turbulent and dangerous. Landlords lived in fear in bad years, and their womenfolk even more so. But, except when they detonated political changes desired by others – as they did in France in 1789 – peasant movements were almost always reactionary. Peasants tenaciously resisted agricultural improvement and capitalist exploitation of land, preferring communal usage and the morcellation of property. In France they were the only considerable social force behind counter-revolution. In Naples in 1799 they had formed the Sanfedist army of Cardinal Ruffo and eagerly set about the lynching of progressive noblemen and middle-class Jacobins; they were the backbone of an insurrection against the French and their Jacobin satellites which took place in Tuscany (to the cry of '*Viva Maria!*', for the Blessed Virgin was supposed to have appeared personally to encourage the insurrectionists). If the Habsburgs had been able to bring themselves to trust any popular force against Napoleon, it was in the Catholic peasantry of the Tyrol that they would have found their staunchest supporters. Peasants formed the armies that followed Napoleon out of Russia and beat him in Germany (and subsequently guaranteed Russia a military hegemony which was for thirty-five years the keystone of European reaction). In 1846 the peasants of Galicia turned on their Polish landlords and massacred fourteen hundred of them, thus nipping in the bud a Polish revolution and ensuring that the province remained quiet two years later when the rest of the Empire exploded. The Habsburg government could hardly feel ungrateful, but was to be embarrassed when the peasants looked to it for reward in the form of lightened burdens.

The truly popular resentment of peasants in so many places at what was happening to them, reactionary in the deepest sense as it was, makes it impossible to depict the great social transformation of the early nineteenth century as just a duel of privilege with legal equality or of progress against obscurantism. A contest between two ages, two concepts of society, was in progress. On one side was the modern world, whether its sources are revolutionary or benign – the world of individualism, liberalism, the market and rationalism. On the other was the Middle Ages. Yet neither existed in pure form nor was the clash often so clearcut as a short account must suggest. There is no tidy picture. The logically prior concomitant of industrialization was the crumbling of what may loosely be termed the feudal order, but in England this had, as we have noted, already happened long before; in the American colonies only a few of its forms had ever been present. In continental Europe it was delayed much longer, but its final collapse, when it came, was much more rapid. Though it was far from complete in 1847, nothing of great importance in it was to survive more than a couple of decades afterwards. This was the measure of the decisiveness of these years.

13 Mentality and taste

Society is ideas as well as institutions. Changes in economics and demography alter these ideas and therefore the way men see and understand the world, but they also take place within a setting of ideas already formed. The horizons set by these ideas provide – if only temporarily – limits to the effects of change because they offer men ways of understanding what is going on which are effective for some purposes and not for others. Ideas in the early nineteenth century had to interpret political, economic, social and technological changes more rapid and widespread than anything yet seen. The roots of the mentality of most Western men then still lay deep in the Christian past, though a minority of them were more aware of the Enlightenment inheritance.

The clearest embodiment of Enlightenment was the continuing and growing recognition given to science. This had been a characteristic of European intellectual life since the beginning of the eighteenth century. Because chemical and electrical experimentation was more spectacular than had been much of the early, more analytical, work of mathematicians and cosmographers, the prestige of science was undoubtedly enhanced by the attendance of the fashionable at scientific (and pseudo-scientific) experiments in the closing years of the *ancien régime*. Science kept its prestige but in the early nineteenth century took a new shape as a central form of human knowledge and a central cultural institution. This was the beginning of the era in which we still live. A change in terminology provides a clue. In 1775 those who investigated nature were still termed 'natural philosophers': by 1847 the word 'scientist' was in use.

The change was perhaps least remarkable in a zone in which science is now reckoned commonly to have its most obvious effects. This was technology. On the whole, science, the systematic investigation of the natural world, still contributed less to technological advance than did empirical experience and the accumulated skills and insights of mechanics and designers. It was much more important that science was more and more quickly changing the mentality and world outlook of the educated.

By the middle of the nineteenth century, there was already available that full, unqualified materialist faith in the infinite power of science to manipulate nature which a later generation would call 'scientism'. The fantasies and speculations of non-scientists often showed this more clearly than the statements of scientists themselves. Saint-Simon's vision of the possibilities of a technocratic society are one example, but the outstanding one is provided by a thinker upon whom he had great influence, though with whom he later fell out, Auguste Comte, who gave its name to the philosophical movement called Positivism. Comte's ideas express more fully the influence and example of science in his age than do those of any contemporary natural scientist. Characteristically, he proposed to the French government (though unsuccessfully) the establishment of the first chair in the history of science at Paris, since he thought that the progress of real knowledge should certainly be taught where the history of dreams and aberrations (that is, religion and philosophy) already had its professors. It was his aim, which he believed to be a practical one, to explain social and moral phenomena as completely and rigorously as science had explained (and would continue increasingly to explain) the phenomena of the natural world. Explanation here meant adherence to what the age took to be the model provided by natural science, the statement of general laws governing the behaviour of phenomena and the relations between them.

The model of scientific knowledge generally acceptable could be found in the work of Laplace, who derived it, substantially, from Newton's world-view, and it was to be dominant until the end of the nineteenth century. It saw the universe as essentially a collection of lumps of matter, whose nature was finite and measurable, since they were made up of irreducible atoms, though they were combined in a great variety of forces and arrangements by regular laws. This material universe was in principle completely explicable and, therefore, subject to manipulation. Man, uniquely, was the free and reasonable being of Enlightenment mythology, able to choose ends in an otherwise determined universe. Some people had aready gone a stage further: perhaps Man was determined, too. But that was a minority view, and Comte's confidence that he could create a science of society by discovering its laws – and he coined a name for it: sociology – was not acceptable to many educated men who would have accepted, broadly speaking, the scientific interpretation of the natural world.

The repute and prestige of science was publicly manifest in institutions and proposals for educational reform. This was a great age for the renovation of academic structures to give new support to science. The role of the French revolutionary and Napoleonic governments was paramount and exemplary. The Constituent Assembly had plans but no time to reorganize French education around a core of science, and the Convention gave way to clamour against 'aristocracy' to the extent of suppressing the old academies, but under the Directory they were revived and with them was created the National Institute with responsibility for state patronage of learning. Its scientific section was the most important.

The Institute was very much the creation of men in the Enlightenment tradition. The reorganization of French education under Napoleon was a more utilitarian and pragmatic business, but, like other achievements of that regime, it was rooted in earlier plans. Their most famous embodiments were the *Ecole normale supérieure* of 1812 which was to set standards for the whole of French education, and the *Ecole polytechnique*, among whose class of 1814 was Auguste Comte. In these institutions scientists were professors and communicated their ideas not merely to other scientists but to pupils.

These institutions were at the heart of the fact of French pre-eminence in science in the early nineteenth century. It was helped by Bonaparte's preference for scientific over literary intellectuals (Laplace was at one time his minister of the interior). Other Institutes were created in French satellites and provinces abroad. They were imitated in Berlin and St Petersburg. In Prussia, intellectual went along with political and economic reform. Jena posed a challenge to Prussian culture as well as to the state, and one answer to it was the foundation of the University of Berlin, an amalgamation of all the learned institutions of the capital into one great foundation. Within a few years, its example and inspiration were felt throughout the German universities. The first fruits were historical and philological, but by the 1830s it was clear that a great scientific advance was under way in Germany. The symbolic date was 1826, when the chemist Liebig returned from his studies at Paris to open his research laboratory at the University of Giessen; at this moment the baton passed from France to Germany in chemistry, and a century of German pre-eminence in almost every field of natural science began. Yet the most fundamental science of the age was going on in Italy and England, where Galvani, Volta and Faraday carried out between 1780 and 1831 the investigations and experiments on which a later revolution in power – the exploitation of electricity – was to be based.

In these developments may be seen developing the science-centred Western civilization of the next century. It was a matter not only of positive scientific advance but also of the sapping and disrupting of traditional mentality by influences drawn from science. Though this was for a long time a change affecting only intellectuals, increasing literacy and the play of political forces had already spread some of these influences deeply down into the most developed Western societies by 1847. Most striking was the undermining of the authority of the Bible, upon which all Protestant and much Roman Catholic Christianity rested. The first important sources of its subversion were geology and natural history. In the eighteenth century it had already been noted that Biblical chronology could not be made to fit accumulating fossil and biological evidence. In the 1830s these ideas at last began to gain a wider public, and one of the most important agencies of this was the publication of *Principles of Geology*, by an Englishman, Charles Lyell. He explained landscape and geological structure in terms of forces still at work and still observable: wind, rain and so on. They were not, therefore, results of a single act of divine creation. Moreover, Lyell also pointed out, the presence of fossils in different geological strata implied that the creation of new animals had been repeated in each geological age. This raised grave questions, not to be brought to a head before 1847, but undermining the authority of scripture, and therefore the inherited conglomerate of ideas.

The new and growing prestige and importance of natural science was also manifest in the appearance in the early nineteenth century of the first 'social science' and the characteristic mental product of market society, Political Economy. This study was raised on the foundations laid out by Adam Smith by practioners who have gone down in history as the 'classical economists', a term invented by Marx, who combined admiration for their intellectual achievement with an intense dislike of their conclusions and what he believed to be their influence. Most of them were English, and the great names among them are those of Malthus, Ricardo, Senior and James Mill. They created the framework within which discussion of economics was to continue for the next century and this obscures the differences between them. These differences make it harder to summarize what they thought and taught than what they were believed to have thought and taught. There were sometimes acrimonious exchanges within the Political Economy Club where they often met. In spite of their reputation and the vulgarization of what they said, they were by no means worshippers of the market to the point of condemning outright any public and legal intervention with it. Poor Malthus has had almost the worst press of any, but he spoke approvingly of the efforts of Robert Owen, the first great practitioner of the co-operative ideal, welcomed Factory Acts to control the abuse of child labour and proposed that subsidies should be paid for bringing marginal land into tillage.

This symbolizes one of their enduring problems. They knew, or believed that they knew, that the operation of economic laws which they discerned at work around them and derived deductively from self-evident premises produced a conflict between classes because of the operation of 'iron laws' of rent and wages. None the less, they also believed that a self-regulating and harmonious economic system *might* be realized; since it was conceivable, surely it was possible? The means might be discerned in a growing rationality of economic behaviour. This meant in practice that the working-man should be encouraged to behave like an *entrepreneur*, showing thrift, enterprise, prudence and industry in the maximization of his own satisfactions. It is, indeed, reasonable to assume that if this were achieved, then the laws of the market would operate to produce the sort of equilibrium they had in mind. It should be remarked that this idea, though pretty much a practical failure, was deeply progressive and, above all, liberal, in its tendency. It rested on nothing less than the assumption that all men are inherently equal. It expressed uncompromisingly the revolutionary potential of capitalism.

To popularize these ideas was a great achievement, but the classical economists believed they had given economics the standing of a natural science by discovering economic laws like the laws governing the natural world. Malthus' gloomy adumbration of the laws of population was a major cultural step. Oddly, for a clergyman, he asserted that the regulators of society and the economy should not be revelation or moral aspiration, or even will, but recognition of irrefragable, non-human mechanisms. It was an assertion that the boundaries of the possible were much narrower than had been thought and it implied a new delineation of the providence of morality. The *cupiditas* which had been denounced by theologians had become the beneficent mainspring of economic improvement in Adam Smith; Malthus proclaimed that regardless of human aspiration, the fundamental rhythms of economy and society were shaped by laws as implacable as those of, say, gravity. This was a reorientation of the intellect of a whole civilization. Moral and economic categories were to be separated as never before.

Another nineteenth-century debt to Enlightenment was the pervasiveness of the ideas and values summed up in the word Utilitarianism. The famous expression which summed up the utilitarian ethical good – the greatest happiness of the greatest number – has origins which are still obscure. This is symptomatic: much of Utilitarianism was simply deduction from and elaboration of ideas which were commonplaces of Enlightenment. One man none the less dominated Utilitarianism in England, where its success was greatest. This was Jeremy Bentham, whose fecundity and ingenuity of mind were displayed in a huge output of books, articles and letters throughout his long adult life (he died in 1832, at the age of eighty-four). By then, among the many practical matters to which he had given his attention and enthusiastic support were the anti-slavery movement, the reform of penal law, the improvement of poor relief, proposals to cut Suez and Panama canals, the registering of births and deaths, the taking of regular censuses and the well-being of factory workers. These things, too, must be accounted as secondary intellectual interests: his main work in his own eyes, and possibly his most important legacy, was his writing on jurisprudence, which, said an admirer, he found a chaos and left a science.

The summary list of Bentham's activities reveals the predominant bias of Utilitarianism: it was a reforming philosophy. Broadly speaking, the psychology upon which it rested assumed that men could normally judge best for themselves what would maximize their own happiness. The task of the statesman, therefore, was to remove the legal obstacles in the way of the individual's search for happiness; only those obstacles were to be allowed to remain which were necessary to assure that the greatest number could seek happiness with the least interference. It was a paradoxical outcome of this liberating, cheerful creed that, like the market system, it should have come later to be seen as a drab, narrow, materialist affair. Perhaps this only shows that the temperament with which a philosophy is joined is as important as that philosophy's content in determining practical results. Bentham was a benign, cheerful man: many Utilitarians were not.

Much ink has been spent on saying what the practical influence of Utilitarianism was. There is a problem here in distinguishing between the vulgarized, vague assimilation by society of utilitarian principles and the conscious deployment of those principles in government. The difference is not unlike that between the vulgarized *laissez-faire* ideas which came to be the creed of nineteenth-century business and the refined teaching of the political economists. This parallel has some interest because both utilitarian and *laissez-faire* ideas generated a powerful push in English society towards the removal of reform of historic institutions and the liberation of the individual from restraint, while at the same time politicians and administrators strove to put theory into practice in ways which led to the extension of state activity and authority. The enthusiastic onslaught of British utilitarian administrators upon native custom in India was one example; another, somewhat more bizarre, was the proposal for standard burials of bodies in standard coffins fitting standard railway trucks which was one of the notions of a great English public servant, Chadwick.

It was in England that both utilitarian ideas and the revolutionizing of society by market principles had gone furthest by 1847, though not without protest. The great triumph of political economy had been the campaign to repeal the Corn Laws; it long gave great prestige to free trade, yet, on the other hand, many found repellent the new Poor Law, which attempted to deal with poverty by setting up a self-regulating price of social machinery. Its theoretical core was the use of the free labour market and the psychological doctrine that men were fundamentally directed by the fear of pain and search for pleasure. To make these work automatically, all that was required was a workhouse for the poor in which conditions, though not as bad as those of starvation and homeless misery outside, were just less tolerable than life on the lowest current wages of an employed man. Such a system, it was calculated, would drive the able to seek work and leave only the absolutely incapable dependent upon public relief. 'Political Economist', we are told, was used as a swear-word in the 1830s to denote an enemy of the common people.

Such social engineering was very remote from the complex bundle of emotions, ideas and images we lump together as 'Romanticism'. Few terms are so incapable of definition, so loosely circumscribed, so abused. Once beyond its emphasis on sentiment, intuition and suggestion, rather than on rationalizing, empirical experience and direct statement, it is each man for himself in saying what Romanticism was. Many contradictions have been discerned within it. One person will seize upon its stress on the individual, another on that on the collective, one on its respect for will and creativity, another on its awareness of the weight of history and nature. Some whom we must call 'romantics' were revolutionaries, but others were reactionaries; Mazzini was a romantic, and so was the young Tory Gladstone.

Chronology is not of much help, though a sense of belonging to a generation whose master-idea is that of freedom can be discerned in those articulate youngsters who were coming to maturity in the decade after 1815. Soon this was to produce colossal and monstrous developments, in the ruthless egotism of Stirner, for example, who ended the preface to his book with the words 'Nothing is more to me than myself!' This foreshadowed the self-indulgences of our own destructive century; here it is more interesting as evidence of how far Europe's intellectals had come since the *ancien régime*. Goethe (who died in the same year as Bentham) had expressed a similar striving for self-assertion within the traditional framework provided by a famous story, that of *Faust*, unhappy in his limitless, unsatisfiable desire. In this great dramatic poem, though the romantic hero is still located in a universe independent of him and still capable of redemption by love.

One of the most characteristic expressions of the romantic quest for freedom and self-assertion was a new attitude to art and artists. Mozart and Haydn had been great masters, and were known to be, but had still operated within the parameters set by a public which saw music as an adjunct to society and provided appropriate forms of patronage. With Beethoven we are at the dawn of another artistic epoch, and music is liberating itself from the drawing-room, church and theatre to become pure art. Beethoven was the first great figure in whom can be discerned the romantic image of the artist, compelled by his internal daemon, owing service to his art above all else; his name is the only artist's name which *cannot* be ignored in any discussion of these years. Even his huge technical skills seem less important in establishing his standing than a spiritual nature he himself felt to be different in kind from that of other men. Another artist, Shelley, also pitched the claims of his own art high, indeed so high as to be preposterous; 'poetry', he wrote in 1820, 'is indeed something divine. It is at once the centre and circumference of knowledge; it is that which comprehends all science, and to which all science must be referred.' He went on to say that composition had about it much that was inspired, unteachable and irrational and thus endorsed again the age's vision of the artist as the man set apart, at least a prophet and perhaps a god.

An ardent taste for freedom was no more likely to be satisfied with the political stabilization which followed 1815 than with the constraints of the artistic world of the *ancien régime*. About that stabilization there was much that was clearly artificial. This attracted criticism from romantics who sought to turn men away from calculation and prudence to the guidance which politics could be given by Will, Feeling, Nature or History. Here was one of the great taproots of modern political irrationalism and in practice it could feed revolution and reaction alike. Appeals to such entities were essentially appeals for faith. Yet the romantic appeal to History claimed to be grounded in fact. It is indubitable that one of the great intellectual achievements of the early nineteenth century was the creation of a new conception of what the study of history might be. It was often rooted in a precise social concern, such as that shown by Burke and Herder for the uncovering of the nature of community, for example, or in reflection on the phenomenon of historical change, manifested above all in the French Revolution, such as that of Hegel. The heart of the romantic revolution in history was not merely a new nostalgia for the past, a more passionate antiquarianism, but a deepening sense of the real differences between peoples and their evolution in time. This was prefigured in the eighteenth century, but in fact opened the way to a relativism deeply corrosive of Enlightenment principles. Gibbon had observed, almost bemused, the oddities of barbarian and early Christian behaviour; with the nineteenth century we enter a time when men seek to understand such individualities, far though history had still to go before acquiring the full panoply of anthropological, economic and social props necessary for it to become truly relativistic. Among the first areas in which this began were the history of legal institutions and philology.

In these cultural changes, the influence of Germany was paramount. German is by European standards a fairly difficult language and it commanded in 1800 nothing like the general acceptability of French, yet Germany dominates the intellectual history of the West in the nineteenth century as had France dominated that of its predecessor. It was soon to be seen in the enthusiasm with which American, English, French and Russian theologians, scientists and historians flocked to attend the German universities whose seminars appeared to offer unrivalled facilities for the student. The popular craze for things German was launched by Madame de Staël, a critic of Napoleon and daughter of Necker, the would-be saviour of the French monarchy. Her book *De l'Allemagne* was banned in France as 'not French' and she was exiled, to publish it abroad. It does not now seem a very remarkable work, but its impact was undeniable in popularizing a vision of Germany as a land of craftsmen, artists and thinkers, where constitutionalism and good simple morality reigned.

The ascendancy of Germans as scholars did more to ground the Germanic hegemony in the opinion of intellectuals than did fashionable literature. Here, the growing repute of Hegel was particularly noteworthy. Inside Germany, the impact of his thought was tremendous. There was no aspect of German intellectual endeavour which remained untouched, for good or ill, by its influence. He manifests more strongly than any of his contemporaries the tendency to see the age in which they lived as crucial, or special. Fichte had done the same, and the main explanation was to be found in the force with which the French Revolution struck men's minds and imaginations. The effects cannot be measured in a phrase – most of this book is by implication about them – but among others they included a blow at the confidence engendered by the Enlightenment. The French Revolution was thought in some sense to be affiliated to it and yet it had brought not peace but a sword, not reason and tolerance but violence and bitterness.

Hegel saw the Revolution as the expression of logical and historical necessity. It marked a distinct evolution in the history of the human spirit. Broadly speaking, his followers retained unquestioningly this part of his teaching and it contributed to the reinforcement of the myth of the Great Revolution. One of the Young Hegelians who went further was Marx, who grasped the link between Ricardo and Hegel, English Political Economy and German Idealism. These thinkers and systems had a common sociological character, both stressing, though in very different ways, the historical importance of society, an entity evolving

227

to its own rhythms. Hegel even took an English phrase to make his meaning clear (one familiar to Adam Smith): Civil Society. This he translated as *bürgerliche Gesellschaft*, from which it was to re-enter English via anglicized French as a part of Socialist jargon: bourgeois society. Hegel thought that the state, representing rationality and consciousness, should take charge of the unconscious evolutions of society. Marx came to think this impossible. He held that history was the determinant, expressing itself through the level of organization reached by the economy, which set limits to the kinds of state and society which were possible. Curiously, though he logically derived from these views the proposition that revolution *would* follow, Marx combined with this the moral precept that men *should* advocate and seek to bring about such revolutions. His career as a revolutionary prophet was, however, barely started in 1847.

There is so much that is novel about the mental world of the early nineteenth century that it takes conscious effort to recall how strong in it still was the power of traditional religion. To be sure, the term is slightly misleading. Religion too was renovated. Something of this can be guessed at from Châteaubriand's announcement in his *Génie du Christianisme* of his intention to make use of only the arguments of poetry and sentiment in considering fundamental Christian dogmas. The English Evangelical movement, especially in its expression among dissenters, offers only slightly less unacceptable examples of a new mood. There were already in 1800 looming on the horizon the first clouds of the great quarrel of natural science with religion which was to preoccupy the nineteenth century, but the apologists of religion resolutely turned their backs on the evidence already available that the geological world did not corroborate the scriptural account of Creation. The flight from all that smacked of reason and criticism was carried to extremes in the overtly political arguments of de Maistre. His book of 1819, *Du Pape*, is something like a culmination of a half-century's mounting obscurantism, where the evidence not only of science and empiricism but also of true history is abandoned. Comte admired it as the definitive statement of the religious view of society. In another work, de Maistre's enthusiasm for religious principle and sentiment carried him to the extreme boundary of Catholic orthodoxy itself, when he asserted that 'since there can be no false religion without some ingredients of truth, all impiety attacks some divine verity, however disfigured.'

More informal expressions of religious fervour than the writings of the best-selling apologists of ultramontanism could be found in popular manifestations of religious fervour. In France, *missionaires* circulated as successfully as travelling dissenters in England, or the circuit-riding evangelists of the United States. They found big audiences ready to be provoked or awoken by their eloquence.

Yet fashionable religion, the writings of intellectuals and popular revivalism were not the whole story. On other fronts, organized religion was as threatened in 1815 as it had ever been. The growing autonomy of the individual, reflected in a growing rejection of the formal restraints of religion, was one aspect of a more and more pervasive secularism. The French kept civil marriage and divorce in spite of the Concordat. But in defining the secularizing process, we have to be especially careful. The eighteenth century was, and has remained, reputedly the age *par excellence* of scepticism and moral laxity yet this was none the less, combined with the long survival of traditional views of the interdependence and co-operation of state and church. A new political tendency observable internationally after 1789 is a growing – though far from complete – acceptance that secular authority should not be deployed in the service of religious ends. The state was to become for religion, as for commerce, an umpire, no more. Later, it would even seem an enemy.

The history of this change in England, where practical toleration was already far advanced before 1799, was marked after 1815 by a steady flow of statutes which whittled away the Protestant Constitution and the Anglican supremacy, and intellectually by the growth of rationalist printing and publication. On the other hand, England did not get any formal separation of church and state. The continental confessional states which survived all had to concede a measure of toleration. In Spain the Inquisition, for so long the judicial link connecting state and faith, was abolished (to the disapproval of the duke of Wellington). Finally, and most importantly, churches lost much of their power of practical regulation, either in their courts, or through their laws enforced by the lay courts, of daily life. The great symbolic question was marriage; civil marriage was never to be extirpated from France after 1815. But there were other less dramatic changes of almost equal or greater significance. When, for example, the maintenance of the essential records of society was no longer the obligation only of the parish priest, much of his real influence and power was eroded, even if this did not at once appear.

In spite of the Concordats and ultramontanism of the Restoration, therefore, a Jansenist who survived from the pre-revolutionary century could have found something to applaud in the relations of Church and State after 1815. He would also probably not have been greatly saddened by the actual material and territorial losses the Roman Church had undergone since 1789, considerable though these were. In many countries the regular working of ecclesiastical administration, courts, seminaries and universities had been interrupted. The Papacy had for a long period lost control of its own sovereign territories. Two popes had been imprisoned and prevented from exercising their pastorate, and the College of Cardinals itself was transported to Paris. In Germany the ecclesiastical electorates disappeared even before the Holy Roman Empire, and ecclesiastical principalities were transferred to lay rulers. German ecclesiastical property was sold, monastic libraries being broken up, while schools, convents and charitable foundations were liquidated in a manner reminiscent of the English Reformation. States once wholly Roman Catholic were replaced by new ones with a mixed confessional basis.

Nor did religious revival or a new sympathy for religious modes of thought prove an unqualified benefit to the established churches. It could lead to support for rival or substitute religions, rather than a return to the establishments. Under the urgings of a prophet, Württembergers left for the Caucasus to await the Second Coming, while Englishmen swallowed the extravagance of Joanna Southcott. These excesses had some explicit theological content, but beyond the fringe phenomena of which they were a part stretched a zone where other rivals of established faith operated with great success, the area of the secular religions of humanity, nationalism and socialism so attractive to the nineteenth century.

Yet survivors of the Enlightenment and the *idéologues* would have felt disappointed in 1847. The new bitterness of quarrels over religion after the French Revolution owed much to real advances in the power of the churches which must be weighed against the general legal tendency to curb them. In spite of secularizations of wealth and new legal restraints, they grew visibly wealthier and more powerful after 1815. The word 'anti-clericalism' had not been invented by 1847, but it was a reality long before that because of new advantages which organized religion seemed often to enjoy even when its formal powers were more and more closely circumscribed.

The hopes of the eighteenth-century *philosophes* and civil servants had been cut across not only by a new intensity of religious faith but by the fear of revolution. It is difficult to avoid the conclusion that most of the gains of formal religion visible since the previous century derived from the shock given by revolution to the possessing classes and its political consequences. Religion and politics were more closely intertwined than ever after 1815. Strong Protestants in England had experienced genuine horror at the treatment of the French church in the 1790s and the examples of religious and anti-religious excess which accompanied it. One good result was the goodwill with which the French *émigré* clergy were received and supported in their exile in England by Protestants. Another side of the response was less admirable, a retreat into a bigoted and sometimes merely formal religiosity in the face of any hint of 'infidelity'.

Sadly, there can be no doubt that it was at worst fear and at best prudence which explains much of the new respect given to religion by members of the upper classes everywhere. It was notorious that before the Revolution the great readers of the works of the *philosophes*, the wittiest scoffers against simple faith and the most outrageous flaunting of Christian traditions of personal behaviour were to be found among the *grands seigneurs*. The emigration soon produced a change; the counter-revolution quickly took as its mentors the priests whose teachings had been ignored before 1789. One of the first *émigrés* was the Duc d'Artois, brother of Louis xvi, a rake who treated even the formal observances of religion with contempt. In 1815 he returned a religious bigot and a man transformed. In due course, his beliefs helped to make him a disaster as king. But France was not the only place where such changes were to be seen. In the 1790s, an English clergyman observed that 'all we have seen, all we have feared, all we have felt for these last ten years leads us to promote the furtherance of that religion which teaches the obedience due, from Christian subjects, to Christian magistrates.' For all the distrust Englishmen would still long feel for the pretensions of the bishop of Rome, such language not only provides the background to the English rural alliance of squire and parson but also implies a general change in which all upholders of religion drew somewhat together, whatever their creed.

Their judgment appeared to be endorsed by facts. In France, Italy, Spain and the Tyrol, the Roman Church proved itself again and again the most effective mobilizer of mass forces against revolution. In the United Kingdom, the influence of the Irish bishops was thrown into the scale by the Pope to help a government which opposed Catholic Emancipation. In England the Evangelical revival and Methodist dissent were quickly seen to have a conservative influence and became respectable. In Protestant Germany the revival of pietism and the growth of sentimental religiosity was as early as the 1790s linked with political reaction. The results of the religious revival were far-reaching and, no doubt, contained some unambiguously good elements. Yet it is difficult to look at those features of it which were most conspicuous without a sense of regret. The sanctimoniousness of the new style (emphatically not confined to Protestantism), the obfuscation of philosophy, the regeneration of the power and influence of the Papacy, the cultivation of popular superstition, the aesthetic horrors of *bondieuserie* and Viollet-le-Duc, the restoration of the Jesuits, sabbatarianism and the cult of the Virgin – these were a heavy price to pay and mark a retrogression of the European spirit. When Newman said 'Liberalism –

there is the enemy,' he was quite right; he identified a quarrel which was to last a century. It might be lay appropriation of clerical revenues which was at the moment in question, but what was implied, as was recognized widely at the time, was religion's opposition to the whole tendency of the age.

Such attitudes had effects in politics. In Europe this was expressed after 1815 in such symbols as the return of religious censorship of publications and a famous French law of sacrilege. Ultramontanism had begun its long career in French politics under Napoleon with the assertion of papal authority over the French bishops, and any English government had to take into account the views and votes of the group of evangelically inclined MPs clustered about Wilberforce and known as the 'Saints'. Some leading politicians were sincerely happy to do so. Lord Liverpool is not one of the English prime ministers most easily recalled as an enthusiast, but Châteaubriand was struck by his zeal and thought he had 'almost reached the stage of puritanical illumination'. Perhaps the most notorious example of religion's new power among the rulers of men was to be found in Alexander I.

What this meant to the masses is hard to say. There remain grave difficulties inherent in the nature of all evidence for the history of religion. What was the state of religious behaviour and what does it signify in terms of faith? To judge by the alarm and dismay sometimes shown by religious spokesmen, Europe in the early nineteenth century was slipping rapidly into paganism. Yet it is legitimate to doubt both the implied contrast with what went before – research has suggested, for example, that much of France was in many ways 'de-Christianized' before the Revolution – and also the extent of the deterioration in religious practice and influence if one considers the great authority still exercised by Christian moral and social teaching in 1847. Only a small minority of men would then willingly have called themselves atheists, to go no further.

This raises another question, that of the gap between the mentality of the elite and that of the masses. It is credible that it was narrower in 1847 than 1775, though still very wide by comparison with later times. The two great processes bringing about its narrowing were the spread of education and the improvement of communication. Literacy, thanks to education, improved in all the major countries during these years, thus continuing a trend observable in western Europe since the late Middle Ages. Some people whose parents had not been literate undoubtedly thus obtained access to books which, from the point of view of traditional religion, were subversive. There are good grounds for thinking that 'Enlightenment' penetrated further down the social structure of France than was once believed. Yet most of the newly literate may well have read none of such literature and very little of any, that little being divided between traditional popular forms of writing and the Bible.

Change in communication was changing this picture mainly because of the spread of the newspaper press. This resulted from a confluence of changes operating irregularly in different countries. Readers of *Martin Chuzzelwitt* will recall the uninhibited democratic freedoms of American journalism which appalled Dickens in the 1840s. At that time, the British press was regulated by a stricter law of libel than the American, but was almost entirely free from other legal restraints on freedom of publication which had still existed in the previous century. In France, on the other hand, the July monarchy maintained a cautionary censorship, while in Germany and the Austrian Empire the grip of police on the press was stronger still. Russia, of course, had a severe censorship.

To the spread of information and ideas there was also a technical dimension. Steam-driven presses were installed in the printing-shop of the London *Times* in 1814. Paper was becoming cheaper; with lower printing-costs and faster methods, this helped to bring down the price of newspapers. Their distribution became easier as other countries followed Great Britain in introducing regular cheap postal services (the British Penny Post was inaugurated in 1840). Information travelled by letter more widely and easily after this, but also because of railways, steamships and the telegraph. It was the age of the greatest advance in communication since the invention of writing itself.

14 Government and Politics

Even in the United Kingdom, long the country where government was distrusted and foreigners despised because they lived under what seemed arbitrary power, there were indications after 1815 of a new respect for the state. Elsewhere a change of mood since 1789 was even more obvious. This was an early indication of one of the historical currents to run right through the nineteenth century: the rise of the state to undisputed pre-eminence. It became stronger than ever before, beginning in the Revolution era a process subsequently almost uninterrupted of drawing power to itself. The states of 1847 were, in spite of the misgivings of their rulers, more secure than those of 1789, though still fragile if we compare them with their successors as many of them were to show in 1848.

The roots of this change were complex. They included the internal reforms which gave birth to new institutions such as conscription, police forces and centralized administration. One of the most important was the growing size and expertise of bureaucracies which began to be recruited and trained on more objective lines and worked with better records and greater knowledge. It is no accident that the first novel (an unfriendly one) about civil servants, Balzac's *Les employés*, was written in this period, or that Dickens should have hit upon the inspired caricature of the Circumlocution Office. These were, of course, prompted by corrupt or decrepit examples of the bureaucratic phenomenon. In Germany, the European country with the best and oldest bureaucratic tradition, there was deservedly more respect for civil servants. The recognition of bureaucracy in Prussia by awarding it the status of a fourth estate was one manifestation of this. So was the increasing care given by German states in the nineteenth century to proper regulation of promotion, pensions on retirement and qualification.

Society seemed to demand more and more officials. Railway and telegraph administration, for example, and the new interest of governments in education, multiplied jobs. This expansion of bureaucratic activity and the creation of new opportunities for politics offered great opportunities to men skilled in the handling of complex private affairs, the negotiation of and drafting of documents, the keeping and controlling of records. Lawyers had these skills and so tended to predominate in these new fields; '*ce siècle est aux avocats*,' said young Fabrizio in *La Chartreuse de Parme*. He had a point. From a similar need stemmed the tendency of the embryonic party organizations in England to call on the aid of solicitors, the use of barristers to carry out the practical initiation of the new electoral arrangements after 1832 and the importance of lawyers to the slowly stirring business of central government.

Better bureaucracies led to better tapping of resources by the state; better fiscal devices (such as the astonishing and unique British innovation of income tax) combined with better credit arrangements to put more money behind government. Finally, technical changes in warfare, transport and communication also strengthened it. New institutions such as Peel's metropolitan police forces, or the rural *gendarmeries* of Europe, solved, in most countries, the problem of public order. Often, the countryside was properly policed for the first time in its history, while in the cities artillery could make rubble of the barricades, if directed (by telegraph) and delivered (by rail) to the right place at the right time. Moreover, it became easier to draw the sting of revolt before it occurred; hunger was the traditional detonator of revolt, and the steamship and railway which made this problem soluble by regularizing food-supply were to do as much for order as canister-shot and police barracks.

Necessarily, some of these practical reinforcements of state power aroused antagonisms. Even English property-owners, for all their amazing docility, did not actually *like* governments which taxed them. 'There could be no more dreadful calamity for this country than its continuance,' said Lord John Russell in 1816 of the income tax, and for nearly a half-century after that it was possible for ministers to envisage its abolition. Conscription, as the history of France in the 1790s and Napoleonic era showed, sometimes aroused opposition. New police, such as the Royal Irish Constabulary or the Spanish Civil Guard, brought to bear on the public authority they represented the resentments and hatreds earlier reserved to the landlord. The arrival of a royal justice to stand between an eastern European landlord and his tenants could be as much resented as a similar intrusion in medieval times in the West. Significantly, too, these years, which brought so great a practical increase in the power of the state, gave birth to anarchism too.

A new respect for the State in some countries arose because more people could identify themselves with it after 1815. The enlightened despots had shown to some discerning minds how power could be beneficially used if restraints on sovereignty were removed. But the idea of legislative sovereignty overriding all privilege was accepted in legal theory before 1789 only in England, and even there occasional protests were heard. For many (though not all) of those who desired change, the recognition of legislative sovereignty was the greatest reform of 1789. The next step was the realization that this could strengthen resistance to the Revolution. Linked to the idea of nationality, it was capable of generating a new conservative power. Mirabeau pointed out to Louis XVI that Richelieu would have given much for the advantages presented to the Crown by the Constituent Assembly's abolition of privilege; the lesson was soon learned by intelligent conservatives. French Constitutions came and went but the Prefects and the Departments remained; the hopes of diehards that *parlements* and provinces could be revived were always disappointed.

New ways of thinking about legal institutions were soon reinforced by the romantic idealization of historical realities and by idealist philosophy. Hegel's development of the distinction between society and state gave the state – any state – an independent moral value above that of any subordinate association or individual. Man, selfish in society, could find in the state a moral cause to serve, thought those who read Hegel; it presented him with a sphere above egoism for action in obedience to a selfless, impersonal morality. It could realize the values no other group could realize; ethical purpose justified the law-giver's demands.

People found it easier to accept such views when the state rested on nationality and tapped its passions. When the two did not coincide, of course, state authority was liable to suffer. The doctrine that state and nation should always coincide is called nationalism and has already made its appearance in these pages. After 1815 it was an increasingly important political force, both within states whose borders did not more or less coincide with those of peoples (such as the United Kingdom and all states east of the Rhine) and internationally because it appeared to impose obligations on great powers to try to remake the map to fit national patterns. It is now so familiar an ideal that some oddities in the new situation are easily overlooked. In the first place, a vast change of intellectual fashion had occurred. Cosmopolitanism (as Rousseau had deplored) had been the ideal of the eighteenth century. In 1789 Schiller reflected that 'the patriotic interest is important only for immature nations.' What brought about change was the linking of popular sovereignty to nationalism in the French Revolution, which in the longer run revealed the usefulness of nationalism to conservatives, too. Theoretically, this should not have been surprising; if nationalism rejected prescriptive rights (such as those of dynasties), it based its own claims on historical and collective realities. Though the primary association of the national mythology was with liberalism, there was nothing necessary or exclusive about the connection. Patriotism cut across reaction and revolution. While, in the Revolution, Frenchmen were persuaded to make 'patriotic contributions', Britons loyally stumped up, too, calling their contributions 'voluntary'. Both registered a transfer of emotional loyalty from the persons of rulers to the abstractions of state and nation. The Prussian found that money poured in during the War of Liberation, too. Thus patriotism eased the tasks of all governments. The change was far from complete still in 1847, but the day was then in sight when governments would no longer see themselves as on the defensive towards their own subjects.

The slow reinforcement of public authority by national feeling could even be discerned in the United States, where geography's gift of land and resources for seemingly limitless expansion, the absence of important foreign competition and the existence of the federal constitution were powerful obstacles to it. Yet even in the United States, the issue was being brought forward in politics. It had underlain the struggles of Federalists and Democrats and broke out in a run of quarrels about the rights of individual states. In the end, it was at the heart of the issue of black slavery and would be settled – in favour of the nation state, it may be remarked – only by war.

Changes in the form and concept of the state made also for the emergence of a new politics. To a society such as that of the *ancien régime* which saw itself as a system in equilibrium, 'politics' had been only a marginal affair, at most a matter of shifts in the composition of the ruling group. The regulators of the *ancien régime* were usually not political but judicial forms; the problem of public power was to distribute force in support of legal rights and the fundamental technique was one of assessing the correct relationship of the legal rights of interested parties. Even international affairs were strongly marked by this juridical emphasis. But acceptance, even reluctant, of the idea of change as a social norm required a new machinery for dealing with conflicting claims which could often no longer fit into juridical categories, or could do so only with anomalies and inappropriate distortions.

What came to be accepted more and more, as a result, was that bargaining and discussion ought to decide the direction of public affairs and that a new class of people, politicians, should undertake this. It also came to be held that certain groups in society (the definition of which varied widely, but tended always to grow wider, sometimes even so far as to include all adult males) should identify these politicians by choosing representatives. The outcome of politics was to be the selection of those to wield the law-making power of the sovereign state. Finally, this was all to take place against the background of another new force, that of public opinion.

The machinery as well as the concepts of modern politics began to appear together. Party had been a parliamentary idea in eighteenth-century England; after 1815 it was more and more carried outside the representative assembly to denote an organized opinion in the country. Its development went *pari passu* with the advance of the idea of legitimate opposition. In the 1830s a British prime minister for the first time addressed his supporters nationwide (though, formally, still concerning himself with the electors of his own constituency) by publishing an electoral manifesto. Political action adapted itself to wider audiences, and more and more successful demands were made for the removal of restraints on publication and the right of assembly. The eighteenth-century movement towards the spontaneous organization of societies for cultural, philanthropic and social purposes was also politicized: 'club' became the outstanding symptom of political disorder or index of political maturity according to your point of view.

The year 1789 began modern politics. For thirty years after 1815 politics in every country except the United States and the United Kingdom was dominated still by the French Revolution. With forty years' perspective, Carlyle in 1837 still came to the conclusion that 'it appears to be, if not stated in words, yet tacitly felt and understood everywhere, that the event of these modern ages is the French Revolution. A huge explosion, bursting through all formulae and customs. . . .' In fact, it *was* often 'stated in words'. As we read those of men who experienced this 'huge explosion', it is difficult not to believe them at times deranged by the danger that they felt to threaten. Metternich is said to have used only eight metaphors to talk about society: volcano, plague, cancer, deluge, conflagration, powder magazine, influenza and cholera. True or not, this draws attention to the huge gap between an eighteenth-century, rationalizing mind such as his and the irrational, passionate turmoil of the French Revolution and its consequences. Even so different a man as Burke, whose imagination kindled more rapidly to a romantic glow and who found emotional comprehension easier, was just as violently repelled. The impact on the European mind was such that for a century men talked of *the* Revolution, and meant by it not just the chronologically defined events of any period, however generously its limits might be drawn, but an independent force, released by the events of France and roaming up and down the public life of Europe like a beast of prey or, for a smaller but growing number of fanatics, like an avenging angel, for the myth of the Revolution was cherished on both sides of the barricades.

Curiously, the huge fright suffered by the possessing classes did not simply drive their ideologists back into a restatement of the ideals of the *ancien régime* and the reassembly of its scattered fragments. Though many people would have liked this in 1815, it was impossible. There were external restraints upon them, but internal ones, too. Their own experience had changed them. The fear of revolution itself shows how they were no longer simply men of the *ancien régime* but were thinking and moving in a new political world of harsh polarities. Whatever this was, it was not the thinking of the *ancien régime*. By 1815 there was in existence for the first time a broad agreement on principles between intelligent reactionaries of all countries. Many of them had been articulated first in the context of the French emigration: the counter-revolution's particular cast of mind owed much to this. It was then, for example, that the tie between conservatism and religion was first established. The revolutionary threat clarified the ideas of the upper class all over Europe. The first modern alternative to the progressive social ideal of the Enlightenment had crystallized. Traditional authority was respected in a new way and so were religion and historical and prescriptive rights.

Thus the old order could not be restored in 1815. Conservatism in 1847 was even more remote from it. When all qualifications are made, corporations and estates were no longer then thought to be the only acceptable basis for political institutions; individual members of society, even if they had to be qualified by wealth or education, increasingly were. The great dispute of the nineteenth century (as Stendhal called it), that between rank and merit, the dispute crystallized in the slogan '*la carrière ouverte aux talents*' proclaimed in 1789, had been formally settled in favour of merit in most countries. It was a reality in many countries by 1847 for all the informal power of wealth and social connection.

Nevertheless, it soon suited many people, liberal and conservative alike, to close their eyes to the fact that 1815 had not brought with it sweeping Restoration. And there was this to be said for their view: that 1815 was a setback to the ideals of the French Revolution in every country and that in most countries, attitudes for or against that Revolution were still the bedrock of political distinctions. The mythology and memory of the Revolution went on being copiously fed by rhetoric and publication, and it continued to be a living force. Two years after the judgment already quoted, Carlyle wrote that 'since the year 1789, there is now half a century complete; and a French Revolution not yet complete.'

The Revolution defined most political issues in continental Europe down to 1847. The most alarming of them was Republicanism. It does not now seem a very exciting idea, but more was involved than simply forms. Republicanism at the beginning of the century had dramatic connotations now unthinkable because of the prevalence of monarchy.

When the first French republic appeared, in 1792, the only others in Europe were ossified antiquities such as Genoa, Venice, the German Imperial Cities and small states such as the United Provinces (with a quasi-monarchical stadholderate) or the Swiss cantons. The example of America was irrelevant; it was a long way away, therefore not exposed to the necessities of strong government which a European state had to suffer; anyway, it looked as if it was likely to dissolve under the natural burdens of faction and geography. Bonaparte damaged the idea still more. By 1847, there were even fewer republics in Europe. New states which survived tended to be constitutional monarchies and some of the fossil republics had gone. But feelings about republicanism were much more violent. Experience of the previous half-century suggested (according to your view) either that they opened the way to anarchy and licence (the evidence was France in 1792, the satellite republics of the Directory and Napoleon), or that they made possible a regeneration of the community unhindered by superstition and vested interest (again the evidence was France in 1792, the satellite republics of the Directory and Napoleon). Republicans recalled the virtues and practised the cult of antiquity; Brutus was idealized and 'senates', 'tribunes', 'consuls', scattered by the French, consciously evoked the glories of republican Rome. Conservatives, on the other hand, recalled Cromwell and pointed out that military dictatorship had in the end succeeded Robespierre's reign of virtue. Very soon, Republicanism was habitually referred to by those who disliked it as 'red' Republicanism. It was assumed that republican forms did not merely involve disrespect for heredity and historic right but would also open the way to social anarchy and license either through the deliberate action of republicans or through their intrinsic weakness and insufficiency.

Before 1847, more was heard of republicanism as a danger to the established order than of socialism and communism. Both these doctrines – or at least persons who claimed to adhere to them – existed, but the first half of the nineteenth century is better regarded as the infant or primitive era of what is now thought of as socialism than one in which modern socialists would feel at home, for it was still largely an unindustrialized, unurbanized world. What the early socialists left to the future was an ethical ideal whose roots lay in the previous century, in a hatred and distrust of the private interest lauded by Smith and a dislike of inequality which can be traced to Rousseau; the consequences drawn from these were taken beyond the moral and legal area where they first made an impact and into the material and economic by Babeuf and his followers in the 'Conspiracy of Equals' of 1796. Combined with the general Enlightenment challenge to authority, this produced in the end the greatest moral challenge to the European order since the Protestant

Reformation. Its essence was a rejection of the view that material inequality was either necessary or justifiable.

Much had to be added to this egalitarian creed before it began to look like modern socialism. The most important change required was the recognition of the impact of industrialization and technical change on material and social relations. This was brilliantly grasped by a French nobleman bearing a great name, Saint-Simon. Some have seen in him the first true socialist and some the first fascist. He grasped before anyone else that industrial society would have its own political necessities. For the most part early socialists and Communists had thought, rather, that legislative change – enforced if necessary by revolution – could bring about greater equality without much regard to economic reality. This faith (which came to be generally called 'Socialism' in about 1830) blurred into the revolutionary tradition born of the Great Revolution. Robespierre came to be idolized as a social egalitarian; one of those who helped to bring this about was Buonarroti, once a member of his circle of hangers-on, later professional conspirator and the hagiographer of Babeuf in his book *The Conspiracy of Equals*. By the 1840s, this tradition, though, was no longer appearing to be quite enough. The word 'proletariat' had become current: the depressing tendency of market society to generate poverty seemed more and more striking. More thoughtful social analysis began to appear on the Left, and in Proudhon's works can be found the origin of a distinction to be much drawn later on, that between scientific and utopian Socialism.

Yet outright social revolution was a matter for the few. Most of those concerned in politics were more concerned with another issue, or rather pair of issues: constitutionalism and the idea of popular sovereignty which became entangled with it. Bitter opponents though these ideas were at times (and ought, logically, always to have been) their effect was often surprisingly convergent.

The word constitution was an anglicism imported into French during the eighteenth century and thence re-exported to become the crucial demand of early nineteenth-century liberals. By a constitution they meant defined rights for individuals and juridical guarantees of them against the intrusion of power. This was no new idea. Even before the Estates General met, there had been demands in France for a written constitution and there was the American example. Later the model most frequently cited and demanded was that which Spain gave itself in 1812. It was imitated in the Piedmontese and Neapolitan revolutions of 1821. But the Restoration *Charte*, a conservative document, was a constitution, too, and all successful revolutions after 1821 tended to result in the adoption of constitutions – as they did after 1847.

Constitutionalism strove to restrict power, popular sovereignty expanded it. They could hardly be reconcilable, as de Tocqueville emphasized. Here was the liberal dilemma: popular sovereignty reinforced authority, where constitutionalism sought to guarantee non-interference. Yet popular sovereignty could be a great engine of liberation because of the threat it presented to traditional authority and hierarchy. It greatly reinforced the power of the state, and many people were willing to acquiesce in this when they believed that the working of popular sovereignty might enable them to share power. The issue came to the fore most obviously and most frequently in questions of representative institutions and the suffrage. The idea of democracy was suspect and its concomitant, universal suffrage, was regarded with almost as deep a misgiving by liberals as by conservatives. But there were gradations of disapproval. Once everyone had agreed that what was being talked about was the question of how many men should have the vote – even among revolutionaries almost no one could be found to support the view that it should be given to women – then agreement ceased even on what were principles relevant to drawing a line. Some feared that the rule of the propertyless would be followed by the spoliation of property; not only was the privilege of wealth at stake but also the foundation of independence for the individual. Others thought that democracy would inaugurate the reign of ignorance, but even an educated democracy seemed a threat to cultural values to some. This was the message of that most sane of political commentaries, *Democracy in America*.

In conflicts over such issues there crystallized a way of conceiving political conflict originating in the French Revolution which seized the European imagination with a grip unshaken almost until today. Its essence was the assumption that all political differences had a common nature and formed part of a single ideological universe. It was expressed in the emergence of a new political vocabulary. The terms 'Left' and 'Right' have obsessed political thinking ever since so persuasively that attempts are even made to present the politics of non-European countries in them. Yet they, and the division they imply, were first adopted only to make sense of specific events in France. From there they were extended in their application until they seemed also to have a general relevance for Europe. The polarization which they indicate became even sharper as more and more strenuous efforts were made to comprehend on the same spectrum every shade of opinion, though by 1847 the extremes of socialism, anarchism and plebiscitary dictatorship should already have made it seem inadequate (to say nothing of the difficulty of fitting English political experience into it). In fact, the red-and-black, revolution-and-reaction dualism on which centred the major political issues of the age gave it a usefulness which hid its shortcomings. Though some ideas did not fit into it, the idea of a Left-Right spectrum indicated significant differences between political ideas and politicians while not blurring the general division into two camps.

Although French political ideas were so influential in these years, other countries also contributed. 'Conservative' had a French origin and it originally expressed a different idea from the English translation (in 1831 in England, 'Conservative' was still to Macaulay a new cant word; it defined a trend within Toryism away from old-fashioned reaction). In Europe, it became a general term for the Right. 'Liberal' had a Spanish origin; in 1816 the poet Southey could still speak of the *Liberales*, consciously using the Spanish word. It quickly came to connote the ideas of constitutional liberties, generalized public rights and equality before the law. 'Radical' was more extreme and was England's most important contribution to Europe's new political vocabulary since 'constitution'; it had been used in a political context in its adjectival form in the eighteenth century and now made its appearance as a noun. Republicans, it was agreed, stood to the left of radicals; radicals might, but need not, be republicans.

This set the stage on which politicians had to work. Some were less marked by it than others. English political life moved to rhythms very different from those of Europe in these years. The July Revolution, it is true, had an electric effect in London. It was an additional warning of danger in a great political crisis in which men talked about the dangers of revolution. Parliamentary reform was in fact achieved in 1832 on conservative principles, but in spite of this, it was a change which conceded the principle of reform. Sooner or later, a second instalment on similar lines – franchise extension by parliamentary redefinition of eligibility to vote and the redistribution of seats – was inevitable.

Given the huge social and economic upheavals going on in England, the insulation of its other political concerns from those of the Continent seems remarkable. 'Corn, Currency, Catholics' – the great issues of English politics before 1830 – and Free Trade and government intervention to ameliorate the condition of Englishmen and rationalize administrations – the major issues afterwards – seem almost preoccupations of a different political planet from that of mainland Europe. Nor did English politicians and parties fit easily into the Left-Right, Reaction-Progress or class-war stereotypes, in spite of middle-class exertions. British party warfare had to wait for the disappearance of a Victorian Liberal party not even born in 1847 before it could be about class; in principle the Chartists asked for nothing incapable of realization within the old constitution's resources. As the manufacturers pressed forwards towards Repeal, exhorted by the embittered rhetoric of the dissenting pulpit, and encouraged by the adhesion of the respectable workingman and Sir Robert Peel, they found themselves opposed by High Tory landlords and Evangelical clergymen anxious to remedy social evil by legislating government inspectors into the factories, and by such improbable associates as Lord Shaftesbury and the young Disraeli. Chartists, Melbourne's Whigs, Peel's Conservatives, Liverpool's Tories, Pitt's Young Men, the friends of Charles James Fox – none of them fit easily into the Procrustean bed of Left and Right on which more and more of continental politics were lopped or stretched.

One consequence was the emergence of the unique English working-class movement. Its first youth was already ending in about 1847 and the main characteristics of much of its future were by then determined. English socialists were few and eccentric to this tradition; this is one of the ways in which English and European history diverge importantly in the nineteenth century. The centre of the stage of English working-class history in these years must be conceded to the Chartists, a multi-farious, many-headed band, reflecting widely differing local and occupational concerns. But Chartism was to prove in the end short-lived; for all its drama and turbulence, the future belonged to other working-class organizations. The still primitive trade unions were one. Another was the Co-operative movement. Friendly Societies were another. In these institutions lay the roots of what was to become a widely ramified structure of working-class organization many of whose elements were to be admired and imitated across the world.

Except in their power to win recognition for themselves, it was a long time before such institutions could produce an effect on legislation. For all the actually swift and radical evolution of English society and politics, there was astonishing continuity in their working. The word 'democracy' remained a pejorative term throughout the whole of these years and in 1847 the landed aristocracy looked as secure in the saddle as in 1789. The Anglican Church, even if its privileges were whittled away, still presided imperturbably over the great moments of the life of the rural Englishman; in the cities, some at least of its clergy had begun to fight back against the new poverty and squalour of urbanism and industrialism. The monarchy was still firmly entrenched in unconscious acceptance and less likely to be betrayed by the occupant of the throne than thirty years before. English republicanism was insignificant, badly damaged by the rise of Bonaparte, whether he was seen as betrayer or fulfiller of revolution. The electorate was growing by natural increase, but was still only a minority of the adult male population. The ruling class exercised power through a tactic of concession and with a sense of responsibility that rarely faltered. The continuity of formal institutions was greater than in any European country, and Englishmen gloried in it; when Barry rebuilt the Palace of Westminster, he took as his starting point not the evocations of republican virtue and imperial rule with which Napoleon sought to impress Parisians but the medieval world in which, it was increasingly believed, the Mother of Parliaments had from the start embodied the virtues and practices of Victorian constitutionalism. Even the Chartists respected Parliament, and expected to carry out the transformations they desired by first gaining a majority in the House of Commons.

Taken all in all, it was an astonishing achievement, and Europeans were right to admire. There was only one serious blot, Ireland. If that country were not quite, as Irish nationalists were later to assert, England's Poland, it was bad enough. The legal fiction of Union concealed the social and political gulf between utterly dissimilar nations. Moreover, the gulf widened, not only because England industrialized after already doing her best to cripple such industry as Ireland possessed but because the Irish were caught in the Malthusian trap into which they had been hurried by taking to the potato. Their millions of peasants existed in misery. 'They have nothing to lose but life,' said Walter Scott in 1829, and things were to get still worse.

Misery was made more intolerable because aggravated and (it seemed to many) inflicted by an alien rule and an alien church. The first great Irish success was to win 'Emancipation' for Catholics, and the essence of it was the vote. The next victory was in a struggle against the payment of tithe to the (English Protestant) Church of Ireland. One great English statesman, Peel, thought he might draw the poison from the issue by officially endorsing Catholicism in Ireland as the religion of most Irishmen. He was defeated; Englishmen not only shared in the general tendency of the age which made men distrustful of that alternative to the authority of the State which an ultramontane Pope seemed to provide but, paradoxically, the 1832 reform gave the country an electorate more concerned and more nicely discriminatory over questions of religious principle than its predecessor had been. In the end, it proved, Emancipation only opened the door to further pressure for change. The famine of 1846, on the other hand, terrible as it was, eventually solved Ireland's problems, though only for a time. They would re-emerge, again and again.

The other great state whose politics marched to rhythms different from those of continental Europe was the youngest, the United States of America. If, in the event, Jefferson's presidency proved less revolutionary than had been feared, this was not to say that there was not indeed a democratic revolution going forward in the United States. It proceeded, though, less by political than by social, economic and demographic channels. Poor though he might be, a poor American often enjoyed a higher real standard of living and always a much greater chance of bettering himself than his European counterpart. Moreover, for a long time his country could not throw up the huge accretions of wealth which emphasized the inequalities of rural Europe. Americans built their sense of equality not only on the ideals and institutions of the Revolution but on the facts of an economy which was long local and, if relatively attractive in European eyes, very modest by later standards.

Wealth and material well-being are now so much a part of our conception of the Union (and, it is true, were such powerful attractions to immigrants almost from the beginnings of colonization) that it requires an effort now to grasp its economic condition at the beginning of the nineteenth century. It was a dependent and conservative economy, still tied to Great Britain; shillings and pence were still occasionally used to reckon prices even in 1800. Of manufacturing industry there was little; the economy was agrarian, vitally distinguished from that of much of Europe by its basis in free-holding, but technically out-of-date by English standards, largely because the easy availability of land made extensive and exhaustive cultivation possible. Nine in ten Americans lived by agriculture. Commerce was important in the coastal cities, yet in 1800 there were only four banks in the huge spaces of New York State, two of them in New York City itself, where Wall Street was still an uptown residential area and Broadway a country drive. Only five cities had populations of more than twenty thousand. Signs of the future lay in the small textile factories of New England, which were to grow to give the north an essential character as distinctive as that of the west or south, and the cotton plantations of the south, whose future had been transformed by the invention of the cotton gin. Cotton was to dominate southern politics and society, intensifying sectionalism until civil war was the outcome. Economically, it was by 1847 the greatest of American exports and one whose growth was far from ended.

By that date, transformation was obvious everywhere in the United States. Population was moving towards the twenty-three millions counted three years later. They inhabited an area which since 1845 ran south to the Rio Grande and between the forty-second and forty-ninth parallels to the Pacific Ocean. Most Americans still lived in rural areas but there were fifteen cities of more than twenty-thousand in 1840, four of them with more than a hundred thousand inhabitants. Population had been built up not only by natural growth but by continuing immigration from Europe, though the era of heaviest immigration opened only with the hungry years of 1846–7. Immigrants sometimes joined the native Americans making their way westward in ever increasing numbers. First by covered wagons along the great trails (it was in 1842 that the Oregon trail was established), then by river boat and finally by railroad, there were better and better means for feeding the occupation of western America which was the principal national achievement of the early nineteenth century, though the Great Plains were still to remain a barrier until the 1860s.

This resettlement made American society both stable and dynamic. The ideal of a nation of independent proprietors was made a reality by the availability of land in the west and by the outlet it provided for the discontented. In return, pioneer values and an enterprising ethic invigorated society in the east. Political radicalism, too, flowed back to the east from the frontier, a matter of growing concern as more and more western states joined the Union. Of twenty-nine states in 1847, fourteen lay west of the Appalachians and the republic was still overwhelmingly rural and agrarian in its social and ideological foundations. Only in a few areas, the mill valleys of New England, or the great Atlantic ports, could there faintly be seen the outlines of a great future industrial and commercial power.

Growth on this scale rushed the United States away with dizzy speed from even such similarities and analogies between Old and New Worlds as had existed. Other changes came from the play of institutions, the pressures and channels of principle and constitutional arrangement; through these political struggles had to make their way, being shaped and controlled by them, or creating new political issues by striving to burst through their banks, wearing them away. The most important American institutions were respect for the constitution and the separation of powers it embodied, and belief in individualism and self-government.

The makers of the constitution could not have anticipated the demands soon put upon it. Speedily, it became clear that it could be interpreted in more than one way. This was often the heart of disputes between proponents of nationalism and defenders of the independence of the individual states which made up the Union. This was why control of the federal judiciary, which from the beginning of the Union had the power to disallow the legislation of individual states were it unconstitutional, became a political issue under Jefferson. The outcome was a victory for the federal judiciary; the Chief Justice, John Marshall, contrived to use a case before him to establish the principle that the Supreme Court could declare provisions in an Act of Congress invalid, too. It was fifty years before this was repeated, but judicial review was thus established as a constitutional principle. John Marshall has thus better right than many of those who sat in the constitutional convention to be identified as one of the shapers of America.

Though the struggle over the judiciary kept party bitterness alive (especially when attempts were made to remove judges by impeachment), the first decade of the nineteenth century brought some decrease in it. Federalism recovered during Jefferson's second term, and the Republican party tended to fragment. But Federalism was more and more clearly a sectional phenomenon, rooted in New England. Meanwhile, the west was becoming more important all the time.

Gradually, old party ties gave way, and the four terms (two each) of Jefferson's successors as presidents, Madison and Monroe, gradually settled into a less contentious politics; these were years which became known later as the 'era of good feelings'. Something, no doubt, was due to the national feeling and sentiments of unity encouraged by the war of 1812, but more was due to the fact that the old politics was tending to pass away before a new one had appeared to take its place. The change was masked by Madison and Monroe, both Virginians, like Washington and Jefferson, and evidence of the continuity of the old revolutionary elite. Younger politicians meanwhile emerged to represent new interests. Clay, leader of the 'warhawks' of 1812, was a Kentucky man; Webster came from New Hampshire, scarcely the heart of the old north; Jackson, who was to be elected president in 1828, was from Tennessee. They represented new political forces maturing in the era of good feelings – which were also helped by the diversion of attention as expansion to the west became less contentious. The eighteenth-century politics was dying and nineteenth-century America was coming to birth. Like the mother country, the Union had somehow arrived at the idea of legitimate opposition.

The last kick of Federalism came when the war of 1812 went badly. There was talk of secession (the New England states were now the ones urging the importance of States' Rights) but the Federalists would not go to the brink. When the peace came they were swept away as defeatists, men lacking in patriotism, an ironic outcome. Their electoral support had crumbled. Yet by this time many Republicans were talking Federalist policy. National action seemed the answer to the reconciliation of the sections. A tariff to protect northern industry in return for a growing market for agricultural produce from the west, together with federal improvements to roads and canals and a new Bank of the United States to clear up the mess after a widespread epidemic of local failures all made talk of an 'American System' by Republicans look much like Hamiltonianism.

In the end, social and economic change revealed that the interests of the sections could not be married so easily as some thought. The era of good feelings dissolved into new party struggles. In them, no question was more important or decisive than one which did not exist in 1789, that posed by the rapid growth of black slavery.

The makers of the constitution had recognized a problem in slavery, but one of pure political mechanics, that of deciding how much weight to give to the slave populations of some states in distributing representation. By 1800, the black slave population had grown to a million or so, and the problem was changing its nature. This growth was to continue. By 1808 there were 1·75 million blacks (in that year the abolition of the slave trade was begun), by 1840 2·75 million, and the number thereafter was to rise faster still. This was a huge increase in investment. It had taken place largely because of the greater production of cotton made possible by the invention of the gin, the growth in demand for it from British and later New England mills, and the availability of new land suitable for its cultivation after the Louisiana Purchase. In 1819, these forces had already gone far enough to produce the first of a series of political crises which eventually led to a civil war.

The moral and social problem of slavery became entangled in sectional divisions. In a sense, this had been recognized by the Founding Fathers, in that slavery had been seen as a necessary evil but one which had to be tolerated and allowed for if some of the southern states were to be satisfied with the terms of political union. There was little question that the general bias of American institutions was already against slavery except where it already existed. The Continental Congress had forbidden the further importation of slaves, and several states had abolished slavery within their borders by 1800. In 1787, the North-West Ordinance prohibited slavery in the territories it covered. There was therefore no doubt that the preservation of slavery where it already existed and of the internal slave-trade was more and more a matter of local interest. But in the south these things grew in importance with the economic importance of cotton.

Translated into politics, this meant that the southern states increased their efforts to prevent federal interference with slavery. The constitution made it necessary for them to depend on the Senate, in which each state had two seats, regardless of population, because the faster-growing population of the old and new northern states was in due course bound to give them a majority in the House of Representatives. In 1819, the Senate was exactly balanced: eleven states in which slavery existed were matched by eleven where it was illegal. But in the previous year the territory of Missouri had applied for statehood, and its bill was amended to provide for admission only if Missouri's slaves were assured of eventual emancipation. The Senate threw the bill out and the first constitutional struggle over slavery was on. The upper Mississippi valley was at stake. Slavery already existed under French and Spanish law in the lower valley; but could it be legislated into territories where it had never existed before? Could it be kept out of them by law?

The year 1819 was an electoral year. A great public debate took place. It was clear that only compromise could avert a clear eclipse of the south's sectional power. If the new states to be created from the Louisiana Purchase were to be 'free' – that is, states where slavery was forbidden by law – then the political power of the south was gone, for Texas at that moment stood in the way of any future expansion to make new states in the south. In 1821 the compromise was arrived at. Maine was admitted as a new 'free' state, while Missouri entered the Union as a slave state to balance it. At the same time it was agreed that the southern boundary of Missouri should provide a line above which slavery was prohibited in the territories of the Louisiana Purchase. The Missouri Compromise was to last thirty years, though signs of renewed difficulty were to appear long before its final abandonment. But far-sighted men could see that the central problem of sectional balance had not been removed and was bound to re-emerge, possibly much more disastrously. 'I take it for granted,' said one of them in his diary 'that the present question is a mere preamble – title-page of a great, tragic volume.'

Even in the 1820s sectionalism had already overstrained the party structure and therefore the basis of the era of good feelings. A fragmented Republican party produced four candidates for the presidency in 1824 and only one of them won support in more than one section, though he was not elected. This was Andrew Jackson, hero of the battle of New Orleans. Four years later he was elected president; 1828 was the real end of the eighteenth-century American politics. Jackson was born on the frontier of the Carolinas and had finally settled down, so far as he ever did so, in Tennessee. He was thus the first westerner to reach the White House. He benefited from western irritation with northern banking and commerce, from the feelings of some southern states against the traditional leadership of Virginia and from the increasing democratization of politics in the 1820s as states abandoned restrictions on the franchise and more and more replaced a legislative by a popular choice of presidential electors These forces won Jackson crucial votes in 1828 in the north-west, Pennsylvania and New York. His inauguration was thought by some a saturnalia appropriate to the democratic disaster which had overtaken the country.

Like Lenin, Andrew Jackson did not think the business of government was very difficult. 'The duties of public office', he said, 'are, or at least admit of being, so plain and simple that men of intelligence may readily qualify themselves for public office.' This in part explains his considerable willingness to let his supporters exploit the spoils system with what seemed unprecedented thoroughness. This was democracy of a kind. So was an attack on the Bank of the United States by the President, if by democracy is meant listening to the majority of Americans who lived in rural communities often in debt to eastern financial institutions and in need of cheap money. Another 'democratic' aspect of

Jackson's policy, some thought, was his use of the presidential veto against the national economic undertakings favoured by Congress. Meanwhile, a fundamental realignment of political forces was in train as Jackson's conduct gradually revealed to leading southern politicians that they could not count on him to uphold slavery with presidential authority. At one point it looked as if the President was prepared to use force to compel South Carolina to accept a national tariff. The claim of a right to secede was again heard, but again a compromise followed because Jackson did not want to use force if he could avoid it, and South Carolina stood alone, unsupported by any other southern state in her contemplated resistance. South Carolina's part of the compromise was a gradual reduction of all rates in the tariff; Jackson got the withdrawal of the secession claim. He, like his predecessor, looked ahead. 'The next pretext', he said, 'will be the negro, or slavery question.'

The Jacksonian era brought changes which make it justifiable to speak of a democratic revolution in American politics, obscured though it was to be in the 1840s by the revival of slavery issues. Meanwhile, immigration, migration and expansion changed the social and economic setting of politics. In the north-south division a violent polarization of politics began to appear to which western themes were increasingly subsidiary and irrelevant. It was accentuated by the growing industrialization and faster urbanization of the north and by the greater prosperity of the cotton producer in the south. Almost all attempts to foster industry in the south failed, largely because of poor communications and a shortage of skilled labour, while the southern dependence on one crop made it unprofitable to build the railroads which might have stimulated growth.

The division of the sections was therefore already very marked in 1847, though by no means as intense as it was yet to become. One current at work in the north since the 1830s was a growing support for outright abolition which excited and alarmed the south. Abolitionist propaganda more and more drove men in the south, though only a small minority of them were slave-owners, to identify slavery as the essence of their sectional identity, their 'peculiar institution'. The parties which emerged from the Jackson era had to grapple with this. Broadly speaking those called 'Democrats' were the old Jeffersonian Republicans plus some democratically inclined city-dwellers; the 'Whigs' were the party of wealth. But this was not settled, and the party-lines were crossed many times in the 1840s as politicians sought to grapple with the problem of expansion and the imbalances it might produce between slave and free states. From the two main parties' anxieties to avoid dealing with the slavery issue was to emerge in the end a third party whose *raison d'être* was just that issue. Before that, another crisis had occurred in 1846 when an attempt was made to legislate that slavery should be barred from lands acquired from Mexico. It was thrown out by the Senate. The congressional line was again drawn north and south. But the south was suddenly appalled to be outflanked by the Californians who gave themselves a constitution forbidding slavery. The southern argument had hitherto been that the federal law should not thwart popular sovereignty in states that wanted to have slavery; now she faced the prospect of admitting a California which was already 'free'. Possibly other lands acquired from Mexico might be lost to slavery, too. The situation was temporarily mastered by agreement that California should be admitted as a state, but that New Mexico and Utah should be organized as territories without mentioning slavery; in addition, the south had to accept the abolition of the slave trade in the federal district of Washington, though the northern abolitionists had to swallow a fiercer law providing for the return of runaway slaves to their masters. The real issue of American politics since 1821 was by 1847 only just capable of being contained within the constitution.

The other constitutional states of the Western World also had lively political histories after 1815. Spain and Portugal manifestly found it difficult to maintain their constitutional systems and it was clear that it was not only the minorities of two young queens which provided the trouble. All that emerged clearly from Spain's tangled history after the revolution of 1821 was that liberalism was inseparably linked there to anti-clericalism, because of liberal government's seizures of ecclesiastical property, that once the constitutional regime was reasonably firmly established political struggle was increasingly a competition by a small number of politicians for loaves and fishes, and that the army was a highly politicized force.

In continental Europe, the most important political arena was bound to be Paris, where, under the July Monarchy, a political class chosen by a narrow electorate of rich men intrigued for the posts through which they could dominate the electoral apparatus. There was legislation which was hotly debated, but it was not here that the real divisions between politicians were to be found but in the degree to which they accepted or contested the right of the king himself to play a prevailing part in government. This issue became crystallized in the 1840s in the question of electoral reform. Meanwhile, French politicians had long felt that much of the most important politics of their day were going on outside the Chamber, where it was clear that the aspirations and rhetoric of the revolutionary tradition were very much alive. In the 1830s a series of violent outbreaks had taken place, which culminated in an attempt to assassinate the king (there were others: he once wryly remarked, 'there's no close season for me'). Behind the riots and street-fighting of 1831 and

1834 in Paris and Lyons there was disappointment that 1830 had not brought a more radical revolution and also the simple fact of misery: these were hard times for the Parisian and Lyonnais poor. When they looked at their masters, it was very clear that the beneficiaries of the July Revolution were doing very well out of the regime. Tocqueville and Marx quite independently hit on the same image to describe it: a joint-stock company.

A taint of class exploitation indeed hung over constitutional France. It was the government of the rich and it is not surprising that bitter attacks were launched on the *bourgeoisie*, the better-off middle class, who had replaced the *seigneurs* in popular demonology. Paris was the nursery of dissension. There were to be found radicals, republicans, socialists, communists all preaching their own panaceas to a working-class population highly politicized and conscious of its revolutionary tradition. There was a danger here. The governments of Louis Philippe had buttressed their position with repressive laws which seemed to put an end to trouble in the 1830s. But as 1846 brought business and agricultural depression, bankruptcies and unemployment, some began to scent trouble. The government, none the less, could feel secure. The National Guard, a middle-class force, would provide for the policing of Paris if there was disturbance and had proved itself in the past. Guizot, who became Prime Minister in 1847, had no reason to believe that a crisis was approaching which he could not handle.

15 The World and the West

In 1794, on one of his visits to the kingdom of Hawaii, Captain George Vancouver managed to persuade its ruler to cede the islands to Great Britain. For this he got small thanks from his government which never accepted the cession, though twenty years later it grandly assured the Hawaiians that they would continue to enjoy freedom from any foreign rule. Curiously, the Russian government seemed no more interested in annexing them when the governor of Alaska sent an agent there in 1815. Yet Honolulu was obviously a place of commercial consequence, lying, as it did, at the junction of ocean trade-routes between Asia and the Americas. Its strategic importance had also been clear for decades.

By 1847 some thought that this indifference would soon disappear. American missionaries had by then arrived and had become an important influence in Hawaiian politics. The British and French were irritated: they feared American influence and let it be known that in their view the islands should remain independent (but France herself had annexed Tahiti only in 1842). In fact, their fears were not to be justified for a long time, but the story of Hawaii in the history of imperialism, though an episode incomplete before 1847, is worth a moment's special consideration for it concentrated in a single geographical focus a number of important themes.

One is the British reluctance to be involved. For all the predatory characteristics Western civilization was showing in the early nineteenth century, the old imperialisms were somewhat in abeyance. Indeed, with the great exception of British India, whose rulers were sucked on in part by ambition, in part by a search for security, the territorial imperialism of the old colonial powers was much less marked than it had been in the eighteenth century and was to be again after 1870. The empires of Spain and Portugal actually suffered huge territorial losses between 1775 and 1847, the Dutch were confined effectively to Indonesia and though the British gained much territory, they had also lost much forever. The old British colonies in the Caribbean went into decline with the end of the sugar boom in the early nineteenth century (the production of sugar-beet in Europe was part of the story of agricultural improvement) and their economic eclipse was consummated when slavery came to an end and the success of free trade ideas in England put paid to their protected market. Even the other major step forward by an old colonial power, that of the French in Algeria, whose acquisition began in 1830, was a conquest largely unintended. Charles x had launched an expedition against Algiers in order to win popular favour by doing something about the Barbary pirates; successful Moslem resistance in the 1830s then bogged down the French and opened nearly forty years of fighting in which a colony gradually assumed a size far greater than had been contemplated in 1830.

The two nations which were most successfully and dramatically increasing their territories in these years were, in fact, not the old colonial powers but the states which could advance their empire across land frontiers. Neither Tsarist Russia nor the republican United States had colonial traditions, but each met a tempting lack of resistance on its periphery. Another characteristic they shared was their common interest in Pacific affairs, a matter in which they tended to come face to face.

The advantages of such islands as Hawaii as places of trade and resort for whalers were available to all comers without political responsibility, so long as they remained independent, the attractiveness of this to imperial powers lay in its cheapness. What was important to everyone concerned was that this availability should continue. An open door was really all that the West required anywhere; private enterprise would do the rest. The missionaries theme is significant, too, in the Hawaiian story. They could not be kept out for long, either by western governments or by native rulers. Yet in any non-western society, they were one of the most obvious of those forms of contact with the west which provoked instability – and thus the danger of intervention from the outside – and the corrosion of local culture and institutions.

This helps to separate the phenomenon of western impact on the world from that of western political domination of it. There was in some degree a pause in empire-building. Africa could not really be penetrated until fresh technical means were available; climate and disease stood in the way. In the Far East, what mattered was access to markets. Europe was somewhat inward-looking, preoccupied by her own problems, and Americans and Russians did not see what they were doing as empire-building but as natural growth. British governments were more aware of the expense involved in adding to the empire than the advantages of it. On the other hand, thousands of individuals were interested for their own reasons, good and bad, in promoting western influence over the rest of the world by means other than direct rule.

Thus a period in which western civilization became visibly more dominant and more expansive right round the globe was one in which commerce and cultural aggressiveness counted for more than colonization.

One example was the exploratory vigour of this era. The knowledge of the globe which had been acquired over three centuries by the West was brought virtually to completion in these years. As 1775 began, Captain Cook had just rounded Cape Horn. He was nearly at the end of his second voyage of exploration. Even this great explorer was capable of underestimating the enterprise of those who would follow him. Down towards the sixtieth parallel he sighted snow-covered peaks and pack ice between him and them; 'I can be bold to say,' he wrote, 'that no man will ever venture further than I have done and that the lands which may lie to the south will never be explored.' Forty years later another explorer found that the peaks were islands, and so attractive had Cook's reports proved that by 1820 more than a million fur seals had been taken in South Georgia, which he had surveyed not far to the north. By then, Cook had long since sailed on his third voyage, that of 1776, from which he was not to return, taking with him on a search for a north-west passage from Pacific to Atlantic, Vancouver, then a midshipman but in the 1790s the surveyor of the coasts from California to Alaska. By 1815 there was little of the world's surface which could be reached by water which was not known and charted. The interior of the remaining great land masses was beginning to be penetrated, too.

Simple contact between westerners and others could by itself often produce important changes. Explorers and travellers who were not consciously in the business of being brokers between civilizations had for centuries unwittingly been transforming what they touched. One all-too familiar example was the communication of Western diseases to peoples earlier isolated from them, often with disastrous results. Less material changes could also be important. The celebrated Captain Bligh precipitated a minor cultural change in Tahiti by arriving there in a ship whose female figurehead gave male islanders a new ideal of female beauty.

Some of the go-betweens of culture, though, were brutally and consciously destructive of what they met. Such were the American settlers and trappers who swept the Indian from the hunting lands they coveted, the Dutch planters in Indonesia who wiped out whole populations in the quest for spice profits, the slaving captains who encouraged African kings to sell them their prisoners and even their subjects, the Tasmanians who rounded up the miserable survivors (about two hundred) of the native population of their island in 1835 and packed them off to die of misery somewhere else, or the Boer farmers who in the following year began their Great Trek towards freedom for themselves in republics to be built on dispossessing the Bushman and crushing the Bantu. Some of these representatives of the Western World had at least a semblance of order and organization in what they did, or at least could sometimes appeal to it, because they acted in accordance with policies of settlement. More alarming, in retrospect, seems the cloud of independent skirmishers and *franc-tireurs* who had always hung about the front line of the West's onslaught on the world in one form or another, descendants of the freebooting *conquistadores* and pirates of former times. They were the most ruthless of go-betweens, lawless men owning no master, any scruples surviving the liberty given them by their firearms being quickly dulled by their belief in the superior rights of their culture. Sometimes they followed the flag instead of preceding it; Ceylon was in the 1830s the scene of a plantation boom which drew to the island an appalling riff-raff whose activities first demoralized the administration and then led to a rebellion in 1848.

Such men were first and last out for material gain. This had always been the most powerful drive behind western expansion, even if some did show more scruples in pursuing it than others. Between 1775 and 1847 there was built upon the search for wealth a structure of world trade which linked the other continents to Europe and the Americas in new ways. Broadly speaking, it corresponded to the change in imperial interests which diverted interest from the old plantation colonies of the Caribbean, back to Asia. The new pattern was one of expanding free trade; British maritime and commercial superiority made this bias inevitable. But its direction towards the East is to be explained by the appearance for the first time of valuable products which were wanted in Asia. Bills which had once to be settled in bullion would in the nineteenth century be settled more and more in manufactured goods. It was in this era that the British manufacturer began to dream of a vast market of hundreds of millions of Asiatics: the reality was present in a measure in India, but always eluded him in China.

One notable and economically important sector of Western trade in 1775 which had all but disappeared in 1847 was that in slaves. The overwhelming majority of them were blacks, brought directly or indirectly from Africa. There had always been slaves, so that to traffic in human beings was a crime not unique to the West. Slaves from Africa in particular went through the hands of Arab traders to the Islamic world (where there were also Europeans enslaved). None the less, slavery did not exist over much of Asia in a form recognizable to Europeans, and the Western slave trade and the slave systems which it fed, were unique in two respects. One was their demographic significance: they changed importantly the distribution of colour round the world, so that today great numbers of citizens of American states have African blood. Its other interest lies in the fact that slavery in the West was destroyed by the civilization of which it was part.

The main source of black slaves in the eighteenth century was the western African 'Slave Coast' – a significant name – and the Portuguese colony of Angola which had actually been founded for slaving purposes. From these catchment areas, slave-traders took their cargoes, often under horrible and destructive conditions, to Brazil, the Caribbean plantation colonies and the southern parts of the United States. Huge profits were made and the trade was a major component of world commerce. Its benefits were shared by the shippers – usually British, French or North American – and the plantation owners, who received in this way what was for a long time cheap labour. Of the millions of blacks who were transported to the Americas, the majority worked as agricultural labourers, often under harsh discipline.

Its quality may be judged from the constant fears of slave revolts expressed by eighteenth-century planters. Cruelty was one reason for attacks on the trade in which men of Enlightenment and men of Christian conscience could join. By 1789 there were already notable movements for the abolition of the slave trade and slavery (though it was possible to envisage the first without the second) in France and Great Britain. Two setbacks then occurred. One was the French Revolution. The universality of the principles it proclaimed told in the direction of abolition, though the powerful lobby of French planters prevented anything being done. None the less, much was heard from the *Amis des noirs*, who were connected with the more radical politicians of the Constituent Assembly, and this tended to taint the idea of anti-slavery with a general feeling of revolutionary and Jacobinical principles. Thus it lost support among cautious men even before the Convention freed all slaves in French territory in 1794. The second was a successful slave revolt in the French island of Haiti in 1791. The war made it possible for the first black nation in the Western World to emerge and to survive. Interestingly, the formal structure it gave itself was western rather than African; to this extent black slavery had been a means of assimilating its victims to the Western World, though much that was African survived the process. Napoleon later attempted to recover the island and succeeded in deposing and carrying off to imprisonment (where he died) the black dictator of the island, the remarkable Toussaint l'Ouverture. But Haiti did not go back under the French or any other flag.

Meanwhile the economic fundamentals were slowly shifting against the slave trade. Much has been made of this important point, but it is still not the whole story of abolition, any more than economic change in the United States explains abolition within that country. More was needed, notably that governments should put force behind a policy of abolition. To do this required the mobilization of moral indignation, and this was what the British anti-slavery agitators achieved, just as, later, William Lloyd Garrison and the northern abolitionists did in the United States. A famous judgment of the 1770s had already removed much of slavery's legal protection in England by making it impossible to expect a court to treat a runaway slave on English soil as property which ought to be returned to its rightful owner. What happened next was the outlawing of the slave trade in 1807 in Great Britain. She was the greatest naval power. For the next forty years, the Royal Navy (soon with the assistance of the United States and French navies) was at work suppressing slave-running to possessions of those countries like Spain with colonies still wanting slaves, or to South America. Slavery itself in 1847 still existed over much of the western hemisphere. The outstanding example was the United States. But it was abolished in the British colonies in 1838, and the tide of opinion was everywhere against it. It was on the way out.

The slavers in the Indian Ocean were Arabs who sold to the Islamic states of the Near East and Persian Gulf. The continuation of such an enormity after the admirable (but also somewhat self-admiring) self-cleansing of the Western World was one of the many things which fed the sense of mission which Europeans and Americans took with them to Asia. The missionary impulse was important in abolition itself; one of the many concerns of abolitionists had been that slavery not only was un-Christian cruelty towards the sons of God but also might stand in the way of the propagation of the gospel among them. In the mission field overseas, whatever might be happening to the Churches in the lands where they had first taken root and been nurtured, the nineteenth century was to prove one of the great ages of Christianity. Africa, Asia and the Pacific were seen as fields ripe for such a harvest as Christianity had not enjoyed since the conquest of the Americas.

The aspirations of missionaries were not new, but found fewer obstacles. In India, the East India Company had long resisted the arrival of missionaries. The first English missionary in India, a Baptist who arrived in 1793, found no welcome from his countryman and went to live at a Danish settlement near Calcutta. In the next century the story was very, and quickly, different. Public opinion in Great Britain was brought formidably to bear upon government in the interests of the churches. In other countries, too, notably France, governments respected missionary aims and did what they could to further them.

Naturally, missionaries, and probably most Western people who thought about this huge expansion of influence, saw it in a purely religious light. Missionaries in the field were often very conscious of ecclesiastical or doctrinal distinctions between themselves, and rivalry – for example between Catholic and Protestant missions – was not uncommon. The recipients of missionary teaching and good works, on the other hand, were often more struck by the similarities between different denominations than by differences. To them, it was the general Western-ness of missionary work which was most striking. It was as 'Franks', a general term adopted by the Chinese for all Western arrivals, that they were seen.

This is another layer of the missionary phenomenon. Christianity had been the original and defining matrix of Western civilization. The urge to bring Christian light to darkness and help to the benighted was part of a much more general impulse shared by all those who believed that the Western civilization in which they had been reared was indisputably superior to anything else the world could offer. For one man such as Sir William Jones, the first great English orientalist and a translator of Sanskrit writings, there were hundreds of high-principled men in India who could see little there but barbarism and superstition. Secular and religious currents flowed together. Utilitarian and Evangelical Christian alike were appalled by such practices as *suttee* (the practice of burning his widow alive on a Hindu's funeral pyre) and female infanticide.

The sense of superior enlightenment and morality, fed by the evident success which Western nations had in imposing their will on other civilizations, brought with it changes in old attitudes. The exotic and outlandish was no longer in the nineteenth century to be seen, as it had been in the eighteenth, as something from which there might be lessons to be drawn for Western civilization. China's stability seemed now stagnation. There disappeared the former enthusiasm for its supposed tolerance and enlightenment, for the uncorrupted innocence of the Noble Savages of Tahiti, or for the mysterious wisdom of the Indian Brahmin. Instead, the great crumbling civilizations of the East came to be seen as picturesque ruins from which nothing was to be learned; they were thought ready only for western reform or improvement. They embodied in an acute form obstacles to progress which had been crumbling under the onslaught of revolution and improvement in Europe and had barely existed in America; only the Greeks, remarked Shelley pompously, had prevented Europe from displaying the same 'stagnant and miserable state of social institutions as China and Japan'.

If improvement proved impossible, then these ancient lands should be exploited by those who knew how; such was a reasonable deduction. The mirage of a mass market in China was to prove as illusory as the apostles of Western civilization were to prove one-eyed, but also as persistent. A certain ignoring of facts was going on. It might be true that, considered as totalities, the societies of Asia looked to Americans and Europeans cruel and poverty-stricken, lacking elementary forms of civilized justice, unapt to enterprise and change. So no doubt they were. But those who dwelled on such judgments seemed to find it easy in their self-esteem to forget or overlook the superstition of Europe where men were still executed for witchcraft only a few years before the French Revolution, the savagery of the American 'mountain men' of the Rockies, the horrors of Engels' Manchester or the crippling of children in the early cotton-mills.

Yet the western sense of conscious superiority, and therefore of justification, was one of the most important constituents of the corrosive power everywhere shown by western culture. The pre-Columbian civilizations of America had long vanished in 1775, and the civilization beginning to show the most extensive signs of damage was that of the Islamic buffer zone between Europe and Asia, dominated by an Ottoman Empire in retreat. By 1847 this had gone much further. Centuries of change had by then done their work; the Turkish rulers of the Islamic countries with which Europeans most easily came in contact had long been exposed to western influence even if their own response had usually been an increasing conservatism in the face of challenge. With the French Revolution, the stimuli to change became much stronger. Bonaparte's Egyptian campaign helped to set in train the events which brought to power the westernizing Mehemet Ali. Later came pressure for reform from European countries anxious to preserve Turkey's independence. Meanwhile, the penetration of Turkey's subject populations by Western ideas – sometimes spread by American missionaries – continued.

Farther East, Persia was disputed between the diplomatic forces from the west and north, but did not suffer so much as either the Ottoman lands or the old civilizations of the Far East, the great theatre of Western predators in the early nineteenth century. They could still show great powers of resistance. Even in India, the corrosion and crumbling of the native political structures which had followed British and French advance into the power vacuum left by the decay of Mughal power long had little effect on Indian society and culture. The British had won an Indian future by 1763, but the final assurance that there was to be no resurgence of the rival power of France came only in the Napoleonic period. Meanwhile, there was from 1772 an almost unbroken advance of intervention by British government in Indian affairs; though they were still formally the business of the East India Company in 1847, it had by then become in effect an agent of the British government for the management of the greatest British dependency. The age of free trade did not favour privileged companies and it had lost first its monopoly of trade with India in 1813 and then that with China twenty years later. From that moment, too, settlement in India by Europeans was allowed without reference to the Company. In the background, there survived the formal authority of the Mughal emperor at Delhi, as whose agent, theoretically, the Company acted in government, but even his name disappeared from the Company's coinage in the 1830s. India was in reality more and more a British colony.

The increasing involvement of British government in India and the withering of the idea that the Company was solely commercial, concerned only to make a profit in India, was an improvement. One reason for greater public control of the Company had been revelations of unscrupulous behaviour by some of its servants and suspicion of much more that remained hidden. The 'nabob', or returned Company official, flaunting his wealth, was not a popular figure in eighteenth-century England, and it was morally satisfying to the envious or self-righteous to attribute his riches to crime or corruption. Dubious as some motives for reform were, they steadily increased the disinterestedness, if not the sympathetic quality, of British government in India. It was run by civil servants with a strong sense of mission, responsibility and competence which was by and large justified, whose recruitment by competitive examination was to be a model for the reform of the English civil service in the 1850s. Convinced of their own rightness, these men turned Indian rural life upside down by revenue and land-tenure reforms which drove individualist principles through the communalism of Indian village life, ruining many Indians in the process. They also abolished *suttee*, in spite of a disinclination to interfere with that area of Indian life where religion and social custom blurred into one another.

By 1847 India was of huge importance to British industry. There were now cheap textiles to export; they not only virtually wiped out Indian textile production, but also ended the old imbalance of British trade with India which had required the export of bullion. Almost the whole peninsula had been by 1847 absorbed into the British system, whether ruled directly or as dependencies under native rulers. In 1847, a war with the Sikhs was in progress which would result in the annexation of the Punjab. The Company's armies had twice even got as far as Kabul, the capital of Afghanistan, though the first time it had been with disastrous results; only one man came back. Indians suddenly saw that the British were not invincible after all. Nevertheless, the acquisition of India seemed unshakeable in 1847 and it was unquestionably an event of huge magnitude. For the first time since the sixteenth century, Europeans had an example of an imperialism looking beyond settlement and trade. What was different from the Iberian American empires of earlier times, though, was that for the first time a Western power was ruling through a handful of its own officials and soldiers hundreds of millions of people who were not to be made to adopt either Christianity or western culture.

Developments in India speeded up the crumbling of the Chinese Empire and therefore of the Chinese Revolution which has come to its completion only in this century. When a British mission was sent to China in 1792 to seek the expansion of trade between the two countries, George III's emissary was received with magnificent condescension, and told that China did not lack anything such a remote barbarian kingdom as Great Britain might produce and that there were thus no Chinese needs she could satisfy. None the less, the ambassador was told to thank his master for the loyalty and respect he showed and to tell him that the emperor would continue to regard him benevolently.

In this message and the practical failure of the mission were expressed the traditional confidence of a Chinese civilization which saw itself as the centre of the world, the bearer of a divine mandate to rule other and barbarian peoples. It was a confidence which had preserved China for two thousand years. Two of its institutional expressions may be thought striking. One was negative: China had no Foreign Office or equivalent to one. This was because the whole of the rest of the world was seen as tributary, not as a world of independent states standing on an equal legal footing with China and therefore requiring diplomatic relations with her. Another was the ordering of China's trade with the West. All of it had to go through one small part of the port of Canton. No other trade was allowed.

In the nineteenth century, such facts had to give way before something China had never before had to face, a rival power which the Chinese might consider barbarian, but which was as self-confident as they, possessed irresistible power and would therefore prove impervious to the absorption and taming which earlier barbarian conquerors had undergone. Not only the British were knocking at the door: merchants and explorers from New England were at work in Chinese waters in the late eighteenth century, prospecting for outlets for North American furs. Chinese trade grew rapidly and it was in 1813 that an island in the Marquesas was acquired by the United States and just over twenty years later that the United States Navy set up a separate East India squadron.

By that time, the British trade with China had been revolutionized by the discovery of a commodity for which there was a huge demand in China which could be grown in India: opium. Here was at last something with which to pay for the huge quantities of tea which the East India Company exported from China to Great Britain. Soon, the flood of opium into China alarmed the Chinese government. When an attempt was made to stop this (its social consequences were deplorable), the British ran up the Jolly Roger of free trade and bombarded their way into China in the Opium Wars of 1839–42. The western assault on China thus began just as the conquest of India was being completed. The British were first, acquiring the important trading station of Hong Kong in 1842 and the right to trade at Canton and four other 'treaty ports'. The Americans followed this with a treaty providing for extra-territorial jurisdiction for its subjects in China (this was to be extended to all foreigners) and the French with one providing toleration for Roman Catholicism. In 1845 this was extended to Protestantism.

These concessions unleashed a process which was to have steady extension. Where the British opened the door to commerce, other nations followed. Concessions of trading rights by the Chinese government led to the arrival of more foreign residents. Xenophobia sometimes placed them in danger; this was particularly true of missionaries, whose influence was deeply distrusted by many Chinese. When there was violence, gunboats and punitive expeditions were sent. Thus the Chinese government was further humiliated in the eyes of its subjects and its authority further eroded. This process had not gone far by 1847 but the implications were beginning to appear. Among those who recognized them were some thoughtful men in a neighbouring kingdom, Japan. The control of Japan's relations with the Western World had been much tighter than China's. Only the Dutch were permitted to trade in Japan, and they were confined to a depot on a little island in Nagasaki harbour.

It was becoming clear to some Japanese that this isolation might not be maintained for much longer. The king of the Netherlands warned them in the 1830s. By then, some scholars and intellectuals were already studying 'Dutch learning', the name given to the books imported by the Dutch in which might be found, it was hoped, the secrets of Western power. From this was to come, later in the century, a much more successful response to western challenge than that of China.

Yet even Japan's response to the West was in a measure the admission of defeat. No non-western nation had the option, in the face of the dynamism of western civilization, of remaining as it was. It might resist – and then be driven by force or fraud to accept more interference in its internal life – or it might try to equip itself with what the West could offer in the way of techniques of self-preservation. Either way, it could not remain unchanged. Technology could be mastered only by a society prepared to change itself: this was the general truth behind Thackeray's commendation of the 'civilizing paddle-wheel' as a force which would sweep away the rottenness of the Turkish empire he visited in 1844. This dilemma was not fully apparent before the first half of the nineteenth century. Already, though, signs of it could be seen. The first leader of a modernizing movement within Hinduism, Ram Mohum Roy, backed the use of English against the vernacular tongues in higher education; those who agreed with him admired Western ideas or wanted to learn English in order to get jobs in the growing administration. More than simply the convenience of educational administration was involved and it was difficult not to agree that, as Macaulay argued in his famous minute of 1835, what was implied was a choice between higher and lower civilizations. Roy, for example, was against *suttee*.

The evident defensiveness or impotence of Asian and Pacific peoples (Africa provided fewer examples in this period because of the closing down of slave-trading and the barriers of terrain, climate and disease) enormously strengthened the West's self-confidence. A *tour d'horizon* in 1847 could scarcely fail to flatter self-esteem. Beyond Europe and the Americas lay European communities in South Africa, Australia and New Zealand. The 'white' share of the world's surface was moving like the 'white' share of world population towards a climax which still lay half-a-century ahead. A British Empire renewed since 1783, together with Dutch Indonesia and the still important French, Spanish and Portuguese empires gave the Western World actual physical control of many non-Western peoples. Beyond these colonial boundaries operated the seemingly irresistible forces of commerce and culture. Before these forces, once-great empires like the Ottoman or Chinese seemed to have no choice but adaptation by imitation or decay and powerlessness. Not all the dynamic effects of Western civilization, of course, necessarily told in its favour in the long run. The establishment of a great *entrepôt* at Singapore, launched by Raffles in 1819, helped to stimulate migration from south China which would profoundly alter the balance of nationalities and cultures in the whole of south-east Asia. When some Decembrist conspirators exiled to the East found themselves among the Buryat Mongols, they began the study of their culture and this had the unlooked-for consequence that the Mongols themselves began to think better of it and thus led to later trouble for their Tsarist rulers. But such consequences, like that of imperial rule which created expectations it later failed to satisfy, could hardly be envisaged in 1847.

What is perhaps most remarkable is that one man of unusual vision had already discerned, well before this, another significant pattern in world affairs and one which determined the future of many non-Western peoples. It was in 1835 that Tocqueville included in *Democracy in America* this judgment:

There are at the present time two great nations in the world, which started from different points, but seem to tend towards the same end. I allude to the Russians and the Americans. Both of them have grown up unnoticed; and while the attention of mankind was directed elsewhere, they have suddenly placed themselves in the front rank among the nations, and the world learned their existence and their greatness at almost the same time.

All other nations seem to have nearly reached their natural limits, and they have only to maintain their power; but these are still in the act of growth. All the others have stopped, or continue to advance with extreme difficulty; these alone are proceeding with ease and celerity along a path to which no limit can be perceived. The American struggles against the obstacles that nature opposes to him; the adversaries of the Russian are men. The former combats the wilderness and savage life; the latter, civilization with all its arms. The conquests of the American are therefore gained by the plowshare; those of the Russian by the sword. The Anglo-American relies upon personal interest to accomplish his ends and gives free scope to the unguided strength and common sense of the people; the Russian centres all the authority of society in a single arm. The principal instrument of the former is freedom; of the latter, servitude. Their starting-point is different and their courses are not the same; yet each of them seems marked out by the will of Heaven to sway the destinies of half the globe.

16 1847 and other dates

At the end of 1847, many Europeans felt a sense of impending tempest. The decade had opened badly, in hard times. Good harvests and recovery then gave way in 1845 once more to dearth and business recession. A potato blight was followed by two years of rain and bad harvests. This book must end, as it began, with bread riots. It was a starving time in many countries; some, of which Ireland was the most unhappy, underwent famine and the diseases which followed in its wake. Unemployment and bankruptcies, by that time familiar indicators of crisis in the new commercial world of the nineteenth century, multiplied in 1847 when the troubles of England spread to Europe.

This was the background of growing political trouble. In 1846 a rising at Cracow was followed by an Austrian annexation of the free city in defiance of the treaty of Vienna and connivance by the Habsburg authorities at a *jacquerie* by the peasants of Galicia against their Polish *seigneurs*. In France radicals seeking franchise reform began to raise the political temperature with a carefully engineered programme of banquets which were really protest meetings. Chartism was again gathering like a stormcloud in the United Kingdom. In Italy, 1846, brought an occurrence Metternich had believed impossible, the election of a liberal pope. Pius IX focused both liberal and national aspirations of many of his countrymen, and his election was a bad omen for Austria, within whose sphere of influence Italy fell; it would be difficult to be more papal than the pope in defence of the order of 1815. Mounting troubles inside the Italian states began to push their rulers down the road of reform. The usual demand was for a constitution, a civic guard and free newspapers; some assumed that the removal of Austria would necessarily follow. Finally, in Switzerland there began a civil war in October 1847 when a union of Catholic cantons refused to dissolve on being told to do so by the liberals of the Confederation's Diet.

Some of this was evidence of long unsatisfied and frustrated demands. For all their great conquests in half a century, liberals had still not won the basic constitutional and juridical guarantees in most of Europe east of the Rhine. Even in the United States, some of them were increasingly troubled, though by a different threat, that of the growing power of a democratic national government to infringe historic rights and the practical independence enjoyed by the states of the Union. Nationalists, too, felt thwarted. While they could point to the success of the national principle in Greece and Belgium since 1815, in other countries their aims were unachieved. They could hardly know that for the satisfaction of many nationalist claims they would have to wait until 1919, nor that such triumphs of nationality as were to be won in the near future would be won by the armies and diplomacy of great states, not by popular support. Had they known this, perhaps they would have borne their frustrations with more resignation. As it was, in Germany, Italy and the Habsburg Empire they constituted another threat to order by their very confidence and self-righteousness.

Those who rejected the existing order at more fundamental levels than these were far fewer in 1847. Only at the very end of the year at Engels' suggestion a congress of the Communist League in London gave Marx the task of drafting the document later known as *The Communist Manifesto*. Though it was to be read round the world with effects as great as the reading of the American Declaration of Independence, it awoke immediately no significant response and went almost unnoticed in the uproar of 1848. The views expressed were those of a minority, but none the less represented in one of its most advanced forms the socialist criticism of the existing order, one which cut not only at the roots of the *ancien régime* but also at those of the order replacing it. Advanced socialists (among whom Marx and his co-believers were only one *coterie*) cut deeper than any other critics into nineteenth-century civilization by rejecting any idea of a general interest such as that upon which rested the *Wealth of Nations* and its majestic account of a self-equilibriating society.

The tremblings in the system were widely felt. Most people summed up their fears by the word Revolution. Yet this hardly seemed inevitable and was to prove far from fatal. When Tocqueville looked back on the crisis which broke in 1848, he attributed to chance the downfall of the July Monarchy which at the beginning of that year seemed as solidly based as ever. He, and some others, were more alarmed by less dramatic and more gradual threats to a society whose civilization they esteemed. Men of the Left sometimes felt the same way. It was the radical Louis Blanc who deplored as any traditionalist of the Right might have done, 'what we now see, the social, the individual character debased; Frenchmen utterly indifferent under national misfortune and disgrace; the genius of the country decaying, disappearing; the nation itself dying, exhausted, corrupt and rotten'.

There were some grounds for feeling optimism in 1847, too. First and foremost was the huge success of the previous three decades in organizing international life. Since 1815 none of the great powers of the Western World had fought one another. This was impressive to those – many of whom survived still in 1847 – who could remember the countless wars of the eighteenth century. If a nascent United States may be counted a power, then in the last quarter of that century there had been only three years, 1784, 1785 and 1786, in which there had not been at least one of the major states formally at war. The foundations of the new peace still seemed solid in 1847. Though the Vienna settlement had not survived unchanged, France was still contained by the boundaries it had given to her, the Holy Alliance still seemed intact and the military preponderance of Russia still showed no sign of its approaching decline. Beyond Europe, Britannia still ruled the waves and on her unchallenged battle-fleet rested a worldwide *pax Britannica*.

Many liberals could feel easy, too, over the internal evolution of constitutional countries. After 1830 and 1832 the essential gains of the French Revolution in constitutional liberty and representation were safe, it seemed; there was to be no rolling back of the ideological frontier. 1846 had brought the great symbolic triumph of the repeal of the Corn Laws in the United Kingdom, a new demonstration of what an aroused public opinion could achieve through parliamentary machinery and little less than a statement that the British state was henceforth to serve a new kind of society. In Italy, there was the election of Pius IX. There was also the triumphant survival of the one great republican power, the United States, a triumph which only close and well-informed observers could discern to be flawed by the nagging and growing virulence of the slavery issue. Finally, there was the optimism engendered by an unparalleled long-term surge of prosperity, however punctuated it might be by temporary swings and recussions. Confidence was soon to recover as the impact of the Californian gold discoveries of the later 1840s began to be felt in the stimulus given to commerce.

It is not easy in such a welter of facts and impressions to decide exactly what does make 1847 significant in the history of the Western World. The answer is probably 'nothing in particular'. Historical periods are conventional devices: though useful, they are always in a measure arbitrary. Their definition depends on the assumptions brought to discussing them. Here it has been argued that between 1847 and 1775, where we began, great changes in fact occurred which gave the epoch a clear significance though not resting on any such clear division as is provided by a particular year.

Even more celebrated dates within this era turn out, on examination to have only a limited validity. One way of summing up the great transformations of this era would be to describe them as the ending of the Middle Ages for much of Europe (though not for America, which had never known this past, nor for some advanced parts of Europe). A great symbolic date for this should be 1789, which has also often been taken as the end of the eighteenth century, too – centuries being for historians periods with discernible unities of theme rather than simply units of a calendar delimited at one end by numbers ending in 1 and at the other by numbers ending in 00. Sometimes people are prepared to be very precise and say that it was on 14 July 1789, with the capture of the Bastille, that a new age began. There is much to be said for such a view. But even within an event so important as the great French Revolution itself, there are complexities, and it could be argued (for example) that 1792, the year of the internationalizing of ideological struggle by war, of the emergence of the republic, was just as decisive a break as 1789. Men's minds moved rapidly once the Bastille had fallen. The French of 1789 still saw solutions to their problems in the terms of enlightened despotism or constitutionalism, both of them well-established eighteenth-century ideas. By 1792 they were used to the idea of democracy, even if few welcomed it.

On a different time-scale, 1789 might provide a marker in another process: the Austrians took Belgrade (though they were to give it back to the Turks later) and the questions of eastern Europe lurched one stage nearer to their nineteenth-century forms. But the search for a viable chronological structure no sooner moves to international relations than it has again to return to France, with Napoleon, the titanic figure who dominated them for fifteen years and whose acts continued to shape them longer still. His accession to power in 1799 is another reasonable date at which to divide historical ages. With him, the consolidation of the French Revolution was assured. Yet he was an eighteenth-century figure, too, not merely because he was educated and grew up in its assumptions but because there is also recognizable in his Empire the greatest of enlightened despotisms.

In 1815 came the Restoration – and the word is another hint that we should not be too ready to lop periods with our historical chopper. You must have – or think you have – something to restore before you can have a Restoration; so, in some sense, a past lives on. Past and future were not so easily divided at that moment. Metternich, twenty-one years old when Robespierre dominated the Convention, was only forty-two when the Congress of Vienna opened and he was able to set about conserving as much of the past as had survived the hurricane. There was a great deal of it. Europe had been given a huge succession of jolts between 1789 and 1815 and much had crumbled under their impact, yet she was able to return to many of her old ways, and many of them were still strong in 1847. Millions of men and women lived daily lives virtually indistinguishable from those they or their parents had lived in 1789. We think of the metric system of weights and measures as one of the most obvious legacies of the French Revolution and so, indeed, it is. Yet before 1840 its units were not in normal use even in France.

The evidence of revolution also speaks for continuity. All over Europe, in the revolutionary waves of 1820–1, 1830 and, later, 1848, men rose to realize aims which had first been set out in the French Revolution and were left unrealized in 1815. Continuity across the Atlantic was even greater. There, for all the transformations brought about by the opening of the West, the United States still lived under the constitution of 1789. For all the social and demographic changes they had seen, too, many Americans still lived in a setting strikingly unchanged since their Revolution. In 1845 Thoreau had only to borrow an axe and cut down the white-pine he needed to build a hut, and he could live in solitude by Walden pond within a few miles of the great port of Boston. The great changes to be wrought by technology in American life had begun, but the cotton-gin was the only invention already revolutionizing American society by 1847.

Yet the world of 1847 was a world transformed from that of 1775, where we began. This was strikingly if superficially visible in dress, in the new machines and the spreading railways. In the broadest perspective of all those with which we are concerned, the eighteenth century was already at an end when we began, with the Declaration of Independence which announced an eventual transformation of the balance of world power. It was in this light the beginning of the end – still a long way away – of a European world hegemony which had yet further to go to reach its peak. In the history of another future world power, Russia, there is no such convenient landmark between 1775 and 1847, though 1795 was important, when the third partition extinguished Poland (with minor exceptions) for a century and a quarter, or 1783 when the incorporation of the Crimea made Russia a Black Sea power. Further afield still, there could be found symbolic dates to mark other epochs, in the opening of China, the subjugation of India or the revolutions of South America.

In the narrower, though wide enough, context of the Atlantic world, it seems best to end by noticing a change not pinned to a date but pervading the whole era. It is a complex one, observable in all sides of society and because it settles so much of the history of what was to come, it signifies a greater change than simply the ending of a 'century' or a 'period'. It was a turning-point in world history. In these years, Western society took the decisive steps towards industrialization, towards the reconstruction of social arrangements on the basis of the individual, towards the secularization of its culture and towards a new politics which has since become worldwide. The particular expressions of this were manifold: a new sort of city, new wealth, the change described as the movement from 'status to contract', the replacement of legal ties defining duties by market relationships, the overshadowing of dynastic claims by national ones, the relative decline of agriculture's importance in the economy, the much wider appearance and spread of such institutions as banks, stock exchanges and a commercial Press – an almost endless list could be drawn out. All the items in it would reflect also the two great processes at work in these years which mark them as truly revolutionary, the relatively sudden acquisition by one part of mankind of unprecedented new resources and material power, and the unique acceleration of history this would produce.

In the end, this acceleration was to be evident worldwide, but it first showed itself in the breaking up of the inherited conglomerates of Europe (and even the much younger ones of the United States) by forces more blind and unsparing than any revolutionary wave. Indeed, the idea of revolution had itself become a part of the inherited culture of the West by 1847, as the imitative gestures of the following year, when revolt and rebellion ran from end to end of Europe, were to show. Even in 1848, too, Revolution did not change the world so very much and certainly did so less than had the majestic march of the forces of Improvement in the previous fifty years. That much, at least, is obvious. What is harder to observe and remember is that even in the Western World, millions of men and women in 1847 still lived lives almost untouched by anything we chose to denote by such abstractions as Revolution and Improvement at all. Theirs was still a world where even the idea of change could be suspected.

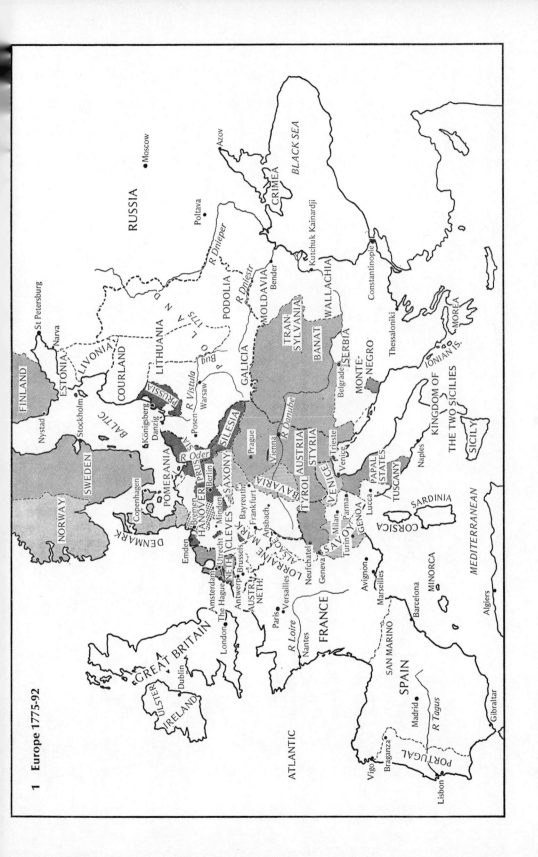

1 Europe 1775-92

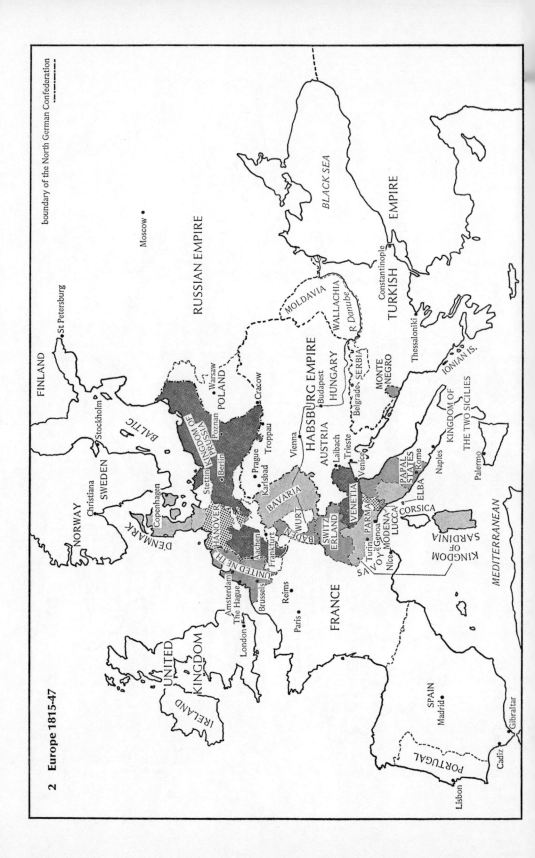

2 Europe 1815-47

boundary of the North German Confederation

FINLAND

St Petersburg

NORWAY

SWEDEN

Christiania

Stockholm

BALTIC

Moscow

RUSSIAN EMPIRE

Copenhagen

DENMARK

Stettin

KINGDOM OF PRUSSIA

Berlin

Warsaw

Poznan

POLAND

Cracow

UNITED KINGDOM

IRELAND

London

UNITED NETH

Amsterdam
The Hague

Brussels

Reims

Paris

FRANCE

HANOVER

Aachen

Frankfurt

BADEN

WURT

BAVARIA

Prague

Karlsbad

Troppau

Vienna

HABSBURG EMPIRE

AUSTRIA

Budapest

HUNGARY

Laibach

Trieste

MOLDAVIA

WALLACHIA

R Danube

Belgrade

SERBIA

MONTE
NEGRO

BLACK SEA

Constantinople

TURKISH

EMPIRE

Thessaloniki

IONIAN IS.

SWITZ
ERLAND

Turin

O Y

Genoa

Nice

SA

MODENA

LUCCA

PARMA

VENETIA

Venice

ELBA

CORSICA

PAPAL
STATES

Rome

Naples

KINGDOM OF

THE TWO SICILIES

Palermo

KINGDOM OF SARDINIA

MEDITERRANEAN

SPAIN

Madrid

PORTUGAL

Lisbon

Cadiz

Gibraltar

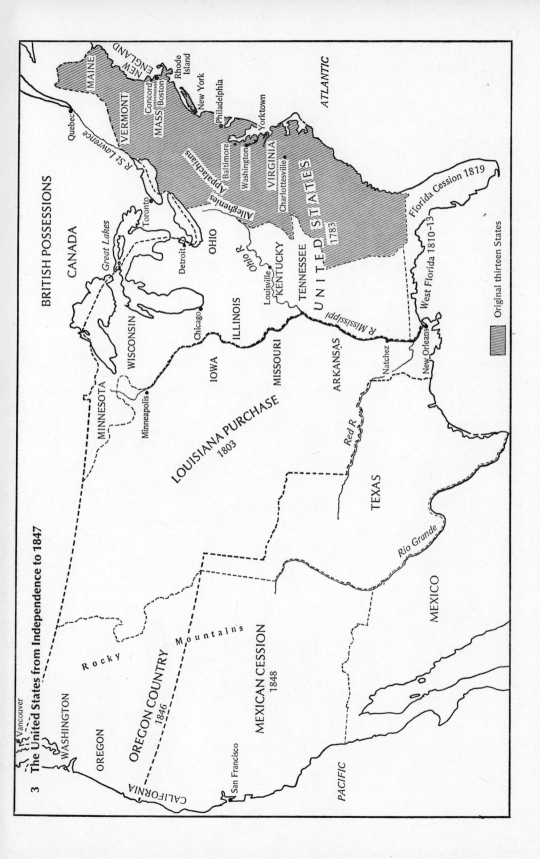

3 The United States from Independence to 1847

BRITISH POSSESSIONS

CANADA

Quebec

R. St. Lawrence

Great Lakes

Toronto

Detroit

OHIO

Ohio R.

Chicago

WISCONSIN

ILLINOIS

IOWA

MINNESOTA

Minneapolis

MISSOURI

KENTUCKY

Louisville

TENNESSEE

ARKANSAS

LOUISIANA PURCHASE
1803

Red R.

Natchez

New Orleans

R. Mississippi

TEXAS

Rio Grande

MEXICO

MEXICAN CESSION
1848

OREGON COUNTRY
1846

Rocky Mountains

WASHINGTON

OREGON

CALIFORNIA

San Francisco

Vancouver

PACIFIC

MAINE

NEW ENGLAND

VERMONT

Concord

MASS Boston

Rhode Island

New York

Philadelphia

Yorktown

Baltimore

Washington

VIRGINIA

Charlottesville

Appalachians

Alleghenies

UNITED STATES

1783

ATLANTIC

Florida Cession 1819

West Florida 1810-13

Original thirteen States

4 **South America 1775-1847**

UNITED MEXICAN STATES

CUBA

HONDURAS

GUATEMALA
EL SALVADOR

HAITI

NICARAGUA

CARIBBEAN SEA

COSTA RICA

PANAMA

Caracas

NEW
GRANADA
1831

VENEZUELA
1830

Bogota

COLOMBIA

GUIANA

ATLANTIC

Quito

ECUADOR
1830

R Amazon

Lima

PERU
1821

EMPIRE OF BRAZIL
1822

PACIFIC

Brazilian Matto Grosso

BOLIVIA
1825

PARAGUAY 1811

Rio de Janeiro

UNITED PROV.
OF LA PLATA
1810-16

Sao Paulo

ARGENTINA

Santiago

CHILE 1818

URUGUAY 1828

Buenos Aires

Montevideo

R Plate

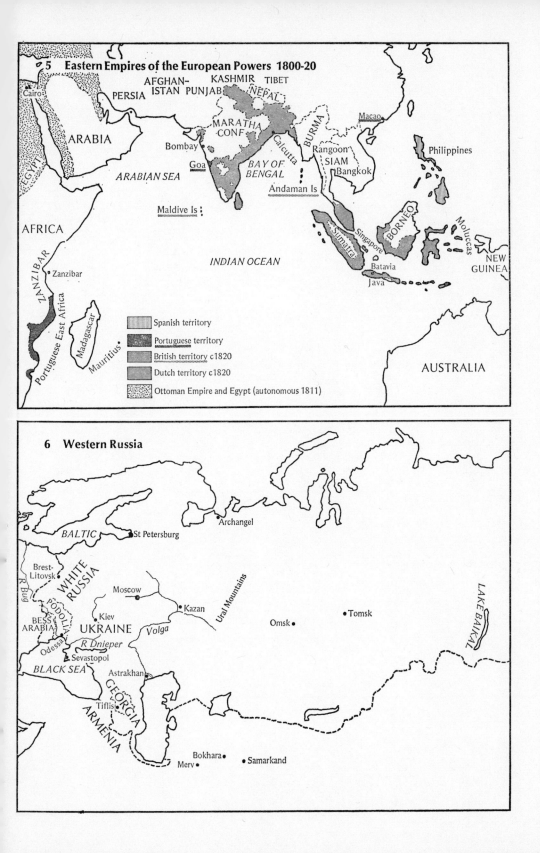

5 Eastern Empires of the European Powers 1800-20

Cairo
PERSIA
AFGHAN-ISTAN
PUNJAB
KASHMIR
TIBET
NEPAL
BURMA
Macao
ARABIA
EGYPT
MARATHA CONF
Bombay
Calcutta
Rangoon
SIAM
Bangkok
Philippines
Goa
BAY OF BENGAL
ARABIAN SEA
Andaman Is
AFRICA
Maldive Is
ZANZIBAR
Zanzibar
BORNEO
Moluccas
NEW GUINEA
Sumatra
Singapore
Portuguese East Africa
Madagascar
Mauritius
INDIAN OCEAN
Batavia
Java
AUSTRALIA

Spanish territory
Portuguese territory
British territory c1820
Dutch territory c1820
Ottoman Empire and Egypt (autonomous 1811)

6 Western Russia

Archangel
BALTIC
St Petersburg
Brest-Litovsk
WHITE RUSSIA
R Bug
Moscow
PODOLIA
BESS-ARABIA
Kiev
Kazan
Ural Mountains
Omsk
Tomsk
LAKE BAIKAL
UKRAINE
Volga
Odessa
R Dnieper
Sevastopol
BLACK SEA
Astrakhan
GEORGIA
Tiflis
ARMENIA
Bokhara
Samarkand
Merv

Index

Adams, John (1735–1826), President of us, 128
Adrianople, Treaty of (1829), 195, 197
Afghanistan, 262
Africa, 255, 258
Agricultural Revolution, 145–8, 150, 210
Agriculture, 144–51, 163, 272
  improvement of productivity, 143, 145–9, 150–1
  and manufacture, 145, 150
  new methods, 147–8, 149, 202
  population engaged in, 149
  and social change, *see* Social change
  wages, 150–1
Alaska, 184, 185
Alexander I, Tsar (1777–1825), 177, 178–9, 184, 192, 232
Alfieri, Vittorio (1749–1803), 60
Algeria, 26, 164, 255
Ali Pasha (?1741–1822), 192, 193
American Declaration of Independence (1776), 5–6, 77, 78, 106, 154, 268, 271
American Revolution, 4–9, 271; *see also* War of American Independence
Amiens, Peace of (1802), 127
Anarchism, 235, 242
Ancien Régime
  assumptions and principles, 34–45, 237
  collapse of, 101, 117, 156, 203, 209
  corporatism of, 34–5, 43–4, 157, 199
  definition, 33–4
  external relations, 46–56
  and feudalism, 42–3
  and legal system, 41–2
  limitations, 38–9, 52
  and locality, 44
  monarchy in, 48, 74–5
  and nobility, *see* Nobility

  privilege and rights, 39–40, 47, 48, 95, 100–1, 134, 201–2, 236
  proprietorial principle, 47–8
  and religion, 35–8, 48
Annals of Agriculture, 147
Anti-clericalism, 53, 71–3, 96, 230, 252
Anti-individualism, 35
Anti-slavery legislation, 87, 249, 259
Anti-slavery movement, 28, 62, 108, 224, 258–9
Art and artists, 225–6
Artois, Duc d', *see* Charles x
Asia, 259–61
Aspern, battle of (1809), 125
Assignats, 159–60
Astor, John Jacob (1763–1848), 188
Austen, Jane (1775–1817), 154
Austerlitz, battle of (1805), 125
Australia, 28
Austria, 51–2
  agriculture, 147
  annexation of Cracow, 267
  and Bavaria, 82
  borders after 1815, 174–5
  and Germany, 137, 175, 176, 197
  and Greece, 194
  Italian possessions, 136, 174, 197
  and Netherlands (Belgium), 51, 52, 82–3, 94, 174
  and Ottoman Empire, 83, 270
  and partition of Poland, 86
  population, 174
  and Prussia, 52, 53, 80, 82–3, 163, 175, 197
  relations with France, 82, 106–8, 114, 118, 124–5
  see also Habsburg
Avignon, 117

Babeuf, François Noël (1760–97), 240, 241